Colección Támesis

SERIE A: MONOGRAFÍAS, 197

MOTHERS AND DAUGHTERS IN POST-REVOLUTIONARY MEXICAN LITERATURE

Nellie Campobello, Rosario Castellanos, Elena Garro and Elena Poniatowska, all born in the first half of the twentieth century, explore in a unique genre – a combination of memoir, autobiography and historical novel – some of the myths about women current in Mexico at the time. Prime among these is that of the *madre abnegada*, the self-sacrificing mother, devoted exclusively to her children at the expense of her own fulfilment. In this study the mothers' dissenting voices are exposed, as are the feelings of the daughters who appear devoted to their mothers but feel resentment at what they perceive as their mother's emotional distance. The antithesis of the *madre abnegada* is the *mujer mala*, the whore, a notion the author also questions by revealing the complexity of the mother-daughter relationship, through which women may perpetuate their own oppression.

Highlighting the voice of the 'other', this book reveals the broad spectrum of people (children, the indigenous, the poor, the impoverished landed gentry, as well as women) who found themselves excluded from the material benefits of reform and progress that followed the Revolution.

TERESA HURLEY is currently teaching at the University of Exeter.

TERESA M. HURLEY

MOTHERS AND DAUGHTERS IN POST-REVOLUTIONARY MEXICAN LITERATURE

TAMESIS

First published 2003
by Tamesis, Woodbridge

ISBN 1 85566 090 3

Tamesis is an imprint of Boydell & Brewer Ltd
PO Box 9, Woodbridge, Suffolk IP12 3DF, UK
and of Boydell & Brewer Inc.
PO Box 41026, Rochester, NY 14604–4126, USA
website: www.boydell.co.uk

A catalogue record for this book is available
from the British Library

Library of Congress Cataloging-in-Publication Data
Hurley, Teresa M., 1953–
  Mothers and daughters in post-revolutionary Mexican literature /
Teresa M. Hurley.
     p. cm. – (Colección Támesis. Serie A, Monografías ; 197)
Includes bibliographical references and index.
  ISBN 1–85566–090–3 (hardback : alk. paper)
1. Mexican fiction – 20th century – History and criticism.
2. Mothers and daughters in literature. 3. Campobello, Nellie.
Cartucho. 4. Castellanos, Rosario. Balún-Canán. 5. Garro, Elena.
Recuerdos del porvenir. 6. Poniatowska, Elena. Flor de lis. I. Title.
  PQ7207.M65H87 2003
  863'.6093520431 – dc21   2003006703

This publication is printed on acid-free paper

Printed in Great Britain by
St Edmundsbury Press Limited, Bury St Edmunds, Suffolk

CONTENTS

ABBREVIATIONS

C	*Cartucho*
EZLN	Ejército Zapatista de Liberación Nacional (Zapatista Army of National Liberation)
FCE	Fondo de Cultura Económica (Mexican publishing Company)
INI	Instituto Nacional Indigenista (Institute for Indigenous Affairs)
MM	*Las manos de mamá*
MI: UMI	Michigan: University Microfilms International
PRI	Partido Revolucionario Institucionalizado (Institutionalised Revolutionary Party)
PRM	Partido Revolucionario Mexicano (Mexican Revolutionary Party)
UNAM	Universidad Autónoma de México

PREFACE

My inspiration for this book came while I was reading Elena Poniatowska's highly acclaimed testimonial novel, *Hasta no verte, Jesús mío* (1969). It was the first work that I had read by a Mexican writer that narrates the life of a woman of humble origins in the first person. I subsequently found that many of the novels and short stories written by women in Mexico had a first-person narrator but were not overtly autobiographical, though there were often similarities between the works and the lives of the writers. This raised the question of what might be the possible motives of the writers for choosing to disguise the narrator in order to conceal the autobiographical nature of the works. The answer lies in something as fundamental as the mother–daughter relationship. This book has, therefore, been both an investigation into women writing about women and a journey of discovery.

Initially I was fortunate to secure research funding from the University of Strathclyde; a further two years' funding arranged by Eddie Moxon-Browne of the University of Limerick enabled me to finish the research.

I am indebted to Nuala Finnegan and Eamonn Rodgers for their enthusiasm for this project. I am also grateful to my friends Claire Lindsay and Catherine Grant for their support in the early stages of the work. Finally I would like to express my heartfelt thanks to Elspeth Ferguson, my editor, for her helpful advice, suggestions and unending patience.

Assistance with publication costs has been kindly provided by Gareth Walters and the Hispanic Studies Department of the University of Exeter, and by the Modern Humanities Research Association.

For Anya and Jack

INTRODUCTION

> As daughters we need mothers who want their
> own freedom and ours. We need not to be the
> vessels of another woman's self-denial and frus-
> tration.[1]

This book examines first-person narrative fiction by four Mexican women writers.[2] The authors whose work is discussed here: Nellie Campobello, Rosario Castellanos, Elena Garro and Elena Poniatowska, were born between 1900 and 1933, and these semi-autobiographical works were their first novels (or in the case of Campobello, novellas). All are concerned with the changes affecting young girls' lives in the process of maturation and all were written against a backdrop of change in Mexico: the eras of 'Reform and Progress' and of 'Modernisation and Industrialisation' and the nation-building associated with those eras.

The first-third of the twentieth century was a period of upheaval in Mexican society, when women's roles inevitably changed from the traditional ones associated with the conservatism of the politically stable *Porfiriato* before the Revolution.[3] However, official policy in this strongly patriarchal society attempted to impose a traditional system of values, with sharply defined male and female roles. This included an undertaking to maintain the status quo (to create and perpetuate stability) by (re)creating the myth which

---

[1]   Adrienne Rich (1995: 247).

[2]   Kay García in her book, *Broken Bars*, has already produced a similar work on four Mexican women writers that coincides in the choice of one of the writers: Elena Ponia-towska. However, while García discusses the ideas of discourse and counter-discourse in Poniatowska's testimonial works *La noche de Tlatelolco* (1971) and *Nada, nadie: Las voces del temblor* (1988*a*), this book restricts itself to looking at first person 'fiction' writing only, which, though more personal, also addresses the notions of discourse and counter-discourse in a more covert way. Later on I borrow Kay García's term 'alternative' discourse to refer to 'a more *positive* narration (than Richard Terdman's "counter-discourse") that deviates from the official discourse by creating a personal (or collective) story that *affirms the vitality* of the narrator and protagonists' (García 1994: 5–6 [my emphasis]).

[3]   The presidency of Porfirio Díaz lasted from 1876 to 1880 and 1884 to 1911, when Gustavo I. Madero was elected to office.

placed the self-sacrificing mother in a binary opposition with the whore or fallen woman. The status quo is challenged in the novels discussed by other or alternative voices – those who are excluded from positions of privilege due to their gender, social class or economic position.

All four of the writers were contemporaries, though not of the same genera-tion. Castellanos and Poniatowska are the most well known and the ones whose work has received most critical attention. Indeed only these two are considered part of the Mexican literary canon. However, the first born of the four, Campobello, although more well known as a dancer and choreographer, is considered among the exceptional writers of the 'Novel of the Revolution' which was at its apogee in the 1930s and Garro, though less well known than Castellanos, is also highly regarded by other Mexican writers and her work has been awarded prizes and received considerable critical attention. Her light was no doubt somewhat eclipsed by the fact that she was at one time married to Octavio Paz.

The first two of the works discussed to be published were Nellie Campo-bello's *Cartucho* (1931), and *Las manos de mamá* (1937) which were trans-lated as *Cartucho* and *My Mother's Hands*. One of the interesting features of these novellas (and of the other works discussed here) is their multivocality – both the presence of many voices and also of multiple discourses in the text. In *Cartucho*, these primarily take the form of the alternative version of the Revolution and the memories the narrator has of the people and events of the time; in *Las manos de mamá*, they also encompass the ambivalent nature of the mother–daughter relationship and the different discourses produced by that ambivalence. Chapters Three and Five discuss Castellanos' *Balún-Canán* (1957), translated as *The Nine Guardians* and Poniatowska's *La 'Flor de Lis'* (1989) respectively. In these novels, where both girl-narrators are brought up as babies by wet-nurses rather than their biological mothers, the relationship between the narrator and the mother or mother-figure is also of primary importance. This crucial relationship and the memories associated with it are often depicted through sensual impressions. The exploration of the way the senses are related to memory and childhood takes precedence, therefore, in Chapters, Two, Three and Five.

My analysis of multivocality in the novels also includes an exploration of the alternative discourse about the post-revolutionary years of reform in Mexico and discusses the concepts of time and memory in *Balún-Canán*, and of nationality and identity in *La 'Flor de Lis'*. Chapter Four centres on the concept of multivocality in Garro's *Los recuerdos del porvenir* (1963), trans-lated as *Recollections of Things to Come*, and explores alternative discourse about the years of Calles's presidency and the Cristero War. However, even here the mother–daughter relationship is vital to the outcome of the novel's plot and the fate of the protagonist whose actions are largely the result of her own experience of being mothered – that is, what she perceives as her mother's attitude and feelings of resentment towards her.

In order to be able to write about a past that is different from that recounted by the official version of the history books, it has been necessary for the writers whose work is discussed in this book to describe events and political, social and economic conditions from a different perspective. They do so by having a narrator who does not fulfil the traditional criteria of the historical witness as an adult (usually white, male and middle-class), educated in the Western philosophical humanist tradition with his associated set of values, preconceptions and prejudices. The stories discussed here are presented through the eyes of an Other (usually female).[4]

In Mexico, particularly between 1930 and 1960, when these writers were young women living there, women were expected to play very precise roles in society. According to Judaeo-Christian ideology, predominant in Catholic societies such as that in Mexico, women were allowed a choice of three roles. In order to depict these roles, Mexican authors have drawn on images of womanhood as represented by religious, historical and literary icons – the Virgin of Guadalupe, La Malinche and Sor Juana Inés de la Cruz respectively. The kinds of roles these offer are those of the pure and self-sacrificing mother (the Virgin of Guadalupe), the whore (*La Malinche* – Doña Marina, the woman who betrayed the indigenous people of Mexico by becoming Cortés's mistress) and the nun or chaste spinster (Sor Juana).[5] All the novels (or novellas) discussed in this book address the concept of transgression of traditional female roles established by patriarchal society and suggest that a certain kind of mothering can perpetuate or challenge those roles.

Debra Castillo has emphasised the need for care in using feminist criticism when referring to Latin American women's writing.[6] Her essays have been indispensable to gaining a new perspective on Mexican writers for the critical approach used in the writing of this book, which also borrows from psychoanalytical feminism and Bakhtinian dialogism, but centres on an analysis of the construction of gender through the use of binary oppositions in the texts. Sidonie Smith and Julia Watson's collection of essays on gender and autobiography has similarly provided insight into the important differences between

---

4   The concept of women as 'Other' in relation to men (i.e. somehow deviant from the norm) was coined by Simone de Beauvoir in *The Second Sex* (Harmondsworth: Penguin 1972). However, it has since been extended to encompass class, race and culture as well as gender. Derrick Price (1997: 59) writes: 'European culture was defined against the "other" of colonised peoples'.

5   For an overview by literary authors and sociologists of the perception of loose woman in Mexico see Debra Castillo 1998: 1–36. Castillo posits the *soldadera* (rather than Sor Juana or the Virgin) as the idealised (chaste) woman during the Revolution (the reality being quite different). Octavio Paz's *Laberinto de la soledad* is now the classic work on the view of Mexican women as descendants of *la chingada* (Malinche). For writings on the Virgin of Guadalupe see Ana Castillo (ed.).

6   Debra Castillo (1992*a*): 242–266, and (1992*b*): 216–259.

male and female autobiographies.[7] For their own work on the mother–
daughter relationship, I am particularly beholden to Nancy Chodorow (1978)
and Adrienne Rich. For its clear presentation and useful analysis of the works
of leading psychoanalysts, Rosalind Minsky's *Psychoanalysis and Gender*
(1996) has been an essential source of reference. In order to substantiate the
claim that a certain kind of mothering can either perpetuate or challenge
stereotypical roles, my discussion draws on psychoanalytical criticism from
Freud to Lacan, as well as on more recent feminist interpretations of their
writing and on the work of the psychoanalyst and paediatrician Donald
Woods Winnicott. During the 1940s and 1950s, Winnicott wrote and lectured
on the importance of the right kind of mother-child relationship for the child's
healthy psychic development. Winnicott thought that a sensation of personal
authenticity (identity) could only be achieved through a special kind of reliable, creative, non-compliant relationship with the mother in early childhood.
He was convinced that all babies have the potential (from birth) to be creative,
to integrate and, eventually, to separate successfully from the mother,
provided she is 'good enough'. He based his theory of identity on the idea of
emotional nurture according to which (ideally) the 'good enough mother'
actively adapts to the needs of the infant rather than the other way round.[8]
Now, however, it is recognised that in most societies it is the child who must
adapt to the (economic) needs of the mother.

Feminist psychoanalysis is the branch of theory that has dealt most thor-
oughly with the mother–daughter relationship. The question of gender, therefore, also assumes particular importance in my analysis, which centres on the
discussion of binary oppositions as established in the work of Hélène Cixous
(following Lacan). Cixous argues that the binary opposition masculinity/
femininity – that is, the meaning of the phallus and sexual difference – is the
basis by which we categorise reality in language and culture (Minsky 1996:
102).[9] This patriarchal binary opposition system (activity/passivity; sun/
moon; culture/nature; day/night and so on) accords certain characteristics to
the feminine and their opposites to the masculine, thereby, according to

---

[7] Smith and Watson (eds) (1987 and 1992).

[8] The term 'good enough mother' was used by Winnicott in Britain during the late
1940s at a time when the status quo was attempting to make women give up the jobs and
independence they had achieved during the War, to return to the home and full-time mothering; so Winnicott has been criticised by feminists for supporting the status quo against
mothers. It is now generally agreed that nurturing by a mother figure, if not the biological
mother, is necessary for the child's healthy development (Minsky 1996: 113–14).

[9] Claude Lévi-Strauss believed that the human mind always thinks in terms of binary
oppositions and that this explained how culture is produced. Ferdinand de Saussure
produced a model of structural linguistics that proposed that all meaning is constructed
through binary oppositional differences. Jacques Lacan offered a post-structuralist decons-
truction of the model by suggesting that one term (the first) is always privileged over the
other – for instance male over female (Phoca and Wright 1999: 34–35, 46).

Cixous, upholding patriarchy.[10] Binary oppositions appear in the text in two guises: the traditionalist, essentialist kind and the transgressive type found in alternative discourse.[11] Transgressive use consists of a subversion of such traditional categorisation by employing humour, irony, mockery or simple reversal of the terms. An examination of the examples of binary oppositions in the texts by Campobello, Castellanos, Garro and Poniatowska reveals how gender roles are both constructed and challenged.

The writers, the narrators and all but one of the protagonists of the novels discussed are female; this fact has precise implications for the interpretation of the works in question. Mary Maynard writes that the current theoretical hype about culture, language and representation implies that a concern with materiality is redundant and that men and women can choose, in a free market, their culture and identity (Maynard 1995: 275). This idea, as Maynard affirms, overlooks intervening factors which might inhibit or restrain them such as material or economic factors or gender.[12] Our lived experience, says Maynard, is mediated not just through discourse or text but also through material structures and relationships. While I acknowledge the central role apportioned to language and discourse by Lacan and the post-structuralists, as, to quote Maynard (269), 'there is no way of comprehending a "reality" which is independent of the language structures through which it is apprehended', yet it is clear that both aspects of language and socio-economic factors (or historical circumstances) need to be taken into consideration when analysing texts. Without language there is no way of analysing the material influences on aspects of the writers' lives, yet the 'ever changing reality' (Maynard) described by the writer's words is informed to a great extent by the socio-economic and historical position she (or he) occupies. These in turn produce diverse modes of speech and result in what Mikhail Bakhtin terms 'dialogism' in the novel.

According to Bakhtin, the novel is by its very nature dialogical (as opposed to the poem or epic which he sees as monological). He writes:

10 I adopt here Adrienne Rich's definition of patriarchy (Rich 1995: 57). In a European context, the above-mentioned middle-class white males would be considered by feminist criticism to form the patriarchy. However, in the context of twentieth-century Mexico, it would consist primarily of the upper middle-class ruling elite (usually white or *mestizo*) male population as the rest of the males were subjugated to the patriarchal system at the same time as they, in turn, subjugated women. Women, according to this definition therefore, are doubly marginalised – within their own class and in society as a whole.

11 Essentialist use comprises an adherence to the terms traditionally applied to the gender constructions male/female which generally associates positive words such as 'culture' (and reason) with the male and those traditionally considered negative, such as 'nature' (and irrationality), with the female.

12 According to Ramos Escandón (1997: 151) the use of gender as an analytical tool has emerged only recently, as has awareness of the need to analyse gender relations.

The novel orchestrates all its themes, the totality of the world of objects and ideas depicted and expressed in it, by means of the social diversity of speech types and the differing individual voices that flourish under such conditions. Authorial speech, the speeches of narrators, inserted genres, the speech of characters are merely those fundamental compositional unities with whose help heteroglossia (*raznorecie*) can enter the novel; each of them permits a multiplicity of social voices and a wide variety of their links and interrelationships (always more or less dialogized).

(Bakhtin 1981: 263)

Through dialogism or multivocality, Campobello, Castellanos, Garro and Poniatowska challenge the official (patriarchal) version of the history of Mexico by presenting what Richard Terdiman terms a 'counter-discourse' to contradict the dominant discourse that is produced by the ruling élite, in this case the Mexican government (García 1994: 5). Thus my analysis of the use of binary oppositions in the texts, and the way these are used to subvert or reinforce traditional patriarchal constructs of gender and historical truth, takes into account the historical, economic and social background against which the novels were written and also discusses the multivocality of the works by alluding to Bakhtin's ideas on heteroglossia and polyphony. I use Graham Roberts' interpretation of Bakhtin's terms to refer to the different types of multivocality in the texts discussed:

'Heteroglossia' [. . .] refers to the conflict between 'official' and 'unofficial' discourses within the same national language [. . .] One way of representing heteroglossia in the novel is by a hybrid construction [. . .] which contains within it the trace of two or more discourses, either those of the narrator and character(s), or of different characters [. . .] 'Heteroglossia' should not be confused with 'polyphony' [. . .] The latter term is used by Bakhtin primarily to describe Dostoevsky's 'multi-voiced' novels, whereby authors' and heroes' discourses interact on equal terms. 'Heteroglossia', on the other hand, foregrounds the clash of antagonistic social forces.[13]

Finally, in my discussion of the mother–daughter relationship and how this in turn is related to the senses and to writing, I also refer to certain ideas pertaining to psychoanalysis. By throwing light on the significance of the senses in the prose and on their connection with memory and binary oppositions, I attempt to explain the relevance of the mother–daughter relationship in the construction of gender. My approach might, for want of a more suitable term, be described as 'psychoanalytically-based dialogism'.

---

[13] Roberts (1994).

1

WOMEN AND WRITING DURING AND AFTER THE MEXICAN REVOLUTION

GENDER AND GENRE

It is useful to consider the existing categories in which the works of authors contemporary to Campobello, Castellanos, Garro and Poniatowska have been placed, as it will be observed that the works by these women writers do not slot easily into any particular category.[1] Rather, they have the characteristics of several of the existing *genres*, as well as being, to varying degrees, autobiographical novels. One reason that the works by these women authors have been given less attention than they merit is that they were not entirely original in style or genre. Campobello's work can be categorised along with other 'novels of the Revolution' in which, to quote Jean Franco, 'in order to give the feeling of violent upheaval, traditional chapter structures and character description disappeared to give way to brief, dissociated scenes' (Franco 1969: 196). Franco may have been referring to Martín Luis Guzmán's *El águila y la serpiente* (The Eagle and the Serpent), but it is also true of *Cartucho* and *Las manos de mamá*, in which the descriptions of the people are physical, rather than of character, and presented in the form of vivid sketches without a narrative sequence. However, Campobello's work differed from that of her contemporaries, such as Guzmán, whose most important work earned him a place as the major novelist of the Revolution, by presenting a picture of the Revolution from the point of view of a young girl.[2] Nellie Campobello writes, 'Las narraciones de *Cartucho*, debo aclararlo de una vez para siempre, son verdad histórica, son hechos trágicos vistos por mis ojos de

---

[1]   According to Julieta Campos' definition, the 'Novel of the Revolution' lasted until 1940 and was characterised by realism. Post-1940 pessimism, as a result of the failure of the Revolution, led to various forms of criticism. Campos defines these as *realismo de las esencias* (Agustín Yañez's *Al filo del agua*) which looks at the world through the experience of the subject and characters; *realismo mágico* (Juan Rulfo's *Pedro Páramo*) revealing the profound nature of Mexican life through a poetic vision; *realismo crítico* (Carlos Fuentes' *La muerte de Artemio Cruz*), and *evocación biográfica* (Castellanos' work) which accentuates the game of social relations insofar as they affect the life of individuals (Campos 1965).

[2]   Campobello had not read Guzmán's work (published in 1928), nor, she claims, any other novel of the Revolution, before she wrote *Cartucho* (Campobello 1960: 25).

niña' (The narratives in *Cartucho*, I must make clear once and for all, are historical truth, tragic events seen by my own eyes as a little girl) (Campobello 1960: 17). Her works also differ from any other novel of the Revolution by challenging two particular myths: that of Pancho Villa as a murderous bandit, and the myth of the Mexican mother as a Madonna figure or *madre abnegada* (self-sacrificing mother).

Rosario Castellanos also, in her novel *Balún-Canán*, debunks the myth of the *madre abnegada*. *Balún-Canán* combines some of the basic concepts of the *novela indigenista* with the theme of the post-revolutionary novel which dealt with the integration (or lack of integration) of the indigenous people into the nation. During the presidency of Adolfo Ruiz Cortines (1952–58) when *Balún-Canán* was published, many writers, disillusioned with the failures of the Revolution and sceptical of the possibilities of social change, altered the focus of *indigenista* writing away from the intermediate world of the government official on to the indigenous community, with more rounded indigenous characters as protagonists, rather than noble savages (Cynthia Steele 1985: 82). After the creation of the *Instituto Nacional Indigenista* (INI) in 1948, some writers, having witnessed the destructive effects of acculturation, stopped supporting the government policy of incorporation of the indigenous people. Castellanos' writing took the approach of using indigenous myth to try to approximate the situation of the indigenous people, which proved more convincing, according to Jean Franco, than other *indigenista* novels – whether the documentary style of Gregorio López y Fuentes' *El indio* (1935), or the anthropologist Ricardo Pozas' 1952 ethnographic study of the indigenous protagonist in *Juan Pérez Jolote* (Franco 1969: 242). Castellanos tended to perpetuate the binary oppositions of civilisation/barbarism[3] (instinct/intellect, superstition/science, dependency/authority, cyclical time/linear time) in her *indigenista* writing but added another dimension which revealed the marginalisation of women in rural Mexico and thus challenged the nature/culture paradigm, whereby education is considered the reserve of men. In *Balún-Canán* she reveals a young girl's non-conformity with her designated future role and, like Campobello, Garro and Poniatowska, challenges the myth of the Mexican mother as *abnegada* and Madonna-like.

Elena Garro's novel, *Los recuerdos del porvenir*, also falls into the genre of post-revolutionary literature (but deals with the *Cristero* war of the 1920s) that addresses the theme of the frustration of revolutionary hopes and 'the rise of a new class of leaders who appeared ready to restore old dictatorial methods' (Franco 1969: 204). Garro, too, subverts the binary oppositions of the

[3] This was an ongoing debate in Latin America initiated by Domingo F. Sarmiento's 19th-century novel *Facundo* in Argentina about the 'conflict between the forces of primitive darkness (the tribe or the mass) and the civilised individual' (Franco 1969: 50). Originally it sprang from the dichotomy Old/New World and primitive indigenous inhabitant/civilised European conqueror.

status quo by challenging first, the role of women in society, with a protagonist who refuses to conform to the feminine ideal and, secondly, the patriarchal view of history as linear and chronological, by presenting non-
indigenous characters who are governed by the concept of cyclical time and
by using a first-person narrator that is collective, and therefore multivocal
rather than monovocal (and patriarchal).

Finally, Elena Poniatowska's work, like Campobello's is both an homage to
her mother and a multivocal text which reveals the unconsciously ambivalent
feelings of the girl narrator towards her mother. In a kind of feminised
Bildungsroman,[4] it presents the view of a young girl who feels herself to be
marginalised, even though her mother is Mexican, because she is an immigrant
to Mexico, growing up amid the climate of cultural nationalism that prevailed
in Mexico in the 1940s and 1950s. Her journey is one of acculturation in her
new homeland. The fact that one of her parents was not Mexican detracted
from Poniatowska's own feeling of being Mexican and augmented her desire
to be accepted; as indeed might have been the case for Garro. This would
certainly have influenced the nature of the authors' writing as would their privileged social background and education. The other factor that clearly affected
their work is gender, particularly in view of the roles women were expected to
play in Mexican society as they were growing up and trying to establish themselves as writers in an almost exclusively male literary establishment.

In the last thirty years there has been a theoretical shift regarding the study
of gender and power relations. Elizabeth Dore writes that, 'At the turn of the
millennium, gender history is still about these things (women's history –
making women visible; why conventional approaches to women's history did
not fit women's past) but they are subsumed within a broader framework
which focuses on how state-building, class exploitation, and racial oppression
construct power relations that are gendered' (Dore 1997: 104–5). Carmen
Ramos Escandón cites Joan Scott as saying that 'there have been three major
approaches to patriarchy within women's history. One sees patriarchy as the
universal cause of women's oppression. A second, the Marxist approach,
explains women's oppression in terms of women's relationship to socialised
production and generational reproduction. A third, the psychoanalytical
school, examines unconscious adherence to gender roles' (Ramos Escandón
1997: 152). 'Gender analysis', writes Dore, 'is about how material and ideo-
logical practices regarding sexual difference reproduce power relations'

---

4   According to German scholars generally, an educational novel. However, according
to Anthony Thorlby (1969: 14), some scholars distinguish between educational novels
proper (*Erziehungsromane*) involving psychological theory; 'novels of development',
where the hero's character evolves; and 'true *Bildungsromane,* in the manner of Goethe,
where an artistic temperament comes to terms with the demands of social life'. For a thor-
ough investigation of the female *Bildungsroman*, see Abel, Hirsch and Langland (eds)
(1983).

(Dore 1997: 114). There is some debate, however, as to how long the gender roles established in post-revolutionary Mexico had actually been the norm, as these change according to historical and social circumstances. Ramos Escandón considers that, 'From the point of view of gender formation, the nineteenth century presents the consolidation of the national state and the nuclear family' (Ramos Escandón 1997: 155). Dore, conversely, affirms that male-headed households in the nineteenth century were not as widespread as was hitherto assumed and that female-headed households were common in both urban and rural Mexico (Dore 1997: 113) (the household in which Nellie Campobello grew up was just such a female-headed one).

There was clearly a need, if the government's nation-building ambitions were to be realised, to promote the (official version of the) patriarchal, male-headed family, established as the ideal during the developmental phase in post-revolutionary Mexico. Dore writes, 'As many believe that female subordination is reproduced primarily in the household, the discovery of high rates of female householders has led historians to suggest that women have been more autonomous in Latin America than previously perceived' (113). This suggests that households headed by strong women (such as that of the narrator of *Cartucho*), or where the father was present but was a weak person-ality (as in *Los recuerdos del porvenir* and *La 'Flor de Lis'*), rather than domi-nated by a patriarchal figure (as in *Balún-Canán*), were more common than is acknowledged by the status quo at that time and that the self-sacrificing, submissive mother is therefore also largely a myth. Above all, however, all four writers challenge the myth of the Madonna/Malinche dichotomy by addressing the question of the status and role of women. In each of the novels this is accomplished indirectly and mainly through the importance assigned to the mother–daughter relationship. Freud links the senses with the pre-Oedipal phase of the mother–child relationship and emphasises their significance in questions of the psyche and the workings of the unconscious. With reference to the mother–child relationship and the senses, Dorothy Dinnerstein writes, 'the crucial fact is that the feeling, the vital emotional intercourse, between infant and parent is carried by touch, by taste and smell, by facial expression and gesture' (Dinnerstein 1991). In the novels discussed here, references to the senses are often associated with the idealised memories of the narrator's mother. This is particularly the case in Campobello's and Poniatowska's works.

The significance attributed to the senses is not merely a post-Freudian preoccupation however. As Lucía Guerra Cunningham observes, Juan Luis Vives advised women to stay as far away as possible from all that which 'escalienta y altera los cuerpos, como son danzas, olores, perfumes, pláticas y vistas de hombres'[5] (excites and upsets their bodies, such as dances, smells,

---

5   Cited in Lucía Guerra Cunningham (1994–95: 49).

perfumes, talk and looking at men). Vives started from the principle that 'toda mujer debe practicar la templanza y la continencia para asemejarse a la Virgen María' (all women should practice restraint and continence in order to be like the Virgin Mary). This attitude became entrenched in what was to become the ideal of the *madre abnegada*.

Women's specific roles in Mexico, even during the era of increased freedom brought about by the Revolution, restricted their participation in what were traditionally considered male pursuits. Their presence on the battle-field was limited to a few exceptional cases and most of the legendary *soldaderas* were confined to accompanying their fighting men from one confrontation to another in order to provide them with food and to do their laundry. Others among the less humble classes (such as Rafaela, Nellie's mother in *Cartucho* and *Las manos de mamá*), devoted themselves to nursing the wounded and sick but, throughout the war and its aftermath, their role as mothers was unquestioned. The myth of the *abnegada y sufrida* Mexican wife and mother has been successfully perpetuated until recently.[6] In an interview in 1990 with Agnes Dimitriou, Poniatowska attributes women's failure to have successful careers in Mexico to the fact that they continue to sacrifice their careers to their families and to the idea that, 'al fin, es mujer. Se va a casar' (when all is said and done, she's a woman. She's going to get married). She sees women as still marginalised, 'Y lo es en la literatura, lo es intelectualmente, lo es en todos los campos' (and she is so in literature, she is intellectually, she is in all areas). Poniatowska ascribes this, in part, to (middle-class) women's indolence and desire for an easy, comfortable life, but also to the patriarchal Catholic tradition, present since the time of the Conquest, according to which, 'pasas de la tutela o el tutelaje del padre y de la familia a la del marido. Tú eres propiedad primero de tu familia y luego propiedad de tu marido' (you pass from the tutelage of your father and the family to that of your husband. First you are the property of your family and then the property of your husband).[7]

All the five works discussed here challenge these myths by presenting a heteroglossic account of the parts played by women (in the home as well as in the context of the Revolution) and the way the daughters of those women attempt to transgress the roles for which they are destined. Through an exploration of the mother–daughter relationship and of the heteroglossia present in the texts, I attempt to show to what extent their challenge is successful.

---

6   See Octavio Paz's *El laberinto de la soledad* (1982) for an account of the myth of woman as Madonna.

7   However, there has been a 'rapid and extensive spread of feminism and women's organizations in the last ten or fifteen years'. See John Beverly and José Oviedo (1995: 8).

WOMEN AND WRITING IN MEXICO

Many of the novels and short stories written by women in Mexico have a
first-person narrator but are not overtly autobiographical, though there are, at
times, some similarities between the works and the lives of the writers. This
raises the question of what might be the possible motives of the writers for
choosing to disguise the narrator in order to conceal the autobiographical nature
of the works. Bertha López Morales writes that the subversive trends of
women's writing comes from women's 'need to affirm their own self-worth and
to value their own writing in the light of that produced by men' (López Morales
1990: 124). This would have been particularly the case in Mexico where there is
a striking absence of literary role models between Sor Juana Inés de la Cruz and
the twentieth century. María Elena de Valdés observes that 'Until the 1950s,
with a few notable exceptions, Mexican women's writing had been traditionally
restricted to "sentimental" fiction and newspaper sections designated as "social
pages" ' (de Valdés 1998: 144). However, even such notable exceptions were
often ignored. A review of anthologies of Mexican literature in the twentieth
century, reveals how little attention has been paid to women writers until
recently; hence the importance given to gender in my analysis.

   Although this book concentrates on women writers, I do not consider them
to be a category apart in Latin America, except for their virtual exclusion from
the literary canon there. The refusal of some Latin American women writers
to see themselves as women writers, or to label themselves feminists (Castellanos and Isabel Allende being notable exceptions), is presumably due to the
fact that they were reluctant to accept definitions that, prior to the 1980s, were
based on the North American and French Feminist models. Such models have
since been found inappropriate when applied to Latin American women,
whose historical situation has been quite different from that of their European
and North American counterparts. In some cases, such as that of Garro (and
also Allende), there exists a desire, as Deborah Shaw writes, to be 'judged
with male writers and accepted on their level' (Shaw 1997: 165). This in itself
reveals the marginalisation of women writers that has existed up until recently
in Latin America. Shaw, in her article 'Problems of Definition in Theorising
Latin American Women's Writing' debates the very existence of a category of
women's writing, rightly pointing out that there are as many categories of
feminine as of masculine writing. For example, she cites Elena Poniatowska
as a writer who finds 'the true nature of women's writing in its social and
political content' (Shaw 1997: 163). Garro's work, too, has elements of
socio-political criticism, but is influenced more by universal concerns, such as
time and the corrupting nature of power or classical themes.[8] Castellanos, on

---

   [8]   Garro's play *La dama boba*, after the homonymous work by Lope de Vega, is one
example of this.

the other hand, depicts the oppression of women, but incorporates this into works heavy with irony and humour (especially her short stories, plays and poems). Also, she has stated the importance of form in her writings – even in the earlier novels set in Chiapas in which she criticises provincial society – contrasting them with the more obviously socio-political nature of truly *indigenista* works.

Seymour Menton, in his article, 'Las cuentistas mexicanas en la época feminista, 1970–1985' (1990) notes the remarkably few references to women writers in anthologies of Mexican literature published between 1946 and 1969. He goes on to remark that in spite of increased opportunities for women as a result of the Revolution, few wrote stories before the 1950s. Indeed, it is true that even the more widely-known and respected writers whose work I discuss in this book, are not mentioned with the same consistency as their male counterparts of the time.[9]

AUTOBIOGRAPHY

There are several possible motives for writers disguising their works as fiction rather than calling them autobiography; among these may be included the fear of ridicule. Many women writers have referred to the negative reception of the work of women who step outside their assigned roles. Virginia Woolf wrote in 1928 of the 'misery and anxiety the patriarchy holds in store for those who express their anger about the enforced destiny of women'; while sixty years later Carolyn Heilbrun affirmed, 'Twenty-five years ago' (at the time the novels discussed in this book were written) 'going public was still a chancy thing' (Heilbrun 1988*b*: 121). She also refers to anger, but as something women are not supposed to feel, 'above all other prohibitions, what has been forbidden to women is anger, together with the open admission of the desire for power and control over one's own life' (3). This desire for control over one's own life has particular resonance with regard to Isabel Moncada, the protagonist of *Los recuerdos del porvenir*. Isabel's transgression is her desire to participate in linear time and become a subject in history, rather than to remain as an object of history by accepting the role assigned her as a young

---

[9] Menton (1990) indicates that, in the two-volume anthology published by José Mancisidor, only Carmen Baez (b.1908) is mentioned, and in Luis Leal's anthology of 1957, only Nellie Campobello; Emmanuel Carballo's three anthologies include Guadalupe Dueñas (b.1920), Carmen Rosenzweig (b.1920), Elena Garro (b.1920), Emma Dolujanoff (b.1922) and Elena Poniatowska (b.1932); in Vols. II and III of an anthology by María del Carmen Millán (1976) only Rosario Castellanos, Guadalupe Dueñas, Amparo Dávila (b.1928) and Inés Arredondo (b.1928) appear. Not one of these writers is mentioned in *The Penguin Companion to Literature – 3: United States and Latin American Literature*, published in 1971.

woman of the privileged classes: that of wife and mother.[10]

There is another possible motive for disguising the autobiographical nature of the novels. Contrary to recent times, when women writers in Latin America such as Isabel Allende have written extensively using the autobiographical format or have merely fictionalised their own autobiographies, at the time that Campobello, Garro, Castellanos and Poniatowska began writing, there were far fewer women writers being published in Mexico. (The success currently enjoyed by Ángeles Mastretta, Laura Esquivel, Carmen Boullosa and Bárbara Jacobs, to name but a few, is unprecedented.) Furthermore, they were writing at a time when women's autobiography was considered trivial, except when written by a person of clearly historical significance. Autobiography, and particularly women's autobiography (which often concentrated on domestic details considered by male critics to be outside the province of autobiography), had only recently begun to be considered as a literary genre worthy of merit. In Mexico during the 1950s, when Garro was writing *Los recuerdos del porvenir*, Castellanos *Balún-Canán* and Poniatowska *La 'Flor de Lis'*, there were no women's autobiographies, so it is feasible that they sought to avoid this genre and chose instead that of the novel.[11] That Garro was less than confident about her writing is revealed by the fact that she kept her manuscripts stored for years in trunks and it was only through the efforts of her family and friends that they came to be published at all (Stoll 1990: 20).[12]

Earlier it was suggested that a discussion of the extent to which these novels may be considered autobiographical was relevant to my exploration of the mother–daughter relationship. Critics generally recognise four different types of autobiography: non-literary, literary, novelistic autobiography, and the autobiographical novel.[13] I would include *Cartucho* and *Las manos de mamá*, *Balún-Canán* and *La 'Flor de Lis'* under the label 'autobiographical novel' – as they are all about the writer even though she is in disguise. Also, they are concerned with what Leigh Gilmore has usefully termed 'autobiographics' (Gilmore 1994). Gilmore uses the term autobiographics to mean that novels and stories are derived from the memory of (largely) real characters and events in the lives of the writers. *Los recuerdos del porvenir*, however, is slightly different as it is about a fictional character who is not equivalent to the author, but draws on the author's own memories and past and therefore would be classified as fictional autobiography.

---

[10] For an explanation of the cultural politics of power between the subjects and objects of history (centre and periphery) see Glenn Jordan and Chris Weedon (1995).

[11] The exception is Fanny Calderón de la Barca's work, but she herself was not Mexican; she merely lived in Mexico with her husband.

[12] In the recently published *Memorias de España 1937*, Garro reveals how Paz, during their marriage was frequently critical of her actions, her 'bourgeois' behaviour and what he saw as her lack of political awareness or commitment to the Spanish Republican cause.

[13] See María de la Cinta Ramblado Minero (1999, Ph.D. thesis) for an explanation of Autobiography in Isabel Allende's work.

Although it is not the objective of this book to discuss autobiography as such, it is relevant to my exploration of the mother–daughter relationship to consider the extent to which the first-person narrator used by the authors in the texts is autobiographical and the authors' possible motives for disguising that fact. A review of other definitions of autobiography and of the scant attention paid to women's autobiographies up until recently is therefore appropriate here. First, however, I wish to draw attention to Richard N. Coe's definition of the sub-genre of autobiography, the 'Childhood', as certain characteristics of that sub-genre apply to the three works discussed here narrated by a child. Coe states that it is closer to the novel than the autobiography proper and that, '[. . .] the balance between literal and symbolic truth is shifted in the direction of the latter. Incidents are given weight in the straight autobiography according to their *factual* significance; in the Childhood, more often than not, according to their emotional, imaginative, or metaphysical significance' (Coe 1984: 79–80). The profusion of sensory details in each of the narrator's accounts adds to this impression. Coe's words are, in spite of his gender-blindness, appropriate again when he says, 'The poet of the Childhood is concerned not so much with the truth, as with *his* [sic] truth' (80).

The narrators of all the works discussed here are female children, with the exception of the narrator of *Los recuerdos del porvenir* – the *pueblo* of Ixtepec – though even this collective voice is composed of a female majority. As writing was not considered a suitable occupation for women in Mexico until relatively recently, it is reasonable to assume that the idea of writing an autobiography, a task usually the preserve of middle-class white males, might have appeared presumptuous; all the more reason for disguising the works as Childhoods.

Paul de Man has posited that, 'any book with a readable title-page, is, to some extent, autobiographical' and has concluded paradoxically that, no text is, nor can be, autobiography (de Man 1979: 919). His view coincides with other critics who apply what Susan Stanford Friedman terms 'Lacanian and structuralist precepts of the self as a fictive entity constituted in images or words that cannot refer back to the "real" world because of the inherently non-referential nature of all signs' (Stanford Friedman 1988: 37). However, Friedman argues that such a definition still gives pre-eminence to the idea posited by Georges Gusdorf, that autobiography is dependent on a 'conscious awareness of the singularity of each individual life' (Gusdorf 1980: 29), and therefore on the existence of a person as a distinct, separate entity (albeit a false one). Such a definition is unhelpful when discussing women's autobiography as it does not take into account the absence of such a concept in the kind of culture inhabited by women (and marginalised beings or *Others* generally), whereby a woman 'cannot experience herself as an entirely unique entity because she is always aware of how she is being defined *as woman*'.[14]

---

[14] Friedman (1988: 38) citing Sheila Rowbotham, *Woman's Consciousness, Man's World.*

However, Gusdorf does concede that such conscious awareness of the self is the 'late product of a specific civilisation' (Gusdorf 1980: 29–30). The way Gusdorf describes the manner in which the individual has seen him- or herself up until this point, in other words throughout most of human history, can be detected in the women's self-writing explored in this book, and might explain the debate about the status of such writing as autobiography, '[. . .] the individual does not oppose himself to all others; he does not feel himself to exist outside of others, and still less against others, but very much *with* others in an interdependent existence that asserts its rhythms everywhere in the community [. . .]' (Gusdorf 1980: 30).

Women writers without a tradition of autobiography are unlike the man referred to by Gusdorf who, 'takes the trouble to tell of himself' because he 'knows that the present differs from the past and that it will not be repeated in the future'. Their writing draws attention to women's absence from official history and the fact that women's present reality very often does *not* differ from the past and *is* repeated in the future. It appears not to be 'true' autobiography to Gusdorf because, for him, women seem not to have 'emerged from the mythic framework of traditional teachings and [. . .] entered into the perilous domain of history' (Gusdorf 1980: 30). In other words, he implies that women have a different sense of self. Nancy Chodorow suggests that (according to object-relations theory) it is the difference in the mother–child relationship between boys and girls that leads to this different sense of self in women. Whereas boys learn to repress their love for their first 'love object' – the mother – for girls this relationship continues throughout the process of individuation – the emergence of a separate identity (Chodorow 1978: 166).[15] Gusdorf's definition of autobiography, therefore, does not encompass women's autobiographical writing.

Estelle C. Jelinek writes that there is consensus among critics that 'a good autobiography not only focuses on its author but also reveals his connectedness to the rest of society'.[16] Thus, women's autobiographies, more concerned with the private space than the public and concentrating on their personal lives, have often been considered 'insignificant' by critics.[17] However, since women's lives have more often than not been radically different from men's,

[15] According to Lacan, the girl-child as well as the boy wants to be her mother's lover but is automatically excluded from this possibility by her lack of a penis and this is extended to the idea, in the words of Rosalind Minsky, that she also lacks 'what is required to be an active, self-determining subject in the world' (Minsky 1996: 159).

[16] Jelinek (1987a: 5–6). Jelinek also states that most autobiographies accepted as such by the canon, emphasise the writer's 'work life, their professional success, or their connectedness to current political or intellectual history' (10).

[17] Though as Marjorie Agosín writes in 'From a Room of One's Own to the Garden', 'in women's culture, there is a marked connection between public and private life' (Agosín 1995: 11).

it follows that their autobiographies should differ in content and style.[18] Jelinek suggests how this difference in attitude to the writing of men's and women's lives might be illustrated:

> imagine how a sampling of women's autobiographies might be described by merely changing their authors' gender [. . .] As men, these women's experiences would be described in heroic or exceptional terms: alienation, initiation, manhood, apotheosis, transformation, guilt, identity crises, and symbolic journeys. As women their experiences are viewed in more conventional terms: heartbreak, anger, loneliness, motherhood, humility, confusion, and self-abnegation. (Jelinek 1987*a*: 4–5)

Another criterion of the autobiographical canon, according to Jelinek, is the fallacy that 'autobiographers write about their inner or emotional life'. In fact, most autobiographies, whether by men or women, do not contain intimate and introspective detail about the author's life nor references to siblings. All of the works discussed in this book contain such references, but it must be remembered that all the writers, with the exception of Campobello, disguise their protagonists either with a name different from their own or with no name at all, and designate the works as 'novels'. Similarly, they all contain references to important historical events in Mexico, or in the case of Poniatowska's *La 'Flor de Lis'*, to important families, as well as to details of the personal lives of the writers.[19]

Castellanos' novel, *Balún-Canán*, has been labelled autobiographical by many critics and this is discussed at length by Catherine Grant in her thesis on Castellanos (Grant 1991: Ch.3). In the case of *Balún-Canán*, the choice of a girl-child as narrator in the first and third parts of the novel implies an interest, on behalf of the author, in representing the voices of the marginalised in Mexican society and is in keeping with her interest in the situation of women and Indians. Also, Castellanos' choice of a first-person voice is attributable to the autobiographical nature of her first novel. In *Balún-Canán*, the protagonist feels guilty for the death of her younger brother; the fact that Castellanos' younger brother in real life died, may be part of the reason – albeit unconscious – why she needed to write her guilt and in confessing, absolve it.

Garro's work, *Los recuerdos del porvenir*, makes no claims to being auto-

---

[18] Jelinek (1987*a*) reveals that the production of autobiographies by men corresponds to important historical events; whereas that by women corresponds to periods of increased opportunities, such as the Progressive era of 1890 to the First World War, and during the late 1960s and 1970s. Jelinek is, however, referring to the United States. In the case of the writers whose work is discussed here, the novels are clearly written in a time of relative peace and stability in Mexico, if not of progress for women.

[19] It is also significant that this novel, though written in the 1950s, was not published until the 1980s because Poniatowska thought her own story insignificant. See Chapter Five for further detail and reference.

biographical although it was based on things that Elena Garro saw. In an interview with Michele Muncy, she said, 'Empecé a pensar, a acordarme de mi
infancia, de todo lo que he visto, de todo, y cuando ya lo había pensado todo,
cuando ya tenía la novela en la cabeza comencé a escribir y la acabé en un
mes' (I began to think about, to remember my childhood, about all that I have
seen, everything, and when I had thought about it all, when I already had the
novel in my head I began to write and I finished it in one month) (Muncy
1986: 68). Although the setting of Ixtepec is based on Iguala in Guerrero
where Garro lived as a child, and the Moncada family is, like the Garro
family, somewhat unconventional, there is no character in *Los recuerdos del
porvenir* that might obviously be Garro herself.[20]

Poniatowska's protagonist in *La 'Flor de Lis'* is clearly autobiographical,
although she herself refers to the work as fiction. Her narrator recalls with
humour and poignancy the relationship with her mother, and the process of
separation from her mother that she undergoes with the help of a priest.
Poniatowska discloses the usefulness of sensual stimuli in recalling past times
and childhood memories. Garro and Castellanos in their novels also explore
the concepts of memory and of time. Castellanos reveals how the pre-Columbian concept of time as circular or cyclical, still organises the lives of the
indigenous people of Chiapas in the 1930s. Garro contrasts the static time she
associates with inaction, with the linearity of dynamic historical time and the
way 'masculine' and 'feminine' characters are governed by each of them.

Thus, the first-person narrators in these works by Campobello, Garro,
Castellanos and Poniatowska become a vehicle for the voice and views of the
authors without rendering the texts mere autobiographies in the traditional
sense. Just as Campobello, Castellanos and Poniatowska do with their child-
narrators in *Cartucho*, *Balún-Canán* and *La 'Flor de Lis'*, Garro disguises her
own voice in the form of the first-person plural (collective) narrator of the
pueblo of Ixtepec in *Los recuerdos del porvenir*. Another motive for disguise
might be an awareness of the too significant presence, or absence, of the
mother figure in their novels and a desire for detachment or privacy. The
importance of the mother figure for each of the protagonists is manifested
through an emphasis on the senses, which in psychoanalytic theory is linked
to the pre-verbal or Imaginary phase of development. The senses are associated, according to such theory, with the child's early relationship with the
mother, and the images reproduced through them in the novels represent the
ambivalent unconscious desires of the narrators/daughters for both greater
closeness to and independence from their mothers.

[20] However, the Moncada children play a game which they call 'la guerra de Troya',
which is also the title of one of Garro's short stories in which she and her sister appear with
the names Leli and Eva. Garro also refers to an incident in her childhood which appears in
Los recuerdos del porvenir (33) where Juan Moncada reminds the protagonist, Isabel, and
her brother Nicolás of when they tried to drown him in the river.

With regard to the writing of autobiography, the traditional reasons for doing so have varied from its being part of the process of development that most writers undergo to an expunging of guilt of some sort. John Updike ascribes writing autobiography to a 'Eurocentric, male, mid-life need to testify to the progress of life in the midst of living it'.[21] Debra Castillo rightly suggests that Updike's comment that it 'possibly stems from a desire to set the record straight before senility muddles in', would sound 'hopelessly foreign to a Latin American woman' who, 'in writing from the margins of accepted literary culture [. . .] must continually, and on all levels re-negotiate the implicit contract between the subjective realms and the sociological and ideo-logical imperatives' (Castillo 1992b: 221). Castellanos, writes Castillo:

> [. . .] is a woman of many, and contradictory words. Accordingly, her intensely personal writing [. . .] refuses to enact the autobiographical pact that would reduce it to a single, if highly elaborate, thread. Her identification of herself, and by extension, all Mexican women with the cause of other marginalised peoples, especially the indigenous peoples of Mexico's provin-cial provinces, would prevent such reductionism. (Castillo 1992b: 221–22)

Garro, by contrast, in choosing the collective narrator of the *pueblo* for *Los recuerdos del porvenir* appears not to achieve a similar identification with the marginalised people of the town, as it is evident that the collective 'yo' of the narrator refers to the old, landed families rather than to the Indians or the pros-titutes. However, those families were to some extent marginalised as they were left behind by the era of progress following the Revolution. Many of them had their lands expropriated; these were distributed to the *caciques* of the Revolution and their unscrupulous supporters, who then became the *nouveaux riches* so despised by the old aristocracy. When choosing the collective narrator, Garro may well have been influenced by the multivocal nature of Campobello's work and also by her contemporary Juan Rulfo's work, *Pedro Páramo* published in 1955, shortly before she wrote *Los recuerdos del porvenir*. Whatever her reasons, the result of her choice of a collective narrator is to enhance the multivocal nature of her own vision of the Revolution and to provide a heteroglossic account from a group whose voice was not often heard in post-revolutionary Mexico.

MYTH AND THE MOTHER–DAUGHTER RELATIONSHIP

Castellanos considered that women are very often instrumental in the perpetuation of their own oppression, and the mother–daughter relationship is the key, therefore, to women's self-development (Poniatowska 1987).

---

[21] Cited in Castillo (1992).

Adrienne Rich supports this view when she writes that, 'it is the mother through whom patriarchy early teaches the small female her proper expectations. The anxious pressure of one female on another to conform to a degrading and dispiriting role can hardly be termed "mothering" even if she does this believing it will help her daughter to survive' (Rich 1995: 243). Marianne Hirsch believes that from Freud to Chodorow to Irigaray what has hardly changed is, 'the presentation of a mother who is overly invested in her child, powerless in the world, a constraining rather than an enabling force in the girl's development, and an inadequate and disappointing object of identification' (Hirsch 1989: 167). The mother–daughter relationship as the key to women's self-development – or lack of such – is confirmed in the works discussed here, but ambivalence is inherent to that relationship in each case. Although the child-narrators admire, or look up to their mothers, these are also consistently absent from the child's existence. This absence takes different forms, however, according to the social situation in which they find themselves. In *Cartucho* and *Las manos de mamá*, Nellie's mother works as a nurse in the Revolution; in *La 'Flor de Lis'*, Mariana's mother has an active social life among Mexico City's élite; in *Balún-Canán*, the *niña*'s mother has become a parent out of duty and a need to survive in provincial society rather than through a desire to mother, so she is absent emotionally from her daughter; and in *Los recuerdos del porvenir*, Isabel's mother is unable to communicate with her as her feelings of love are obscured by guilt. In some cases, care of the child is designated to a nursemaid, or nanny. (The case of *Los recuerdos del porvenir* is slightly different; first, because Garro's novel is not autobiographical and secondly, because the protagonist is an adolescent and, while she does not perceive her mother as being absent, she does not admire or look up to her either.) When referring to memory and the mother–daughter relationship, the works also share an emphasis on nature and the senses. The link between these has been clearly established by psychoanalysis, and is important when considering the autobiographical aspects of the novels. Marianne Hirsch writes with reference to the mother–daughter relationship and creativity, 'For Melanie Klein narrative [. . .] revolves [. . .] around the figure of the mother [. . .] The mother remains an important psychic presence throughout life, motivating even the production of art and culture' (Hirsch 1989: 100).

Thus motherhood – women's enforced destiny – was particularly strongly emphasised during the nation-building era in Mexico during the 1940s and 1950s, as it was in Europe and the United States following the loss of life after the two World Wars. Similarly, the fact that women had worked during the Revolution made it necessary to reinforce the notion of woman's role as mother and homemaker, supporting her working husband, so that the effective industrialisation of the country could take place.[22] Furthermore, the Catholic

---

[22] It also occurred during the Victorian era in Britain and the *porfiriato* in Mexico, both times of industrialisation when the ideal was that women should be the angel in the private

heritage with the figure of the Virgin mother, played an important part in the (re)creation of the myth of the *madre abnegada*, particularly after the anti-Catholic attitude of the government had been replaced by one of religious tolerance. This ideal was juxtaposed with the other type of woman – the whore – epitomised by the Malinche figure and with the cultivation of the third archetype, based on the model of Sor Juana, which formed the triad of roles to which women were expected to conform. The child-narrators/protagonists of the works discussed here are too young to be seen to have deviated from these models (with the exception of Isabel in *Los recuerdos del porvenir*, where this is indeed the case), though they are all depicted as different from other children, so it may be inferred that they will be different as women. However, all their mothers do indeed deviate from the ideal.

Nellie must vie with brothers, sisters and the fighters of the Revolution for attention from her mother whom she adores, but by whom she feels rejected. The *niña*'s mother is a distant and unapproachable figure so she must identify with her *nana* (wet-nurse) and her *nana*'s indigenous culture to procure maternal love and a sense of identity. Mariana worships Luz, as does Nellie, but sees herself as unworthy of such a glamorous mother and must compete with many other people for her attention. Isabel despises her mother in a typically adolescent way, apparently because she sees her as weak and conforming to her maternal role in trying to oblige her daughter to marry.

However, there is a more profound reason for the various types and degrees of estrangement between mothers and daughters. The mothers appear differently when seen objectively rather than from the point of view of their daughters – that is, when given a subjectivity largely denied them by psychoanalytic criticism (Hirsch 1989: 170).

In Garro's novel, the protagonist's mother, Ana Moncada, resents her daughter, Isabel, for what she sees as Isabel's betrayal of her own (Ana's) sexuality. Isabel's exuberant behaviour, which later is seen as promiscuous, reminds her of her own lasciviousness, of which she is ashamed, so she rejects her daughter and destroys any possibility of closeness between them. (Isabel, sensing this rejection as a young child, confides to her brother that she does not love her mother and it is clear that she prefers to spend time with him.) Mariana's mother is loving but distant. An active woman, who finds the restricted social role of her Mexican counterparts frustrating, she prefers to indulge in a variety of activities, from driving around Mexico to horse-riding and cards, until she believes she finds meaning in her life when she meets a radical priest. The *niña*'s mother, a reluctant mother, under social pressure to produce a male heir and estranged from her husband, hands the care of her daughter over to a *nana* and concentrates her attention on nurturing her son.

---

space of the house for the husband returning from his work in the public spaces of factory and office. The reality of course, was always different for working class women who also worked in the factories.

Nellie's mother is seen to be an independent woman who works as a seamstress to support her children (and indeed, has more children after her husband
dies) and also works as a nurse to help the wounded of the Revolution.

From the child's point of view, this pattern conforms to Carolyn Heilbrun's
idea that, 'The heroines of most novels by women have (either no mothers, or)
mothers who are ineffectual or *unsatisfactory*' (Heilbrun 1988*b*: 118, [my
emphasis]). All of these representations, whether intended or interpreted as
positive or negative, suggest the fundamental importance of the mother in a
girl's life. However, Hirsch writes of an 'ideal psychoanalysis' which would
not always see the mother–daughter relationship from the child's viewpoint,
from which daughters speak for mothers, but from a mother's perspective, in
which mothers speak for themselves (Hirsch 1989). I would argue that, the
heteroglossia of the texts discussed here, does allow the mothers to speak for
themselves, albeit with voices given to them by their daughters (as authors).

The importance of the mother–daughter relationship has become a focus
for recent (often feminist) psychoanalytical criticism, which has revised
Freud's apparent reluctance to broach that topic. It appears that the child must
participate in a contradictory struggle which entails simultaneously fighting to
hold on to the mother and mother-love, while trying to escape being part of
the mother rather than an individual. Linda Ruth Williams writes that Luce
Irigaray's 'And One Doesn't Stir Without the Other' 'depicts a difficult
version of the notion of fluid boundaries between mother and daughter,
against which the daughter must struggle if she is to gain any form of independence' (Williams 1995: 1180). Irigaray's own words would seem to sum
up the feelings of the writers rather than those of the narrators/protagonists of
the works discussed in this book, 'Don't engulf yourself or me in what flows
from you into me. I would like both of us to be present. So that the one doesn't
disappear in the other, or the other in the one. So that we can taste each other,
feel each other, listen to each other, see each other – together' (Irigaray 1981:
61).

The words of Heilbrun spring to mind again: 'The heroines of most novels
by women have either no mothers, or mothers who are ineffectual or unsatisfactory.' In the case of Poniatowska's and Garro's heroines, the question
arises as to whether the narrators' mothers are indeed ineffectual and unsatisfactory or merely appear so in the eyes of their daughters. It seems to be the
case that the daughters in each of these novels make their mothers seem unsatisfactory, although they are not viewed as such by other characters in the
novels, because they are unsatisfied in their desire for their mothers.
According to Adrienne Rich, we can never have enough of our mother's love
however much she is prepared (or able) to give: 'Few women growing up in
patriarchal society can feel mothered enough; the power of our mothers, whatever their love for us and their struggles on our behalf, is too restricted' (Rich
1995: 243). Although difficult and painful for the child, nevertheless the
passing from the Imaginary and dependence on the Mother, to the Symbolic

and independence in the world of the Father, is seen by psychoanalysts as essential to healthy psychic development. Lacan uses the term the 'Imaginary' or the 'Mirror Stage' for our first fragile identity because although it *feels* real it depends on an image of ourselves which is reflected back from someone else (usually our mother), from whom we are separated (Minsky 1996: 141).[23] He uses the term 'the Symbolic' to describe the stage when language is learnt and the realm of the Father takes over from that of the Mother.

Thus Nellie's versions, for example, of her relationship with her mother and her witnessing of the Revolution can be read as metonyms for the realms of the Imaginary 'where identity has been based on a search for the same' (as when Nellie sees herself and her mother as one being), and of the Symbolic (where subjectivity is based on difference). In other words 'a transfer from the world we see, of the senses, to the world we speak, of the signifier, from the domain of the specular to the domain of the social' (Minsky 1996: 156).

Linked to the mother–daughter relationship then, is the idea of citizen/ mother-country (nation). In *La 'Flor de Lis'* in particular, the dual concept of mother/motherland emerges. The use of the mother-tongue is seen as having significance for the concept of belonging. Women, as Denise Kandiyoti observes 'bear the burden of being "mothers of the nation" '. She cites Yuval-Davies and Anthias as 'convincingly arguing that the control of women and their sexuality is central to national and ethnic processes' (Kandiyoti 1994: 376). According to Kate Millett, the mythification of Motherhood (the myth of women's mothering, nurturing and empathetic capacities) represents a strategy of subjugation (Millett 1991: 26). In *Los recuerdos del porvenir*, Isabel, in rejecting marriage and respectability, is thus transgressing not just private patriarchy (in the social tradition of small town families) but public patriarchy also, as her activity could be seen as destabilising society as a whole and therefore the nation.[24] With reference again to Carolyn Heilbrun's statement about the desire for control over one's life (Heilbrun 1988: 13), one possible way of gaining control is to *write* that life, as Isabel's mother and the narrator of *Balún-Canán* both attempt to do and as the four writers whose work is discussed here succeeded in doing.[25]

[23] Melanie Klein, affirms Minsky, 'writes about "positions" rather than "phases" of development to emphasise that both infant and adult can move from one psychical structure to the other' (Minsky 1996: 79).

[24] Kandiyoti also cites B. S. Walby (1990), as distinguishing between these two main forms of patriarchy: 'Private patriarchy is based on the relative exclusion of women from arenas of social life other than the household and the appropriation of their services by individual patriarchs within the confines of the home. Public patriarchy is based on employment and the state; women are no longer excluded from the public arena but subordinated within it'. She adds, 'Walby argues that the twentieth century has witnessed a major shift from private to public patriarchy' (Kandiyoti 1994: 377).

[25] Linda Ruth Williams notes that Cixous 'evokes a creative power into which women can tap if only they can relocate that "first attachment" to the mother within the self'

Thus, the two concepts of Motherhood and Multivocality though seemingly unconnected, are in fact related in a significant way. The heteroglossia found in much writing by marginalised people is a response to patriarchal society which is reproduced by mothering, that is, by the way mothers bring up boy children differently from girls. This ensures that females become the primary carers of children and the system is perpetuated: girls are brought up to be the mothers of future mothers and of citizens of the nation.[26]

HETEROGLOSSIA AND HISTORY

I will now consider the part played by heteroglossia in undermining official discourse about the events of the Mexican Revolution and about motherhood in Mexico at that time. Alan Riding writes of the Revolution, 'even this social disruption did not release women from their assignment as abnegated wives and mothers' (Riding 1987: 249). This is not strictly true, as the case of Nellie's mother in *Las manos de mamá* demonstrates, and as Debra Castillo explores in her book *Easy Women*. First, however, I shall clarify what is meant by the revolutionary era, as the Mexican Revolution has been dated in several ways.

The first date used with regard to the Mexican Revolution: 1910–1917, refers to the period of fighting that took place between the *revolucionarios* led by various charismatic generals and the *federalista* troops who supported the conservative government of Porfirio Díaz. It is in this period that Nellie Campobello's novellas *Cartucho* and *Las manos de mamá* are set. These works describe the relationship between Nellie and her mother against a background which shows the fighting men of the Revolution and the women who supported them during the struggle. At the same time, Campobello challenges the official discourse which subsequently arose, denigrating the northern protagonist of the Revolution, Pancho Villa.

A second phase of the Revolution took place between 1917 and 1935. This was a period of political instability marked by assassinations and the struggle for power by different factions of the victorious revolutionary side.[27] A particularly turbulent period, during the presidency of Plutarco Elías Calles (1924–1928) known as the Cristero Wars (1926–1929), came about in response to the

(Williams 1995: 1180, citing Cixous 1975 'Laugh of the Medusa').

[26] This is particularly well demonstrated by the example of the Nazi and Fascist States in Germany and Italy respectively, in the first half of the twentieth century, where myths were utilised to this end.

[27] It was the creation of the PNR (*Partido Nacional Revolucionario*) by Calles in 1929, and his (indirect) period of strong rule known as the *Maximato,* lasting until 1935, that finally diminished the power of the *caciques.* See Lorenzo Meyer (1976: 1194–96).

official persecution of the Church by the revolutionary government.[28] Bloody battles took place between the allegedly secular revolutionary troops and Catholic factions, *cristeros*, who defended both their right to worship and the power of the Church over – among other things – education.[29] Rosario Castellanos' novel *Balún-Canán* and Elena Garro's *Los recuerdos del porvenir* are both set during this period of *caciquismo* when political power in the provinces was in the hands of local petty tyrants, either ruthless military *caciques* or rich landowners with their own paramilitary forces.

A third revolutionary phase took place, according to certain historical accounts, between 1935 and 1960. The end of political wrangling and assassinations saw the firm entrenchment of the *Partido Revolucionario Institucional* (PRI) in power and the consequent institutionalisation of the Revolution, as Mexico attempted to consolidate its sovereignty. This led to a period of economic growth and stability as Mexico affirmed its place as an industrialised nation in the capitalist economy.

During the second phase of the Revolution, from 1920 onwards, a programme of Cultural Nationalism was begun, propagated by education as thousands of schools were set up in rural areas and typified by the Muralist movement with its great public homage to pre-Columbian culture, which became known as the 'Mexican Renaissance'. During the 1930s and 1940s the Golden Age of Mexican cinema and music was at its height. However, Mexico itself, during the 1940s under presidents Manuel Ávila Camacho (1940–46) and, more particularly, Miguel Alemán (1946–52), was engaging in international capitalism.[30] Alemán saw participation in the capitalist system

---

[28] Lázaro Cárdenas (1928–1934) was the first President to enjoy the six-year term in office which became the norm. See Skidmore and Smith (1989) and Lorenzo Meyer (1976) for an excellent overview of historical data.

[29] This was the theory at least, though the emblem worn by the troops of the Revolution was the image of the Virgin of Guadalupe, as seen in a painting by Fernando Leal, *Zapatistas at Rest* (1921), where the central figure wears an image of the Virgin on his *sombrero*. See Dore Ashton (no date: 585).

[30] Ávila Camacho moved away from Lázaro Cárdenas' left-wing land redistribution and nationalisation policies; supplied the US with raw materials at government-controlled prices; and began the *bracero* programme which allowed workers to go north to replace American field-workers fighting in World War II (Skidmore and Smith 1989: 234). Mexico's entry into the Capitalist system was due in part to the Second World War. Lorenzo Meyer (1981), writes that 'the history of the changes that took place in Mexico from 1940 onwards is basically the history of the development of a modern industrial base with all the consequences characteristic of this type of process: subordination of agriculture to industry, increase in urbanisation, growth of the tertiary sector, etc. [. . .]. In the 1950s it was an internationally accepted fact that the Mexican economy had begun a process of irreversible qualitative change [. . .]. As a consequence of world conflict, Mexican exports increased by 100 per cent between 1939 and 1945 [. . .]. In 1940 the country received 50 million dollars from tourism, in 1950 the sum was 233 million, which was equivalent to almost 50 per cent of the value of goods exported by Mexico that year' (Meyer 1981: 1277–82 [my translation]).

as the way forward but in order to accomplish this it was necessary to create
the idea of a Mexican nation, with a strong central government and political
and economic stability. Due to the reduced demand for so many migrant
workers when the Second World War ended, a solution was required to end
the endemic poverty in Mexico, and industrialisation was seen as that solution
(Skidmore and Smith 1989). In spite of the efforts of the *Secretaria de
Educación Pública*, by the 1950s the country was beginning to lose some of
its *mexicanidad* with the growth of the middle classes who were dissatisfied
with being on the margins of international culture and contemporaneity. 'Lo
mexicano' was seen as commercialised folklore and the importation of
consumer goods and films from the USA led to a desire for the 'American
way of life' (parodied in *La 'Flor de Lis'*). The discrepancy between official
and alternative discourses became clear and, as Carlos Monsiváis writes,
'Denostado en la prensa, el *american way of life* impera en la práctica'
(Reviled by the press, the American way of life prevails in practice).[31]

The idea of official and alternative discourse is also manifested in the
novels discussed in this book and this is observable in the two main characteristics that distinguish the first-person narrators. First, those narrators are not,
in the strictest sense, autobiographical; that is, they do not profess to be
recounting a factual and accurate account of the authors' lives nor of the
historical events that took place during and after the Mexican Revolution.
Secondly, the narrators do not concentrate entirely on the personal, unlike in
some self-writing by women, but rather present a wider critical view of
society, the Revolution and its consequences on a national level. This is the
heteroglossia of the texts.

It was not until the 1930s that Campobello's novellas appeared, and the
1950s when Garro and Castellanos were in their thirties, and Poniatowska in
her twenties, that their novels were written – in other words, between fifteen
and thirty years after the events they describe. Whether semi-autobiographical, as are *Cartucho, Las manos de mamá, Balún-Canán*, and *La 'Flor de
Lis'*, or mostly fictional, as is *Los recuerdos del porvenir*, all four accounts are
written through the reconstruction of the authors' memories and experiences.
This is inevitably done through the prism of a particular world view and
historical perspective.

As women writing in the conservative 1950s in Mexico, and having been
brought up as girls in the post-revolutionary 1930s, Garro and Castellanos, as
women, would necessarily have a different perspective on life from the more
well-known Mexican writers at that time, such as Juan Rulfo and Carlos
Fuentes (though their first novels *Pedro Páramo* (1955) and *La muerte de
Artemio Cruz* (1962) were also heavily heteroglossic). The same is true of
Poniatowska, educated to be part of an élite in which women were not

---

31 Monsiváis (1981: 1487–88). Television did not arrive in Mexico until 1957.

expected to work or write. Apart from a brief post-revolutionary period, when Campobello was growing up, and when women had greater freedom of opportunity, the narrow official view of the roles women were supposed to play in society had changed little since the times of Sor Juana to the mid-twentieth century when Garro, Castellanos and Poniatowska started writing. After the years of political wrangling and instability following the Revolution, the governing party (the then PRM – *Partido Revolucionario Mexicano*) saw economic development based on industrialisation and urbanisation as the way to establish Mexico within the capitalist system.[32] However, in spite of the availability of consumer goods, only a minority actually benefited from the distribution of wealth. This led to a change in the type of novel being written in Mexico around 1940, from the Novel of the Revolution, to the expression of pessimism as a result of frustration at the failure of the Revolution (Julieta Campos 1973: 144–45).

Urban congestion and consumerism (satirised by Castellanos in her plays and short stories) were considered, writes David G. La France, a necessary part of development. This process, along with a renewed emphasis on political centralisation, had begun in the nineteenth century under the leadership of Porfirio Díaz, but in the 1940s and 1950s, particularly under Miguel Alemán (1946–52), it was consolidated. The official party was by this time firmly entrenched, Alemán having reorganised it, renaming it the PRI. The apparent stability did not depend on democratic participation, however. Society, as I have indicated, was at its most conservative since before the disruption of the Revolution; women's roles were clearly defined and most women were still marginalised insofar as participation in the power structures was concerned.

DIFFERENCE AND BINARY OPPOSITIONS

Among the similarities that the novels I discuss here share, are their use of the first person 'yo', and the condition of marginality of the narrators. Other common denominators are the reconstruction of events or situations triggered largely by memory, and a plot based on a series of incidents which give the works a cinematographic quality. However, in turn, this raises questions regarding the accuracy or inaccuracy of memory, including the degree to which distortion occurs as memories are recalled and recounted and the (unconscious) process of selection and embellishment or elimination of certain details and events. The answer to these questions surely lies in Coe's suggestion that the writer of the Childhood is concerned with *his* (or her) truth rather than some kind of universal truth.

Bound up with the Other's difficulty in expressing his/her truth is the

---

[32] Skidmore and Smith (1989: 233–35).

notion of silence. Silence is usually associated with the marginalised as they are seen as the ones who do not have a voice; and speech with 'los que mandan' (literally: those who give the orders/command). However, silence, as well as being a condition enforced on the weak by dominant patriarchal figures, has also been appropriated by them and used for subversive ends. Hugo Gutiérrez Vega, writing about silence in *Pedro Páramo*, sums up the reason this silence has come about among the peasants of central and western Mexico, where *Los recuerdos del porvenir* also is set:

> Los campesinos de esas regiones son grandes ahorradores de palabras [. . .]. Los muchos siglos de lucha con la tierra, con los amos feudales, los elementos adversos, la demagogia, la corrupción y el abandono, los han hecho callados y los han llenado de una explicable desconfianza. Tal vez por estas razones huyan de la verbosidad. (Gutiérrez Vega 1969: 75–82)

> [The peasants of these regions are great savers of words [. . .]. The many centuries of struggle with the land, with feudal masters, adverse elements, demagoguery, corruption and abandonment have made them silent and have filled them with an understandable mistrust. Perhaps for these reasons they shun verbosity.]

Debra Castillo explains the origins of this silence with reference to *Balún-Canán*:

> Marginalised peoples are excluded from the great conversation that makes up national discourse; their voices and their very being are erased as an unpleasantly dissonant background. The Indians, says the Elder Brother, are walled up in their silence at the time of the conquest; the contemporary landowners continue to enforce this historically established linguistic tradition. (Castillo 1992b: 234–35)

This 'linguistic tradition' is seen in the way César Argüello, the landowner in *Balún-Canán*, speaks to the Indians, using the few phrases of Tzeltal he knows, ignoring with the impunity of the powerful anything they say beyond what he expects to hear. Women are given little more status as they too 'are condemned to silence and invisibility. Unheard and unseen, they offer, on another level, the dominant class's unacknowledged counterpart to the repression of the Indians' (Castillo 1992b: 234–35).

All the novels discussed here refer to the ways in which those in power in society use myths to hold on to that power and to the effect this has on people's lives: Campobello addresses the post-revolutionary government's demonisation of Villa; Garro adopts classical myth and turns her heroine to stone; Poniatowska gently mocks ideas of European superiority and Castellanos considers how certain myths about the indigenous people are used to perpetuate their oppression. The way in which women and indigenous people

are characterised has been a major subject for the attention of critics, particularly of Castellanos' work. Violence and death in Mexican culture play a
central role in Campobello's, Castellanos' and Garro's novels. Campobello
was a young girl during the fighting years of the Revolution, as were Castellanos and Garro during the era of *caciquismo*. So memories associated with
the violence would have been in the conscious and unconscious minds of
these three writers.[33] Poniatowska arrived in Mexico fifteen years too late to
witness the persecution of the priests during the process of secularisation of
the state following the Mexican Revolution, but she does witness the deep
suspicion felt towards a priest, which she records in *La 'Flor de Lis'*.

Reference to historical events is normally linked to the notion of linear
time. The binary opposition linear/cyclical time associates (positive) linear
time with the masculine and (negative) cyclical time with the feminine. A
striking similarity appears between *Balún-Canán* and *Los recuerdos del porvenir* in the expression of differing concepts of time. In both novels (masculine) linear time is allied with the historical process and progress and cyclical
(women's) time is linked with the inescapable nature of (women's) fortune (a
turning wheel in classical mythology) and with the repeating cycles in the
unchanging world inhabited by the indigenous people. Different levels of
reality and alternative worlds, including the realms of death and human
memory are also invoked by the notion of different types of time. In *Balún-
Canán*, the child-narrator, identifies both with the linear time associated with
her *ladino* world and the cyclical time analogous to the indigenous world. Part
of her crisis of identity relates to her being torn between the two worlds which
originate in her love for her indigenous *nana* and her *desire* to be loved by her
biological mother. In *Los recuerdos del porvenir*, Isabel, the protagonist,
identifies with the linear time she associates with the occupying military force
led by General Rosas (patriarchal historicity) and with the cyclical time
(indigenous fatalism) she is submerged in, due to her upbringing by her atyp-
ical parents, in a small provincial town where little has changed in her life-
time. Both linear and cyclical time may be seen as positive – the former being
associated with action and the latter with imagination, but, equally, both may
become static time which is seen as negative and stultifying and in opposition
to action. For example, violence in *Los recuerdos del porvenir* is linked with
the notion of static time. Chapters Three and Four will explain my views on
how the concepts of circular and linear time are used in *Balún-Canán* and *Los
recuerdos del porvenir*. The two concepts of time are related to the different
characters to show the ways that some of them transgress their designated
male and female roles.

A further binary opposition appears in the emphasis on time and memory.
This ties in with the importance in the novels attributed to fiction, storytelling

---

[33] As are, for example, memories of the hiding and subsequent killing of the priests;
events which occur in both *Balún-Canán* and *Los recuerdos del porvenir*.

and writing (and what is often considered the childlike quality of a belief in magic and illusion), and the writing of 'factual' accounts of historical events. 'Child' and 'memory' are linked in the notion of 'Childhood' writing. According to Coe, the writing of the Childhood started with Rousseau, developed with the Romantics, and culminated in the archetypal novel of remembrance by Proust. It is known that Castellanos read Proust and it seems likely that Garro, while perusing her father's extensive library, also encountered his work. Armand F. Baker suggests that Proust used Bergson's theory of time, whereby, to reunite today's with yesterday's self – one only needs to *remember*.[34] Furthermore, states Baker, Proust 'was more interested in (the idea of the fusion of different temporal planes in the consciousness and) the use of the senses to evoke time' (Baker 1968: 22). The relation between the senses and memory is clear in all the works discussed in this book but plays a definitive role in *Los recuerdos del porvenir* and *Balún-Canán*, where different notions of time are suggested by images relating to the senses. I have already discussed the importance of the senses as a trigger for memory.[35] The mirror is another device used in Garro's work to symbolise the passing of time and memory, and by both Garro and Castellanos, as a door into another world or the reflection of an alternative reality. However, it is also a trigger to memory through sight. Memory is stimulated by the association of a past-recorded experience with a present percept; thus sight, sounds, smells, and touch are used by all four writers to evoke memories. The influence of Freud and Jung on literature of this period is well-documented and psychoanalysis was starting to become popular from the 1950s onwards in Mexico.[36] Freud's work on dreams revealed that some of the symbols in dreams are the same as those that have influenced human consciousness throughout history and also

---

[34] Baker's clear and concise account of the history of theories of time since the Ancient Greeks clarified my thoughts on this area. I have borrowed from his text, to illustrate the link between Heraclitus and Proust. According to the theory put forward by Heraclitus (540–470 BC), the Universe exists in a state of constant change so that a man cannot put his foot twice into the same river and permanence is an illusion. This theory was redeveloped by Bergson (1859–1941) who believed that not only is the river different but so also is the person extending his (or her) foot. Intervening theories were postulated by Descartes, Pascal and Hume. These ideas culminated in the late eighteenth century with a reaction against continuous flux due to the discovery of the *affective memory* – the faculty that recuperates feelings and emotions from the past and relives them. Through memory, human beings can escape from the present and form a link between the present and past self. This is where Rousseau comes in, as he explored the use of memory to write his own 'Childhood' (Baker 1968).

[35] Genevieve Lloyd (1993: 20) in 'Being in Time', writes that St Augustine 'compares memory to a "great field or a spacious palace . . . a store-house for countless images of all kinds which are conveyed to it by the senses" ' (X; 8; 214).

[36] In 1959 Santiago Ramírez published *El mexicano, psicología de sus motivaciones*, and the Asociación Psicoanalítica Mexicana was founded in 1960. Castellanos was very aware of this interest in psychoanalysis and mentions Ramírez in a letter to Ricardo, her husband (*Cartas a Ricardo*).

appear in myths and folk-tales. He also revealed that 'our perceptions are linked with one another in our memory [. . .] We speak of this fact as "association" ' (Freud 1991: 524). Also relevant here is Jung's theory that there exists a direct contact between a person's subconscious and the universal consciousness of the whole human race. This contact, according to Jung, explains why in the subconscious of all men there is a tendency to the recreation of myths and images which are repeated throughout history, creating a type of circular time (cited in Baker: 26). Maureen Ahern (1989) writes that Castellanos had discovered that one way of understanding a culture's attitudes toward women was by studying its myths.[37] Simone de Beauvoir affirms that, 'Cyclical time can be associated with stultifying "immanence" or with the danger of petrifaction' (de Beauvoir 1972: 94). This concept is particularly appropriate with regard to *Los recuerdos del porvenir*, in view of the fate of Isabel Moncada.

One of the advantages of having an alternative narrator is that she/he can be identified with a notion of time which is outside the historicity associated with the 'rational, white, adult male'. There are two reasons for this. The first is the obvious exclusion of women and 'Other' narrators from the writing of history, and the second, the idea that, due to this very exclusion, these alternative narrators avoid being governed by, or living in, a world of chronological time. Circular time, says de Beauvoir (1972), could be described as the space to which women are banished when they are exiled from history.[38] Some Other subjects, particularly children and indigenous people, are believed to possess a different notion of time anyway. Whether this is of a cyclical nature or in some way outside the linear time of history, it is believed to afford them doors to different worlds or realities. In Garro's and Castellanos' novels it is symbolised by the gift of illusion which is often lost by the time adulthood is reached.

---

[37] 'Otra vez Sor Juana', presents Castellanos' ideas on women as 'myth and silence' in Mexico.

[38] De Beauvoir adds, '(Julia) Kristeva describes it spectacularly differently, reclaiming it as a space dizzying in its vastness rather than as "confinement or restriction to a narrow round of uncreative or repetitious duties" ' (de Beauvoir 1972: 63).

2

MOTHER, MEMORY AND MULTIVOCALITY IN NELLIE CAMPOBELLO'S *CARTUCHO* AND *LAS MANOS DE MAMÁ*

> [. . .] there is no bottom, none, to a child's bound-
> less love and demand for love, there is *no* satis-
> faction possible [. . .].[1]

INTRODUCTION

Cartucho, Nellie Campobello's first novella, was published in 1931 and
Las manos de mamá was begun in 1934 and published in 1937.[2] Both have
been the subject of discussion by critics for having (at the time of publication)
an unconventional narrative technique and construction – there is no plot.
There has also been considerable debate about their status as novels and as
memoirs or autobiography.[3] However, Campobello's biographical details
clearly reveal the autobiographical nature of *Cartucho* and *Las manos de
mamá*.

Nellie Francisca was born in Villa Ocampo, Durango, in the north of
Mexico on 7 April 1900, though, in an interview with Emmanuel Carballo she
gives her date of birth as 7 November 1909.[4] Her family had owned a large
hacienda in Villa Ocampo since 1680. Her ancestors had helped found the
town where she was born and Campobello was proud of her indigenous roots.
The family lived in Durango, then Chihuahua, where she heard stories and

---

1   Juliet Mitchell (1990: 57).
2   Second editions of *Cartucho* (expanded and altered) and of *Las manos de mamá*
(less altered but illustrated by José Clemente Orozco) appeared in 1940 and 1949 respectively. A third and final edition (in Spanish) appeared in 1960 under the title *Mis libros*.
The two works were translated and published in the same volume as *Cartucho/My
Mother's Hands* in 1988.
3   Valeska Strickland Nájera (1980: 53–58) refers to the works as Campobello's 'dos
novelas autobiográficas' and has observed that the changes to the second and third publica-
tions indicate her desire to make the works more novelesque and less like memoirs. I am
indebted to Strickland Nájera (1980) and Catherine Nickel (1990: 117–127) for most of the
biographical details on Campobello.
4   See Poniatowska (1988*b*: viii), and Carballo (1965) respectively. Dates cited in
other sources, for example Michèle Muncy (1990) vary between 1909 and 1913.

witnessed events of the Revolution, its battles and soldiers until they moved to Texas, after the death of her father.[5] Her mother later remarried an American doctor called Stephen Campbell. When her mother died in 1923 Nellie and five of her siblings moved to Mexico City where she and her sister Gloria, attended the English Institute. She retained a love of the outdoors, rural life and indigenous culture and traditions and this was reflected in her interest in folk music, dance and the *corrido* (ballad). After working for several years in the Ministry of State Education (*Secretaría de Educación Pública*), Campobello was the first woman to be named Director of the National Dance School (*Escuela Nacional de Danza*) in 1937. She had no formal education, having been taught by an aunt and her mother, but she was a novelist, poet, journalist and essayist as well as dancer and choreographer. A love of freedom was inculcated in her by her mother, Rafaela Luna, who, recognising her daughter's reluctance to be confined by formal schooling, took on the task of educating her, with the help of an aunt. Her indigenous heritage with its traditional respect for nature is evident in her artistic expression (prose, poetry and dance).

The two novellas describe a vision of the Mexican Revolution and a mother. This is achieved by various means including: through the *eyes* of a little girl called Nellie (who is the first-person narrator)[6] and of her mother; through her mother's *hands* and the associations these bring to Nellie's mind; and through the *voices* belonging to the people of the north of Mexico. Thus the senses play a significant part in this analysis. Although Campobello wrote them after she moved to Mexico City, it is the north of Mexico which provides the background to these novellas.

Cartucho, unlike other novels of the Revolution, such as Martín Luis Guzmán's *El águila y la serpiente* (*The Eagle and the Serpent*), does not go into detail about its battles or heroism. Instead, it presents short pieces described variously as *cuadros, estampas* and *vignettes* which, in a few lines, provide a vivid portrait of the heroes and villains of the Revolution and the often terrible circumstances of their deaths. Stark yet poetic they depict a series of impressions, tinged with nostalgia and engraved on Nellie's memory. Although essentially happy, Nellie's childhood was, at the same time, darkened by the shadow of violence of the Mexican Revolution and by the premature death of her beloved mother. *Las manos de mamá*, continues the series of impressions in a more lyrical and personal mode in which Nellie pays homage, even more than in *Cartucho*, to her mother. In this chapter I

---

5   According to Michèle Muncy (1990), he was one of Villa's generals and died in the battle of Ojinaga in 1914.
6   Nellie is Nellie Campobello; the mother is Rafaela Luna, Campobello's own mother. Henceforth I shall use 'Nellie', when referring to the narrator and 'Campobello' when referring to the writer.

shall discuss the two works together as *Las manos de mamá* is, effectively, a continuation of *Cartucho*.

The objectives of this chapter are twofold: to explore the ambivalent nature of the mother–daughter relationship and to reveal the presence of multi-vocality (heteroglossia *and* polyphony)[7] in Nellie Campobello's two novellas. This will be achieved by an analysis of the way the senses work in the texts and through a discussion of the use of binary oppositions. The opposition sight/touch is the one which appears most frequently. It suggests the process of looking, associated with the male gaze and desire, language and writing and that of touch, associated with the relationship between mother and child during the pre-verbal phase in childhood.[8] My exploration of the mother–daughter relationship proposes to reveal the complexity of that bond and how it influences the memories Nellie has of her mother.[9] It will expose the heteroglossia that emerges in the dissenting voice of the mother, who transgresses her role as *madre abnegada*, and the ambivalence of Nellie's filial love, as she attempts to come to terms with the feelings of loss produced by her mother's death. It will also reveal the way Campobello presents the mother's discourse as woman (not just mother) through the character of Rafaela. Finally it will describe how a multivocal account of the Revolution is produced through the polyphony of the different voices of the people of the north.

ALTERNATIVE VOICES

Campobello chooses to narrate through the voice of her childhood, but with the inevitable intrusions from time to time of the adult/authorial voice. Even within the child's discourse, the disclosure of Nellie's ambivalent feelings produces different discourses. Nellie reveals that the feelings of overwhelming love and admiration for her mother conceal resentment for what she perceives to be a lack of maternal attention towards her. Heteroglossia is also present, therefore, in the clash of these two discourses: that of Nellie's ideal-ised view of her mother as *madre abnegada* (as personified by the Madonna

---

   [7] The clash of antagonistic social forces and discourses interacting on equal terms, respectively (Roberts in Morris 1994).
   [8] Griselda Pollock (1988) writes, 'Lacanian theories of desire and the imaginary introduce a function for the image as a means to regain visual access to the lost object' (147). Feminist theory applied to the reading of images identifies the male gaze as a means of possessing the (female) object; see Mulvey (1975). By looking at her mother, Nellie attempts to maintain the closeness that existed during the pre-Oedipal phase of their relationship.
   [9] According to Julia Kristeva (1987), there is an inextricable link between a subject's linguistic and psychic processes.

figure), and her expression of feelings of neglect by a mother who appears to transgress that myth.

At the same time, heteroglossia appears in a third, maternal discourse, represented by Nellie's mother, which, by its very presence counteracts the silence which psychoanalysis posits as the lot of mothers. Marianne Hirsch writes, 'The adult woman who is a mother, in particular, continues to exist only in relation to her child, never as a subject in her own right. And in the maternal function, she remains an object, always distanced, always idealized or denigrated, always mystified, always represented through the small child's point of view' (Hirsch 1989: 167). Rafaela does not live up to the image of the ideal mother as she has a life of her own as a woman, as a seamstress and as a nurse to the casualties of the Revolution. Campobello depicts, then, a mother–daughter relationship modelled on her own relationship with her mother, that does not conform to the ideal as it gives her mother a voice that is not exclusively maternal.

As well as dialogic from the point of view of mother–daughter or daughter–mother discourse, Campobello's novellas can be read as dialogic in a national context.[10] They also present an alternative discourse to the official history of the Revolution, as does Castellanos' *Balún-Canán*. During the 1930s, when Campobello wrote these novellas, official discourse denigrated Pancho Villa by casting him in the role of unruly barbarian. Campobello clearly felt an obligation to set the record straight regarding the calumny that had been heaped on Pancho Villa subsequent to his assassination in 1923. In an interview with Emmanuel Carballo in 1958, she states that she wrote *Cartucho* 'para vengar una injuria' because the other novels written about the battles of the Revolution 'Están repletos de mentiras contra los hombres de la Revolución, principalmente contra Francisco Villa' (They are full of lies about the men of the Revolution, principally about Francisco Villa) (Carballo 1965: 336). She wanted to redeem Villa who was reviled in the post-revolutionary period when Mexican history was being re-written by the Revolutionary Party (by then institutionalised as the PRI). Campobello states: 'Escribí en este libro lo que me consta del villismo, no lo que me han contado' (I wrote in this book what I know first hand about the Revolution, not what I have been told) (Carballo 1965). In the *Prólogo* to *Mis libros*, Campobello reveals the reasons she felt compelled to write her own alternative version and her feelings about the new leaders: '[. . .] amante de la verdad y de la justicia, humanamente hablando, me vi en la necesidad de escribir' (a lover of truth and justice, speaking as a human being, I felt it was necessary for me to write). She also explains why she chose to have a child-narrator for her novellas:

---

[10] Dialogic refers here to the dialogue produced between two discourses. Bakhtin (1981: 279–80) argued that every utterance or discourse is a response to another utterance or discourse.

Busqué la forma de poder decir, pero para hacerlo necesitaba una voz, y fui
hacia ella. Era la única que podía dar el tono, la única autorizada: era la voz
de mi niñez. Usar de su aparente inconsciencia para exponer lo que supe
era la necesidad de un decir sincero y directo. (Campobello 1960: 12–13)

(I searched for the way to be able to speak, but to do it, I needed a voice,
and I eventually found it. It was the only one that could give it the right
tone, the only one authorised to speak: the voice of my childhood. By using
its apparent unawareness to expose what I knew was the need for a sincere
and direct way of speaking.)

She refers to the injustices and betrayal of the Revolution and to the deliberate denial of the truth by those who are in power 'lo que no desean saber los
que día a día nos oprimen y nos castigan, negando a nuestros padres y negán-
donos' (what those who daily oppress and punish us, disavowing our ancestors and disavowing us, do not want to know) (Campobello 1960). However,
she knew her task would not be easy as she also explains in the *Prólogo*:

Mi tema era despreciado, mis héroes estaban proscritos. A Francisco Villa
lo consideraban peor que al propio Atila. A todos sus hombres los clasifi-
caban de horribles bandidos y asesinos. Yo leía esto día a día, escuchaba las
odiosas calumnias y comprendía la injusticia, la barbarie de estos nuevos
ricos mexicanos,[11] hartos de dinero, del dinero que robaban, a este pueblo
al cual tanto defendió aquel glorioso señor general don Francisco Villa, y lo
atacaban sistemáticamente con el solo propósito de desvirtuarlo y destruirle
su personalidad de gran mexicano y de guerrero genial.

(Campobello 1960: 14)

(My subject was despised, my heros were banned. Francisco Villa was
considered worse than Attila himself. All his men were labelled horrible
bandits and murderers. I used to read this day after day; I listened to the
hateful calumny and understood the injustice and the barbarism of these
new rich Mexicans, with too much money, money that they stole from the
people that that glorious general Don Francisco Villa defended so
staunchly. They attacked him systematically with the sole intention of
ruining his reputation and destroying his character as a great Mexican and
general of genius.)

Campobello knew her frankness would not be well received by those in
authority and realised that her alternative discourse would inevitably turn
them against her. She new that she was making herself vulnerable 'to being
utterly squashed herself' (Campobello 1960). Such alternative discourse

11 Campobello's family had owned a large *hacienda* since 1680 and the social milieu
she frequented was that of the aristocracy. However, she despised the *nuevos ricos*, those
who had made their fortune with the Revolution at the expense of the *pueblo* (*Prólogo*
1960: 12–13).

regarding Pancho Villa provides, in the words of Doris Meyer, an 'oppositional challenge to the historiography controlled by Mexico's ruling classes'
(Meyer 1996: 48).[12]

Campobello is considered by Max Aub to be the most 'interesting' female
novelist of the Revolution and María Luisa Ocampo (*Bajo el fuego* 1947) is
the only other one he lists (Aub 1985: 21). Given the position of women at the
beginning of the twentieth century in Mexico, this has precise gender implications. Campobello alludes to the lack of liberty of females (of her social class)
to express themselves or to engage in physical pursuits, when she refers to her
exquisite feeling of freedom the first time she rides a horse:

> Aquel paseo, que sólo duró unos instantes, me hizo sentir una seguridad
> casi permanente de bienestar. Capté un aire nuevo, creí haber ido por un
> mundo desconocido, inmenso y libre. Ni las miradas directas de regaño, ni
> las opresiones psicológicas, ni la autoridad salvaje, ni las ropas ajustadas,
> ni nada que obstruyera la acción libre del movimiento físico y mental
> podría detener el impulso de que yo tuviera la parte de bienestar que me
> pertenecía. (Campobello 1960: 10)

> (That ride, which only lasted a few moments, gave me an almost permanent
> feeling of well-being. I took on a new air, I thought I had been to an
> unknown world, one that was immense and free. Neither direct scolding
> looks, nor psychological oppression, nor brutal authority, nor tight clothing,
> nor anything that obstructed freedom of physical or mental movement could
> stop the feeling that I was experiencing the well-being I deserved.)

If Campobello wrote *Cartucho* to set the record straight about the Revolution, she wrote *Las manos de mamá* for another reason: 'Lo compuse para
pagar una deuda que tenía contraída con Ella, con Mamá ' (I wrote it to pay a
debt I had with Her, with Mamma) (Campobello 1960). Campobello's ambivalent feelings for her mother are revealed in the following extract which bears
a striking resemblance to Castellanos' description of her lack of freedom to go
outside the house following the death of her younger brother. It shows how, in
spite of her love for her mother, she also longs for freedom:

> El placer de ir al encuentro de la brisa para tenerlo en el aliento me llevaba
> constantemente a buscar una ventana *de escape* para mi deseo imperante, y
> así fue como una mañana de primavera, estando en una huerta exuberante,
> donde el aire se cortaba pletórico de perfumes por la inmensa cantidad de
> flores, *me escapé de junto a mi mamá* y me deslicé a la orilla de un río [. . .]
> voy al encuentro de mi libertad, a la que amo más que a las olas del mar, y
> más, mucho más, que el amor. (Campobello 1960: 10 [my emphasis])

---

[12] Meyer's chapter proved most useful to my discussion on multivocality. Since she
discusses dialogics in *Cartucho*, I shall concentrate mostly on *Las manos de mamá* when
discussing that aspect of Campobello's work.

(The pleasure of going to find the breeze to be able to breathe it in led me to search constantly for a window of escape for my overriding desire, and so it was that one Spring morning, standing in a lush orchard, where the air was brimming with perfume due to the huge quantity of flowers, I escaped from my Mamma's side and slipped away to the river bank [. . .] I am going to meet my freedom, which I love more than the waves in the sea, and more, much more, than love.)

Although essentially autobiographical, then, these novellas do more than present only the visions of the child-narrator and textual author: they are at the same time multivocal. Campobello reflects a vision of the Revolution that belongs to herself, her mother and the people of the north, that is often opposed to the official version. The oral quality of the writing (confirmed by both Rand Morton and Nickel)[13] is linked to the polyphonic effect of the different voices heard by Nellie as a little girl.

FEMALE AUTOBIOGRAPHY AND MULTIVOCALITY

In women's writing from Latin America, as explained in Chapter One, the use of the first person is more often present in the form of testimonial writing, due to the dearth of autobiography by women. Campobello's work may be seen to prefigure such testimonial writing, as it is clear that she is bearing witness to events that took place during the Revolution. It is also a character-istic of women's writing, particularly in a Latin American context, that the writer's own voice is sublimated (so that the autobiographical nature of the writing is disguised). This may be due to the instability of the woman as subject due to women's historical condition as objects, or as subjects with low self-esteem. The consequence of such low self-esteem among women writers meant that they were unable to be at the centre of the text in a consistent way. Such inconsistency in positioning the self at the centre of the narrative is revealed, in Campobello's case, in the way the 'I' appears and disappears from the text. *Cartucho* begins with the first section, HOMBRES DEL NORTE and a description of 'Él' – the revolutionary fighter known as 'Cartucho' after whom the novella is named. Most autobiographies begin with 'I' or a sugges-tion that the narrative revolves around the first-person narrator. In *Cartucho*,

---

13 Rand Morton (1949: 164) writes that they have to be read as if they were spoken language and if you only take note of the punctuation you will get lost. Nickel (1990: 122), states that, 'virtually every piece in the book [. . .] combines various levels of past time with direct dialogue, producing the sensation of a past event told with the immediacy of an eternal present, a technique firmly rooted in the ancient art of story telling. The entire book is pervaded by the impression of the past being evoked as if memories were being plucked from a dream world'.

after the opening description of the man called *Cartucho*, the narrator's voice appears from under the table, '*Cartucho* no dijo su nombre. No sabía coser ni pegar botones. Un día llevaron sus camisas para la casa. *Cartucho* fue a dar las gracias. "El dinero hace a veces que la gente no sepa reir", *dije yo jugando debajo de una mesa*' (Cartucho didn't tell us his name. He didn't know how to sew or put buttons on. One day his shirts were brought to the house. Cartucho came to say thank you. "Money sometimes makes people forget how to laugh" I said, from where I was playing *under the table*) (*C*.929 [my emphasis]).[14] Thus Campobello's first-person narrator begins the 'autobiography' that is at the same time a biography of her mother and the other people of the north that she knew and observed as a child.

Gabriella de Beer writes that Campobello's contribution to the genre of the *memoria* or *estampa* 'is the personal testimony of the writer as observer or bystander' (de Beer 1979: 14). Campobello also gives a voice (by presenting their collective testimony) to the people of the north of Mexico at the time of the Revolution. She was writing from the perspective of her own experience, though she included not only what her own child's eyes and ears witnessed, but also what she overheard or was told by her mother and others. Hence, her perspective of the Revolution, and of life in the mountains of Chihuahua and Durango for the humble families of the north, becomes a multivocal view in that it does more than merely reflect her own childish impressions of that time and place. With regard to this collectivity Doris Meyer writes:

> Campobello turns the classical notion of autobiography – the writing of a timeless, private self – into the shared experience of a public, grounded self. The child's testimony acquires meaning and depth through ratification by other witnesses in the shifting optics of the text. Through this multi-focused approach, Campobello collectivizes her testimony and shares the narrative function with others. The true protagonist thus becomes the pueblo. Although individual voices speak through her memory, they all represent one group – the common people of the north who collectively witnessed the Revolution. (Meyer 1996: 53–54)

Multivocality (both heteroglossia and polyphony) in the texts works on two levels in *Cartucho* and *Las manos de mamá*. The first (a testimony that represents the many voices of the people of the north)[15] involves the instability of

14 Nellie Campobello (1937), *Cartucho*, in: Antonio Castro Leal (ed.) 1970. *La novela de la Revolución mexicana*, Mexico City: Aguilar (933). All subsequent textual references to *Cartucho* and *Las manos de mamá* will be to this edition, with the page number preceded by *C*. and *MM*. respectively.

15 In this way it is an early example of testimonial writing which prefigures both Elena Poniatowska's testimonial novel, *Hasta no verte Jesús mío* (1969) and her journalistic style testimony *La noche de Tlatelolco* (1971). It also prefigures the collective narrator of Ixtepec in Garro's *Los recuerdos del porvenir*.

the subject and leads to the apparent disappearance of the 'I' from the text. This, in turn, leads to strategies of concealment or disguise – the second effect of the heteroglossia and polyphony in both novellas. Multivocality conceals or disguises, by masking the jealousy that Nellie feels towards her brothers, the soldiers of the Revolution, her little sister, Gloria, and indeed, anyone who is a rival for her beloved mother's attention. Nellie's testimony alone would be that of what Wayne Booth terms a 'reflector'. However, in his chapter on the unreliable narrator Booth writes, 'a reflector whose own jealousy affects the action is no longer a mere reflector' (Booth 1961: 341). In other words, the reflector becomes involved and loses his/her impartiality and reliability. Put another way, the multivocality in *Cartucho* and *Las manos de mamá* disguises the fact that Nellie is an 'unreliable' narrator.

However, while Nellie may be an 'unreliable' narrator according to the traditional definition, such unreliability is merely a symptom of her instability as a subject. There is evidence that Campobello is an unreliable narrator of the facts of her own life, as the discrepancy between her claimed and recorded dates of birth reveals. Booth refers to the reader's 'all too frequent identification of author with first-person narrator', but such identification is often justified, as the large number of self-writing and autobiographical works by women (and recently by men also) demonstrates. Furthermore, traditional (largely male) definitions of autobiography do not necessarily apply to feminine autobiography. By feminine I do not refer exclusively to writing by women but rather to a form of self-writing which does not fit the description of autobiography as defined by Georges Gusdorf, in which the writer expresses a 'conscious awareness of the singularity of each individual life' (Gusdorf 1980: 29). For those deprived of selfhood or a subject position, such awareness does not exist. In what, then, does the particularly feminine nature of most autobiography written by women reside? According to Shari Benstock, it is in the instability of the subject that came about generally with the rise of Modernism, and is particularly apparent in women's writing after the First World War (she refers to European writers, citing Virginia Woolf, Isak Dinesen and Anaïs Nin, among others). Susan Stanford Friedman, on the other hand, suggests that it is the sense of '*identification, interdependence* and *community*' that Gusdorf dismisses from autobiographical selves' that are the main factors in the development of a woman's identity (Stanford Friedman 1988: 38). In Campobello's work these two characteristics: the instability of the subject brought about by the traumatic experience of the Mexican Revolution, and the narrator's identification with her mother and others in their community, combine to form Nellie's narrative.

This is where the senses come into the equation. The many different voices of the people of the Revolution, as well as Nellie's ambivalent feelings for her mother, emerge in the text through a combination of sensory impressions transposed into descriptions related to what the protagonist sees, hears, smells and touches. According to Lacan, the unconscious develops along with the conscious mind, shaped by sensory input (that is, it is not something the child is born with); indeed, the unconscious is composed of these initial perceptions.[16] Language, in Lacan's view, is a defence against unconscious knowledge but is not wholly effective, as the messages from the unconscious that attempt to break down the barriers between the conscious and unconscious show. Benstock explains that those who occupy positions of exclusion within the culture, socially or economically marginalised and existing on the margins of society in the position of Other, may even deny the existence of such a barrier. In Campobello's works the presence of supressed feelings from the unconscious is suggested by Nellie's fixation on, and covert resentment towards, her mother. This effect is produced through the multiple voices that come through the text in the guise of the first-person narrator. While it is clearly true then, that Campobello's works are based on her childhood, the heteroglossia and polyphony in her writing suggest that Campobello attempts to undermine official discourse in several ways.

By speaking through the tales told by the men of the Revolution in *Cartucho*, and through her mother's voice in *Las manos de mamá*, Nellie not only offers the alternative vision of the little girl, but also others in the voices of adults. These provide a source of 'reliable' witnesses to fill in the gaps and give credibility to what she herself sees, hears and tells. Indeed, the different voices produce the effect of storytelling – by its very nature, multivocal. What was Campobello's purpose in creating this collective vision of the Revolution? On one level, it can be read as a need to stress the 'truthfulness' of her story by emphasising that it was not 'merely' a personal, subjective vision coloured by the concerns and limitations of a young girl. Nájera, in her study of Campobello's work, observes that the second and third editions of *Cartucho* play down the autobiographical elements, the intention being to make it more impersonal, more novelesque and to give it the epic quality of the Revolution. Campobello, she explains, puts emphasis on the collective rather than the personal, thus reducing its quality of chronicle (Nájera 1980: 53–58). Campobello goes further, linking this to a collective desire for liberty, which although only implicit in the novels, gives them a universal dimension (Nájera: 108).[17]

The polyphonic effect in the novellas is achieved through the use of direct speech by the protagonists of the Revolution, including Pancho Villa, and by

16 Benstock (1988: 18) cites Ellie Ragland-Sullivan: 'In *The Agency of the Letter* (1957), Lacan says there is no original or instinctual unconscious. Everything in the unconscious gets there from the outside world via symbolization and its effects [. . .] earliest perception is inseparable from the effects of the outside world, both linguistic and visual [. . .] Since the primordial subject of unconsciousness is formed by identification with its first images and sensory experiences, it will thereafter reflect the essence of these images and objects in identity'.

17 Given Campobello's expression of her own love of liberty in the *Prólogo* to *Mis libros*, this is a logical reading.

those not directly involved in the fighting such as the women of the north, including Nellie's mother. Most of these examples of direct speech, which are further collectivised by being written in colloquial Mexican Spanish, are to be found in *Cartucho*. The soldiers who remember Antonio Silva, the general who punished his men when they misbehaved by lashing them with a belt, is one such example. The insertion of phrases such as 'Le contaron a mamá' and 'cuentan que' precede the colloquial language used by Silva himself, '[. . .] mis hijos necesitan la cueriadita a nalga pelona y dada por mi santa mano' (My boys need thrashing on their bare behinds and by my own blessed hand). Another example is that of the gravedigger who recounts the appearance of one of the Portillo brothers prior to his execution (using a characteristically Mexican repetition of adjectives) 'Luis Herrera traía los ojos colorados, colorados; parecía que lloraba sangre' (Luis Herrera's eyes were bright red; it looked as though he were crying tears of blood) (*C*.935).

Another device used is contrast. The use of contrast emphasises the squalid nature of war but also indicates that the different voices of the people of the north do not necessarily form a single (political) voice. When one of Nellie's aunts says, 'José Díaz es el muchacho más bello que conozco' (José Díaz is the most beautiful lad I know) (*C*.938), this portrayal is closely followed by Nellie's own description of him when he later dies, 'devorado por la mugre' (devoured by filth) (*C*.939). Similarly, her great uncle says of Tomás Urbina, 'Son mentiras las que dicen del chapo [. . .] era buen hombre de la revolución' (What they say about El Chapo is lies [. . .] he was a good revolutionary) (*C*.947). This reiterates the theme of the denigration of Pancho Villa. In the section entitled MUJERES DEL NORTE Chonita emphasises the bravery of another of Villa's men, Martín López: 'aquel muchacho tan muchacho, que parecía un San Miguel de los combates' (that lad and a half who was like Saint Michael in combat) (*C*.966). A further example of the collective voice adding to the polyphony of the text is when the sister of one of the fighters comes to find out how he died, ' "Parecía pavo real [. . .] la hermana de Bartolo de Santiago" *dijeron las voces*' ('She looked like a peacock [. . .] Bartolo de Santiago's sister' *the voices said*) (*C*.931 [my emphasis]).

The polyphony of many different speakers, combined with Nellie's own testimony, produces an alternative version of history which makes Nellie a transmitter of information as well as a 'reflector'. However, multivocality also manifests itself in the texts in the presence of the authorial voice which exists alongside both of the above. The following statement about the women awaiting the return of their men, ' "¡Pero ellos volverán en abril o en mayo!", dicen todavía las voces de aquellas buenas e *ingenuas* mujeres del norte' ('But they will return in April or May' say the voices of those good and *ingenuous* women of the north) (*C*.967 [my emphasis]) reveals a breakdown in the child-narration as another voice appears. The sophisticated and distanced adult, authorial view is expressed in the ironic use of *ingenuas* when referring to the women waiting patiently for their men who are unlikely ever to return from battle.

In *Las manos de mamá*, there is less use of dialogue than in *Cartucho*. However, there are a few examples of reported speech which are important as they reveal another aspect of multivocality in this work. An 'other' voice that is revealed is that of the revolutionary fighter, the romantic and aptly named officer Rafael Galán (*galán* meaning handsome young man or gallant), who gives flowers to Rafaela. His monologue reveals the complexity of those who fought in the Revolution; they were not merely hardened fighters or desperate peasants (as depicted in Mariano Azuela's *Los de abajo,* translated as *The Underdogs*), but ordinary people who needed love and poetry in their lives. He says to Nellie's mother, 'Vengo a platicar con usted. ¿Me lo permite? La luna invita a detenerse aquí, en esta puerta, donde una mujer se adormece con un cigarillo en los labios. Mire la luna. Piense en su primer novio. Usted ha amado. Todos amamos aunque sea un imposible' (I've come to chat with you. Do you mind? The moon invites one to stop here, in this doorway, where a woman with a cigarette between her lips is getting sleepy. Look at the moon. Think of your first boyfriend. You have loved. We all love even though it is hopeless) (*MM*.982). Campobello's authorial voice also appears here to support Rafael Galán's own words, and to reveal that there is more than one Rafael Galán, 'nardos, pedazos de luna, sentado en la puerta gris [. . .] le deja todas las bellezas y delicados perfiles de su yo, el yo que era para las mujeres y que él no utilizaba para echar balazos' (spikenard, pieces of moon, sat in the grey doorway [. . .] he leaves her all the beauties and delicate profiles of the self which he kept for women and which he did not use for firing bullets) (*MM*.982).

A further example of multivocality in *Las manos de mamá* is the inclusion of the maternal discourse. To begin with, there are the two extracts of reported speech which involve Nellie's mother fighting for her children. They provide a response to the idea of the submissive woman which is reinforced by Nellie herself when they are on their way to Parral by train (*MM*.978). Once they arrive, Rafaela is telling a man about how she prevented the court from taking her children away, for allegedly 'indecent' behaviour, by faking sexual assault, '[. . .] mostré mi blusa rota y dije: "Vean aquí; ésta es la prueba," habló la ley: "Éste es el delito" ' (I showed my torn blouse and said: 'Look, here is the proof,' then the law spoke: 'There is your crime') (*MM*.979). She saves herself and keeps her children with a lie which she sees as justified, since it was a lie that brought her to the court in the first place. This extract is important as it shows how Rafaela knows enough of legal discourse – that the truth may be less important than technical details – to be able to manipulate it to suit her own ends. In other words, she becomes a subject in her own right.

Rafaela's independence is further emphasised when she is describing how she refused a pension offered her by her companion's Commanding Officer, as he fought because he wanted to and nobody can replace him (*MM*.979).

Campobello's awareness of the vulnerability of women (regardless of their social class) is also revealed in the affirmation that follows, 'Sus palabras sencillas, dichas con el pudor de las mujeres que solo tienen una clase, hicieron el milagro de no convertirnos en protegidos de un jefe de la revolución' (His simple words, said with the modesty of women, who have only one social class, achieved the miracle of not putting us under the protection of a revolutionary leader) (*MM*.979).

Rafaela stands up for herself with absolute serenity on two further occasions. The first time is when she is helping wounded men from the opposing side (*MM*.980); the second, when she goes to the town of Jiménez to reclaim her son from the fearsome officer whose hard angular face and flinty eyes might intimidate anyone. She protests, 'Es un niño. No quiero que lo maten tan chico. Esperen a que sea hombre' (He is just a boy. I don't want them to kill him so young. Wait until he is a man) and is allowed to take her son home (*MM*.985).

It would be understandable if Rafaela were angry in these situations, but she realises that the best way to achieve what she wants is to conform to her role as *madre abnegada y sumisa*. According to Hirsch, her position (as mother) prevents her from being able to show anger. She writes:

> anger may well be what defines subjectivity whenever the subject is denied speech [. . .] inasmuch as women can be subjects at all, the subjectivity of mothers is different. [. . .] as a mother, her subjectivity is under erasure [. . .] to be angry is to assert one's own self, not to subordinate it [. . .] A mother cannot articulate anger *as a mother*; to do so she must step out of a culturally circumscribed role which commands mothers to be caring and nurturing to others, even at the expense of themselves. (Hirsch 1989: 170)

Nellie's mother in the novels is independent, working as a seamstress and nursing the wounded, and refusing to accept a war pension to which she is entitled following the death of her husband.[18] Her role as nurse, was not particularly unusual, however, as Shirlene Soto describes:

---

[18] Shirlene Soto (1986: 19), writes: 'Despite the advances during the Porfiriato, women, irrespective of social class, suffered heavy legal discrimination. Their lives were severely circumscribed by laws prohibiting them from professions and locking them into marriage and family life. In addition, the Catholic Church reinforced institutionalised sexism by encouraging women to confine their existence to family and home'. Campobello's decision to remain single was therefore extremely unusual. As a young woman in Mexico in the 1930s, there was even less opportunity outside marriage than in Europe. Nájera writes of Campobello with respect to working rather than marrying, that she was dedicated to the improvement of cultural life in Mexico and this was why she never married (Nájera 1980: 16). Add to this fact that after Rafaela died in 1922 and five of her children, including Nellie, moved to Mexico City, Campobello looked after her half-sister, Gloria, until she died in 1968' (Nájera 1980: 4).

From the outset of the Revolution, women undertook new occupational and social roles and faced political challenges [. . .] During the post-Porfiriato era, increased numbers of upper-class women worked for health and charitable organizations, middle-class women served in a wide variety of revolutionary support roles, and many lower-class women served as *soldaderas*. (Soto 1986: 19)[19]

Soto's research, therefore, also reveals the conflict between the official version of what women's roles were and the reality of women's lives during the Revolution.

BINARY OPPOSITIONS AND GENDERED MEMORY

Given the particular forms of repression in Western culture which women experience, feminist psychoanalysis has a special interest in investigating how memory structures concepts of the self. It argues that memory preferences are gendered. Mary Jacobus claims that women's memory is a revision or representation of an ultimately irretrievable past – our memories of our mothers. (Maggie Humm 1989: 134)[20]

Nellie's memories of her mother are gendered (that is, initiated by sensual impressions, then poetically transcribed as references to nature and the senses) through being influenced by the relationship she has with her mother as a daughter (rather than as a son). The greater closeness that, according to some Freudian psychoanalysts, exists between mothers and daughters and which makes separation and individuation more difficult for girls, may lead to obsession with (the memory of) the mother, or to distorted or exaggerated feelings of neglect by girls.[21]

Campobello's memory of her mother became almost an obsession to the extent that she was unable – or consciously decided not – to embark on a loving relationship with another adult:

---

[19] The protagonist of *Mal de amores* by Ángeles Mastretta (1997) trains as a doctor (without ever gaining a medical degree because, as a woman, she is not admitted to Medical School) and practises at the revolutionary front.

[20] Humm cites Jacobus (1987).

[21] Incomplete individuation is the inability to separate completely from the mother at the age when this is supposed to occur; that is, following a good relationship with her which allows the infant to develop a separate sense of self (Chodorow 1978, 68–69). According to Freud (1996: 221) 'in some cases the attachment to the mother lasts beyond the fourth year of life'. This is because the 'reality principle' according to which the child 'comes to recognise that its mother is a separate being with separate interests and activities' is incomplete.

Conservo la última ropa que usó. A Mamá no le gustaba que la tocásemos;
nos permitía, cuando mucho, que le adoráramos la mano con la punta de la
nariz. La quise tanto que no he tenido tiempo de dedicarme al amor. Claro
que he tenido pretendientes, pero estoy muy ocupada con mis recuerdos.

(Carballo 1965: 336–37)

(I have kept the last piece of clothing she wore. Mamma didn't like our
touching her; she allowed us, at the most, to adore her by touching her hand
with the tip of our noses. I loved her so much that I have not had time to
devote myself to love. Of course, I have had admirers, but I am very taken
up with my memories.)

I referred earlier to the indigenous people's repect for nature which was
inherited by Campobello.This is reflected in the many references to nature
found in the two texts, in particular in the short poem which appears at the
beginning of *Las manos de mamá*, which has been described by critics as a
hymn to her mother or to motherhood itself (Magaña Esquivel 1965: 144), but
which is also a hymn to nature:

> *Mu–Bana–ci Maci Reyé*
> *Busa Nará Mapu Be–Cabe*
> *Jupi Cureko Neje Sinaa.*   (*MM*.971)

This Tarahumaran *Hai-kai* is roughly translated as 'Your face of light,
mother awakens and cries, like before, when I shout for you today'. (The
placing of this piece of indigenous writing at the beginning of the text is paralleled by Castellanos' use of extracts from the *Popol Vuh* and *The Book of
Chilam Balam* at the beginning of the sections of *Balún-Canán*.)

Of the references to nature and the senses, the most significant, obvious
and frequently ocurring is *ojos* but other words associated with the child's-eye
view of the world around her, such as *color, lágrimas* (tears) and so on, are
also important. Words related to the other senses, particularly touch and
manos are also discussed, as the senses appear to be the vehicle through which
Campobello expresses her ideas and memories about the Revolution from a
gendered perspective. In view of the restrictions on little girls' physical
freedom the senses assume major importance in the narrator's psyche and in
my reading of her accounts of her life during the Revolution.

It is clear that Nellie greatly loved her mother. However, her often exaggerated praise of her mother conceals unconscious feelings of resentment
towards her for what, as a child, she experienced as a lack of attention. Yet
Rafaela was, to use D. W. Winnicott's term, a 'good enough mother'.
According to Winnicott, in order for separation from the mother to take place
successfully, the period of 'illusionment' (what Freud called 'desire' and
Klein called 'phantasy') must be followed by the 'opportunity for disillusionment'. Winnicott explains that this entails her adapting to the baby, 'less

exactly so it gradually confronts the fact that it cannot omnipotently control the world'.[22] Nellie evidently experiences a prolonged period of disillusionment, as does the narrator of Poniatowska's La 'Flor de Lis'. This is revealed in her references to her feelings of being excluded by her mother. However, Rafaela's behaviour, or the way she mothered, was clearly normal in a situation of conflict, where she had to support herself and her children as well as contribute to the (civil) 'war effort' by nursing the casualties of the fighting. Nevertheless it is Nellie's perceived rather than actual neglect that is relevant to her memories and the way she depicts these through sensual references.

Encompassing the emphasis on the sensual is an acclamation of nature. Nellie's overwhelming love for her mother is equally a tribute to nature and the traditional, 'natural' way of life she associates with the indigenous people (and her ancestors).[23] According to such a tradition, the mother figure is caring and nurturing, but, like Mother Earth herself, she can also be aloof and self-interested, even neglectful or destructive. There is plenty of evidence in Campobello's work to support this ambivalent view of motherhood. Through the memories evoked by the sights and smells experienced by an older Nellie returning to the setting of Cartucho, Campobello's alternative view of the Revolution focuses this time on her mother's role in the conflict, and on her relationship with her mother, seen with hindsight.

The use of poetic language is regarded by Kristeva as a way for the semiotic to disrupt the symbolic.[24] In Campobello's writing this ties in with the lauding of her indigenous heritage with its oral tradition of storytelling. This oral tradition can be related to mother/earth and representative of the Oral stage in the child's development (based around the senses), until the acquisition of language and entry into the Symbolic with its access to the written word.[25] Kemy Oyarzún writes: 'it has been said that the domain of the eye and the gaze, which coincides with the appearance of writing, is essentially patriarchal and, to a large extent, expresses the masculine way of

22 Quoted in Minsky (1996: 113–15).

23 Carballo (1965: 338) quotes Campobello as stating, 'La gente es difícil de trato porque es muy pura en su manera de ser y actuar. Una debería encontrarse con sus antepasados, ser como fueron los mayores' ([The] people are difficult to deal with because they are very pure in their ways of acting and being. You should meet with your ancestors, be as your elders were).

24 Kristeva (1984: 50 and 81) and (1987: 136–137). See 'The Semiotic and the Symbolic' and 'From One Identity to Another'. Kristeva's semiotic is the pre-Oedipal stage (Lacan's Imaginary); she contrasts this with the Symbolic of the post-Oedipal phase and argues that male-dominated thought resides in the repression of the semiotic and the pre-Oedipal mother. Disruption of the Symbolic, therefore, represents a reaction against such repression.

25 According to Lacan, separation from the mother is followed by acceptance of the Law of the Father and the acquisition of language, that is, the passing from the oral position of the 'Mirror' stage of development in childhood through to the 'Symbolic' and language (and the written word); see Minsky (1996: Ch. 4, 'Lacan: The Meaning of the Phallus').

expressing desire' (Oyarzún 1996: 188 [my translation]). Thus, Nellie's versions of her relationship with her mother and the incidents of the Revolution she recalls – often through the voices of others – can be read as metaphors for the worlds of the Imaginary (where, as Minsky claims, 'identity has been based on a search for the same' – as when Nellie sees herself and her mother as one being) and for the Symbolic (where subjectivity is based on difference) (Minsky 1996: 156). Construction of the self as subject, according to this theory, involves a transfer from the semiotic/oral stage of the world of the senses (the oral tradition associated with the mother) to the world of the signifier (the written word associated with the Father).

However, if *Las manos de mamá* is a hymn to Campobello's mother, it is a sensual and pantheistic hymn. The poem at the beginning of the novel is full of allusions to the senses, as are both the texts of *Cartucho* and *Las manos de mamá*. *Mamá* herself is the embodiment of nature as the opening lines of the text, which also emphasise all five senses, reveal:[26]

ASÍ ERA [. . .]
Esbelta, como las flores de la sierra cuando danzan mecidas por el viento.
Su perfume se aspira junto a los madroños vírgenes, allá donde la luz se abre entera.
Su forma se percibe a la caída del sol en la falda de la montaña.
Era como las flores de maíz no cortadas y en el mismo instante en que las besa el sol.
Un himno, un amanecer todo *Ella* era. Los trigales se reflejaban en sus ojos cuando sus manos, en el trabajo, se apretaban sobre las espigas doradas y formaban ramilletes que se volvían tortillas húmedas de lágrimas.

(*MM*.971)

(Slender, like the mountain flowers when they dance swaying in the wind.
Their perfume blends with the aroma of the strawberry trees, there where the sky opens up,
Their shape is visible at sunset at the foot of the mountain.
She was like the uncut maize flowers at the very moment they are kissed by the sun.
All of her was a hymn, a dawn. The wheatfields were reflected in her eyes when her hands, at work, squeezed the golden sheaves and formed bunches that became tortillas moist with tears.)

Nature is present in the form of the red earth and white dust of the north, the sun, moon and stars, the wind, the mountains, the flowers, the trees and ears of maize and wheat. Here, the picture is of a benevolent, bountiful nature

---

[26] Laura Cázares writes: 'The poetic presentation of the character in the first fragment brings together the visual (flowers that dance), smell (their perfume) hearing (the hymn) touch (hands on the ears of corn) and taste (the tortillas, wet with tears)' (1996: 53 [my translation]).

and contrasts sharply with the descriptions of nature in *literatura regionalista*, such as that of Horacio Quiroga (1878–1937) in which nature is hostile and human beings must struggle constantly to survive in it; or that of Juan Rulfo (1918–1986), whose images of the provinces in *El llano en llamas* (1953) (*The Burning Plain*), came to epitomise the harshness of the Mexican landscape for those who lived on the land.[27]

Campobello in the *Prólogo* to *Mis libros*, writes about her choice of a title for her second prose work:

> Para mí fue fácil encontrarlo porque de todo lo que recibimos de la madre, las manos son, a lo largo de la vida, lo que está en contacto permanente con los hijos. Sabemos, sin embargo, de los ojos, hablamos de la voz y del regazo[28] que nuestra madre nos da y nos vuelve a dar; nadie lo ignora: pude haber preferido otro título: debí haber pensado en los ojos de Mamá; pero en aquel momento vi sus manos, las sentí sobre mis hombros y, claro está sus manos se convirtieron en mi libro. (Campobello 1960: 32)

> (For me it was easy to find it because of everything we receive from our mother, her hands are, throughout our lives, what is in permanent contact with her children. We know, however, about eyes, we talk about voice and lap which our mother gives to us over and over again; everybody knows that: I could have preferred another title: I should have thought of my Mother's eyes, but at that moment I saw her hands, I felt them on my shoulders and of course, her hands became my book.)

The child's two discourses in the novellas, which centre on the binary opposition eyes/hands and the two senses, sight/touch associated with them, begin here. Nellie gradually moves from the Imaginary to the Symbolic, with the latter (represented by the visual) gradually becoming dominant. The twin emphasis on the tactile and the visual, associated by Irigaray with the female world and the male world respectively, are integral to my binary reading of *Cartucho* and *Las manos de mamá*.[29] Doris Meyer (1985) affirms that the title's emphasis on her mother's hands reflects Campobello's recollection of being guided and comforted by her mother in a particularly physical way.

This would explain Campobello's emphasis on both hands and eyes. Living in a man's world – particularly in Mexico at the beginning of the twen-

---

[27] *Literatura regionalista* was the attempt to describe the unique experience of Latin Americans and their geographical and historical situation, by writers who rejected the *modernista* tradition based on a European model. Those that attracted international attention included Rómulo Gallegos' *Doña Bárbara* (1929), Ricardo Güiraldes's *Don Segundo Sombra* (1926) and Eustasio Rivera's *La vorágine* (1924) (Franco 1969: 193).

[28] *Regazo* is an important site of maternal comfort and nurture as will be discussed further in Chapter Three where the child-narrator of *Balún-Canán* refers to her *nana*'s lap.

[29] For Irigaray (1993), the way sight is associated with the masculine and the other senses with the feminine in our culture and the fact that sight predominates over smell, taste, touch and hearing, has provoked an impoverishment of bodily relations.

tieth century – she nevertheless has been brought up by an independent and freedom-loving woman who has inculcated these same qualities into her daughter in a variety of ways. Nellie is torn between the tactile world she associates with her mother, and the visual world she associates with men, in particular with Papá Grande, her grandfather; hence the almost equal emphasis on eyes and hands. Rafaela is both masculinised – in that she is strong and independent and therefore transgresses the myth of the weak, passive, Mexican mother – and essentialised, by being aligned with Mother Nature according to the binary system, which places male and culture in opposition to female and nature. The essentialising of women by associating them with nature relegates them to a position of inescapable biological destiny as mothers (a destiny which Campobello rejected) and denies them the faculty of reason associated with culture (and creativity). Campobello, in her portrayal of Rafaela, thus subverts the simplistic gender categorising of males and females as 'masculine' and 'feminine' with attributes exclusive to either (as does Garro in her portrayal of Isabel, the protagonist of *Los recuerdos del porvenir*).

Through the senses, then, Campobello expresses her own ideas, convictions and, in particular, memories about the Revolution. Her memories are triggered by the senses and those memories form the basis for her vision of the Revolution.[30] Also, as is the case with Castellanos' *niña* in *Balún-Canán*, an emphasis on the senses lends verisimilitude to the child-narrator. Benstock (1987: 23) describes two scenes from Virginia Woolf's fragments of a memoir, 'Moments of Being', where the memories are comprised of sound and sight and states: 'We know that the unconscious is comprised of just such "memories" – of images and sounds – and that later identity reflects these first sensory experiences.' Campobello reconstructs the Revolution through the senses and through the technique of the child-narrator; by doing so she enhances the verisimilitude of the text as the two techniques become interwoven, the one supporting the other. My emphasis on the senses stems from the belief that they are vital to the child's process of remembering. This is particularly true in the case of a child like Nellie, who was so aware of the feeling of freedom gained from being outside because she had to spend so much of her time indoors. Much of Nellie's observation of her world and the Revolution is conducted (as is that of her counterpart in *Balún-Canán*) through windows and doorways and by watching the adults who peopled it, from positions of concealment inside the house, such as under the table.

Nellie's love of nature would seem to be the key to the emphasis on the sensual. However, on a psychoanalytical level, both confinement to the domestic female sphere, and Nellie's incomplete individuation and separation from her mother, increase the importance of touch as a tool for her under-

---

30 For the relationship between memory and the senses, see Freud (1991: 687).

standing of the world; hence the importance given to *hands* in the texts, and the emphasis on *las manos* of so many of the characters described, including her mother. At the same time, the child-narrator's visual powers develop through her capacity as silent observer to much of what went on around her. This is revealed in the way Nellie notices colours and in particular how clean or dirty, fair- or dark-skinned the people she describes are, as well as in the multiple appearances of the word *ojos*.

The eyes are alluded to in the expression of loss and sorrow, brought about by the Revolution and by the death of Nellie's mother, found in the words *llorar* (cry) and *lágrimas* (tears). Both of these experiences – direct contact with nature, and its antithesis, being shut indoors – contribute to the significance of sounds for Nellie. In both texts the sounds that are most often heard are *gritos* (shouts) and *disparos* (gunshots) in relation to the men of the Revolution; and *cantar* (sing) and *risas* (laughter) in relation to her mother. The evocative smells associated with Nellie's memories of her childhood are similarly positive – *perfume* and *flores*, when associated with her mother and negative – *hospital* and *orinas* (*C*.939) when she describes memories of the Revolution.

The first time *olor* appears in Cartucho it refers to the flowery smell of a woman's skirt (*C*.931). Although the woman is not Mamá, this is significant because of the juxtaposition of *falda,* the word used to signify femaleness and *flor*, the epitome of ephemeral beauty. From this point on, these words are used when Nellie is alluding to her mother. The other smells which Nellie mentions in connection with the Revolution are urine, in the alleyway leading to the El Águila inn (*C*.939); gunpowder, when she describes the doctor who tends to her brother (*MM*.980), and the smell of hospitals. The natural perfume of plants and flowers which generally characterises *Las manos de mamá*, represents, for Nellie, the clean freshness of nature. She associates this with both Papá Grande (*MM*.972), and with her mother. The narrator also relates how the street was filled with perfume one night when the romantic Rafael Galán gathers an armful of spikenard to bring to Rafaela (*MM*.982).

The second section of *Las manos de mamá*, following the dedication to her mother in ASÍ ERA . . . (That's how she was . . .) begins with the adult returning to the place of her childhood and seeing everything with adult eyes, 'La calle la veo más angosta, más corta, más triste; [. . .] La tierra es roja, las banquetas desdentadas, los focos cabezas de cerillos. A las puertas asoman las gentes; son las mismas; no necesito cerrar los ojos para imaginarlas' (The street looks narrower, shorter, sadder; [. . .] the earth is red, the pavements have stones missing, the lamps are like match-heads. People lean out of their doorways; they are the same; I don't need to close my eyes to picture them) (*MM*.971). Here the Symbolic is dominant, with sight having primacy over the other senses in what is clearly an adult view of a scene remembered since childhood. The narrator in the next sentence, however, is once again the child playing on the ground, close to nature and part of the red earth itself. Here the pre-verbal or Imaginary intrudes as emphasis is placed on touch and physical contact with the earth, 'Ando en la tierra, mis manos rojas, roja mi cara y el sol y mi calle, todo rojo como el panorama de los niños' (I'm playing with the earth again, my hands are red, my face, the sun and my street are red, all red, a child's-eye view) (*MM*.971). This is restated a few pages later: 'La tierra era nuestra compañera: con ella jugábamos bajo el sol. Aquella tierra roja como la palma de nuestras manos y nuestros talones nos abría sus brazos y nos protegía hasta que volvía mamá' (The earth was our companion, we played with her under the sun. That earth, red like the palms of our hands and our heels opened her arms to us and protected us until Mamma came home) (*MM*.975). 'Mother Nature' is indeed a substitute for the mother in her absence. But unlike Nellie's real mother, whose hands often push her away, Nature opens her arms and protects Nellie. Irene Matthews goes even further, saying that the hands of the mother, 'as well as (instead of?) being a metonym for the intimacy and connectiveness of mother and child, in the daughter's narrative recollection [. . .] like the tears of the Virgin forever remain within the realm of the symbolic, as a metaphor for absence and an index of lack' (Matthews 1993: 166).

Other people's hands are referred to in terms of their colour, size, and state of cleanliness. Sometimes they carry life or death in them. A rider turns the corner of San Francisco street (mecía en *su mano trigueña y mugrosa* un papel blanco; traía aprisionada la vida de Gerardo Ruiz' (he cradled in his *golden-brown, dirty hand* a piece of white paper; it carried, imprisoned, the life of Gerardo Ruiz) (*C*.936 [my emphasis]). Similar, is the account of the sleeping sentinel who carries 'the thread of life in his eyes' but also holds the death-dealing weapon – his rifle – in his hands (*C*.940). These two images, contrasting with that of the mother's nurturing hands, illustrate a universal idea; the ambivalence of human nature which allows that hands can both sustain life and eliminate it. This idea also appears in the inset in italics which is an indication of Nellie's attitude to city and country people, '*Una mano fina y blanca, la otra tostada y dura. Son dos manos distintas, pero pueden ser iguales*' (One hand soft and white, the other sunburnt and hard. Two different hands, but they can be the same) (*MM*.976). Nellie's mother, like other women from a privileged background, contributes to the difficult physical task of caring for the wounded of the Revolution as well as for her children, a point illustrated by Soto in her study.

MY MOTHER'S EYES

The importance of the eyes in popular culture and myth is indisputable. In Mexico, *mis ojos* is a commonly used term of endearment for loved ones. Nellie's frequent references to eyes suggest that these are the way that she, as a small child, is able to identify the people around her and to 'read' them. In other words, not only do eyes figure in the physical descriptions she gives of the men and women around her but the association of the word *ojos* with vocabulary other than adjectives of colour, reveals that for Nellie they hold the key to the thoughts, feelings, memory, character, personality and even the fate of their owner. This is clearly illustrated in the much quoted passage describing *Ella* which, as well as being a loving portrait, also reveals the complexity and variability of her mother's personality:

> [. . .] asomada al postigo de la puerta gris: sus cabellos negros, sus ojos dorados, que en la mañana eran amarillos y verdes, indecisos a las tres de la tarde; después, como por magia, se le volvían de oro. En ese momento los tenía verdes, vistos desde los rieles del tranvía; más cerca danzaban los puntos cafés; amarillos, grises; su piel ocre, su boca dibujada con un ligero respinguito en el lado izquierdo. (*MM*.971)

> (leaning out of the grey doorway: her black hair, her golden eyes which in the morning were yellow and green, indecisive at three o'clock in the after-noon, afterward, as if by magic, turned to gold. At that moment, seen from the tramlines, she had green ones; closer up brown, yellow, grey dots danced in them; her skin was ochre, her mouth well-defined with a slight curl in the left corner.)

The narrator's mother is referred to variously as *Mamá, Madre, Usted* and *Ella*. This is another example of Nellie's many voices. *Mamá* suggests the normal intimacy that is expected of the mother–daughter relationship; *Usted* is the respectful form of address of children to parents that is current even now in rural communities, and *Ella* implies both distance and reverence. In the section entitled AMOR DE 'ELLA' (Love for 'Her'), Nellie eulogises her mother, 'Era esbelta, fina, ágil; sus ojos vivos y claros, se grabaron en nuestro corazón' (She was slender, fine-boned, agile; her bright and lively eyes were engraved on our hearts) (*MM*.973). She speaks for her brothers and sisters but is really expressing her own sentiments when she voices her admiration for her mother, 'Su esbelta figura, con el caer de los pliegues de su enagua, hacía que nuestros ojos vieran una mamá inolvidable' (Her slender figure, with the fall of the folds of her petticoat, made our eyes see an unforgettable mother) (*MM*.976). Nellie also extols her mother's closeness to nature, emphasising here her mother's eyes, 'La luz de sus ojos era nuestra vida. Ojos de mujer joven, capaces de orientarse en la noche sin estrellas' (The light of her eyes was our life. Young woman's eyes, able to find their way in a starless night) (*MM*.977). Later on, after the death of her youngest child, Rafaela loses the will to live and, Nellie writes, 'Sus ojos se secaban [. . .] No podía vivir' (Her eyes dried up [. . .] She could not live) (*MM*.987). Nellie adores her mother with her own eyes, describing her with the loving detail of an artist, 'Yo pensaba: "Mamá es muy bonita", y corría mis ojos de la punta de su nariz a su boca y a sus ojos' (I thought: 'Mamma is very pretty' and I ran my eyes from the tip of her nose to her mouth and her eyes) (*MM*.983). In the last section of the novella, CARTA PARA USTED, Nellie describes her mother's death in terms of her *eyes* resting, rather than her body, 'la tierra donde descansaron sus ojos' (the earth where her eyes rested) and her memory of her mother centres on this, her most important attribute, along with her hands (*MM*.988).

Nellie also uses eyes to describe people's relationship to their external world and as an indicator of their internal world. The effect of the war on her mother is recorded through her eyes, which have the timelessness of the natural world:

> Así pasaron frente a los ojos de Ella escenas salvajes [. . .] Los cantos y danzas de guerra, las heroicas defensas, las mujeres hermosas, las hogueras brillantes – símbolo de la vida de estas gentes – los odios feudales; todo esto y más le fue revelado. En sus ojos se grabaron las visiones exactas [. . .]. (*MM*.972)

> (In this way savage scenes passed in front of Her eyes [. . .] The songs and dances of war, heroic defence, the beautiful women, the bright fires – symbol of the life of these people – feudal hate; all this and more was revealed to her. In her eyes were recorded the exact sights [. . .].)

Left alone when her husband dies in the war her tears are dried by nature, not by some sympathetic person (*MM*.974). Then, when *Mamá* herself dies, Nellie describes her eyes as dying (as if they were a fire) (*MM*.988).

Nellie thus clearly associates the eyes and what they absorb with the inner world of a person (his/her thoughts and feelings) as well as their relationship with the outside world. This is particularly the case with her mother and herself, 'Y estaba allí, la vieron mis ojos, mis ojos míos de niña' (And there she was, my eyes saw her, my own little-girl's eyes) (*MM*.972). Nellie's depiction of her mother may be seen as essentialist in the way it associates her mother with nature and emphasises what appears to be her 'innate' femininity and motherliness. Yet at the same time this image is frequently contradicted when Nellie stresses her mother's independence and strength and the way she herself feels rejected by her mother, who would therefore not be fulfilling her role of *madre abnegada*. The portrayal of Rafaela is complex therefore; she does not fit into any of the one-dimensional categories established by patriarchy for women.

THE PEOPLE OF THE NORTH

The binary opposition *civilización/barbarie* is reversed in the negative depiction of the city of Chihuaua given by Nellie/Campobello (here the narrator *and* the textual author's view is represented). This view conforms to post-revolutionary rhetoric of the 1930s which, in order to try and combat the mass migration to cities, embraced the idea of the country, and romanticised the country people.[31] In the section CUANDO LLEGAMOS A UNA CAPITAL (When we reach a Capital City) the narrator describes the city in negative terms which reveal her preference for country life and people. She describes the long, sad streets of Chihuahua, which receive them 'with open arms'. But they are 'Brazos fuertes que devoran' (strong arms that devour) (*MM*.986). Nellie sees the negativity of city life reflected in people's faces, especially in their eyes, '*Ojos indiferentes* que matan, que empequeñecen el espíritu [. . .] Afuera las caras de la gente tienen tristeza, *ojos apagados*, bocas apretadas' (*Indifferent eyes* that kill, that shrivel the spirit [. . .] Outside the people's faces have sadness in them, *dull eyes*, tight mouths) (*MM*.986 [my emphasis]). This contrasts with her idealised view of country people. Campobello reveals her admiration for certain traditional values she associates with the indigenous people of the north of Mexico, such as straightforwardness and integrity, which she sees as characteristics of her grandfather. Here, as in all references to the grandfather, emphasis is on the visual, 'un hombre alto, de pelo recortado hasta el cuello, de ancha capa, tehuas en los pies y *mirada de ojos exactos*' (a tall man, hair cut to his collar, broad cape, sandals on his feet and an exact gaze in his eyes) (*MM*.972 [my emphasis]). Nellie identifies with *Papá Grande,* a countryman of indigenous descent, who loved nature and shunned elegant society, 'Me hallo en mi abuelo: él amaba los ríos y las grandes llanuras. Se llevó en sus ojos los panoramas de la naturaleza y se salvó de la elegancia de las tertulias caseras' (I find myself in my grandfather: he loved the rivers and the great plains. He took with him in his eyes the vistas of nature and saved himself from the elegance of social gatherings at home) (*MM*.972). She addresses him with affection and respect, 'Usted conocía la verdad de todos los rincones del alma y sus gentes. Su alegría en los ojos revelaba sus relaciones con el alba, los ríos y las huertas' (You knew the truth of all the corners of the soul and your people. The joy in your eyes revealed your relationship with the dawn, the rivers and the fertile fields) (*MM*.973).

The eyes *are* the person as far as Nellie is concerned. In the section entitled USTED Y ÉL (You and Him), where she relates the time prior to her parents' meeting she says, 'Los ojos de él no habían llegado' (His eyes had not arrived) (*MM*.973). Not only are the eyes the person, but each person's future is visible in his or her eyes according to Nellie. This is the case with Luis Herrera, who before being shot at five in the afternoon, 'traía los ojos colorados, colorados; parecía que lloraba sangre' (his eyes were bright red, it looked as though he were crying tears of blood) (*C*.935).

In a similar vein, Nellie describes how, on returning from a journey to Chihuahua to visit her wounded brother in hospital, she sees a woman, her

---

[31] This romanticisation of the country is apparent in Mexican cinema of the time such as the *Ranchera* comedy *Allá en el Rancho Grande* (Fernando de Fuentes 1936), and right through the 1940s with films such as *María Candelaria* (El 'Indio' Fernández 1943) (Monsiváis 1981: 1515–17).

body wrapped in her petticoat, lying dead by the railway line next to a young man. Nellie's remarks, while apparently reflecting her childish ignorance about death as she thinks that the dead should have their eyes closed, emphasise not only the man's open eyes, but his gaze, in other words, his life and personality, and the way it is eliminated by a handful of earth: 'Le echaron un puño de tierra y se le borró la mirada' (They threw a handful of earth over him and erased his gaze) (*MM*.981). Nellie is accustomed to seeing broken and bloodied bodies with their eyes closed but this man, pale and with no marks of violence, his eyes open, looks as though he should be alive. In LA SENTENCIA DE BABIS, the account of the death of her friend in *Cartucho*, the death of Babis is anticipated in this description of his eyes as Babis speaks, 'El día que me dé de alta – y se le hundían los ojos echando fuera los dientes – voy a pelear muy bien' (The day they get rid of me – and his eyes sank into his head as he bared his teeth – I am going to fight very well) (*C*.937). Nellie only hears about his death after not seeing him for what seems to her, in her child's time frame, a long time, 'Hacía un mes – un año para mis ojos amarillos – sin ver a *Babis*' (It was a month – a year for my yellow eyes – since I saw Babis) (*C*.937). Nellie also counts people in terms of eyes. When she is describing the number of people being killed in the war she asks, 'How many kilos of flesh would they make all together?' '¿Cuántos ojos y pensamientos? [. . .] ¿Cuántas lenguas? ¿Cuántos ojos?' (How many eyes and thoughts? [. . .] How many tongues? How many eyes?) (*MM*.983).[32]

Eyes, then, are also the mirror for thoughts and memories. In the section LA PLAZA DE LAS LILAS (The Square of the Lilacs), Nellie describes the dusty town of Jiménez, 'Sus focos hacen un canto triste a los ojos cuando en la noche lacrimosa besan las caras' (Its street lamps sing a sad song to eyes when they kiss faces in the tearful night) (*MM*.985). This is the setting for the death of Emilio, an officer in love with Rafaela, doomed from the start because of his romantic nature: 'El romanticismo era otra enemigo, el más peligroso. Generalmente los que preferían el perfume de la flores y los cantos de amor morían con más rapidez que los otros, porque ya estaban envenenados.' (Romanticism was another enemy, the most dangerous one. Generally, those who preferred the perfume of flowers and love songs died more quickly than the others, because they were already poisoned) (*MM*, 985). He is sentenced by the local garrison commander, Maclovio, 'Un hombre muy malo [. . .] Su cara era dura, angulosa, los ojos vidriosos' (A very bad man [. . .] His face was hard, angular, his eyes glassy) (*MM*.985–86). Emilio's eyes are glassy too, but for a different reason: they reflect memories that only bullets are able to erase, 'Sus ojos vidriosos se movían de un lado a otro [. . .] Pocos segundos después las balas lograron deshacer eso que él no lograba borrar de su memoria' (*MM*.986).

---

[32] The question '¿Cuántas lenguas?' here, emphasises the multivocality in the text.

Nellie refers to the collectivisation of the eyes of her brothers and sisters and herself, once again, when their mother goes away. The children, left behind at their aunt's house, find some consolation in various objects left on a bench. Their joy and sorrow are both expressed by their eyes, ' "¡Tesoro!", dijeron nuestros ojos, y nos abalanzamos [. . .]' ("Treasure!" our eyes said, and we fell upon it) (*MM*.977). But when Pirala shares it out and keeps the most coveted objects for himself: 'Nuestros ojos sangraron de tristeza' (our eyes bled with sadness) (*MM*.?). Thus the collective voice of the people of the north contains the diversity of the group. Nellie refers to the collective eyes of the dogs that represent, and are part of, the town and its collective voice:

> Quedó solo Parral, y, cuando se quedaban solas las calles, era cuando los perros lloraban a sus dueños. Una desesperación salvaje se apoderaba de ellos [. . .] Sus ojos polvosos, lacrimosos, buscan los ojos de las gentes [. . .] A veces, en su carrera loca, con el cuerpo encogido y los ojos rojos por el llanto, encontraban a sus amos [. . .]. A veces los perros y los niños son iguales. Pero los perros no cambian. La desesperación limpia; el verdadero amor, la adoración, están en sus ojos. (*MM*.984)

> (Parral was deserted, and, when the streets were emptied, that was when the dogs cried for their owners. A wild desperation took hold of them [. . .] Their dusty, tearful eyes search for the eyes of people. [. . .] Sometimes, in their mad race, their bodies cringing and their eyes red with weeping, they would find their masters [. . .] Sometimes dogs and children are the same. But dogs do not change. Desperation has a cleansing effect; true love and adoration are in their eyes.)

In *Cartucho,* references to eye colour are mostly devoid of any obvious reference to character, unlike in the description of Nellie's little sister Gloria in *Las manos de mamá*, '[. . .] ojitos azules de salvaje' (blue eyes of a little wild thing) (*MM*.981). More often they are merely descriptive of physical appearance. However, such descriptions are often slanted by the addition of a reference to the skin colour, hands and pulchritude of the person described; or are used to reflect the emotional impact on Nellie and the other characters of the war. When Nellie hears that a certain General, who had mistreated her mother, has been shot she tells herself: ' "Lo mataron porque fue malo con ella" Los ojos endurecidos de mamá los tenía yo' ('They killed him because he was bad to her' I had Mamma's hardened eyes now) (*C*.941).[33] Two years after the General mistreats her mother, when she sees him again, she recalls how that day everything went wrong for her, she could not study and she spent the day 'pensando en ser hombre, tener mi pistola y pegarle cien tiros' (thinking about being a man, having my pistol and shooting him a hundred times) (*C*.941). Nellie here reveals her awareness that men have more free-

---

[33] This also reveals the way Nellie sees herself and her mother as one and the same; it shows, in other words, her incomplete individuation.

dom of action. Although Rafaela is far from passive, as a mother she is expected to restrain her emotion. As Dennis Parle writes, 'Throughout much of the novel, the mother's emotions are expressed indirectly through her actions rather than words, thus suggesting a well of restrained emotion' (Parle 1985: 203). But Nellie also realises that when it comes to expressing emotion, men are as restricted as women – and equally unhappy. Dogs, however, 'pueden aullar en las calles con todo lo que su pulmón les da; son más libres que las gentes, deben ser más felices' (can howl in the street for all they are worth, they are freer than people, they must be happier) (*MM*.984).

However the frequent references to tears reveals that people do cry even when hardened by the horrors of war that surround them. Tears are prominent in Nellie's tale about her mother and her role in the Revolution. In both *Cartucho* and *Las manos de mamá* the words *llora/r, llanto, lágrimas*, appear frequently, both in the context of Mamá and of the men and women of the Revolution. When the much respected general Antonio Silva, 'a man who loved order', dies, 'mamá lloró por él; dijo que se había acabado un hombre' (Mamma cried for him; she said a man had died) (*C*.933). Similarly, when the gentlemanly Catarino Acosta, who would ride by the house tipping his hat at Rafaela with a little smile, meets a horrific death, his ears severed and bleeding profusely from several wounds in his side, Nellie describes her mother's reaction thus: 'Mamá lo bendijo y lloró de pena al verlo pasar' (Mamma blessed him and cried in sadness on seeing him pass by) (*C*.933). In the section LOS OFICIALES DE LA SEGUNDA DEL RAYO (The Officers of the Segunda del Rayo), Captain Gándara relates the death of the romantic Rafael Galán to some girls and, as he tells the tale, the girls' crying becomes sobbing. However, Nellie notices that it is not only the women who cry in the macho world of fighting and bloodshed. Or, as the popular saying goes, 'los hombres no lloran pero los machos sí' (men don't cry but macho men do). Captain Gándara also relates that when he himself and the soldiers bury Rafael, 'se nos salieron las lágrimas cuando echamos la tierra' (we shed tears when we threw the earth on him) (*C*.962); and when the young General, Martín López, scourge of the *carrancistas* dies, even Villa cries and 'more than anyone' (*C*.965). I have already described how the dogs in Parral cry and in Jiménez, the night itself cries (*MM*. 985). It is interesting that Nellie spends a lot of time describing how other people cry and then is accused of aloofness. I believe this may be merely another disguise, those tears representing her own tears of neglect and abandonment, but it also demonstrates the textual author's (temporal) distance from the events.

Finally, another way that the eyes are used in Campobello's writing, more directly related to the senses, is in the observation of colour. I have already mentioned the way the narrator uses eye colour to denote character traits, as in the case of the descriptions of Nellie's mother and little sister, Gloria. Another example of this is the case of José Ruiz who has 'Los ojos exactos de un perro amarillo' (*C*.929).[34] Generally, eye colour appears devoid of any apparent significance in the descriptions of the fighting men. However, while these descriptions reflect the diversity of the Mexican people and undermine the official discourse of the Revolution, which sustained that those fighting on the side of the revolutionaries and against the government were mainly peasants and Indians (therefore dark-eyed), some of the portraits are sympathetic and others plainly not so. On the first page of *Cartucho* there is a description of Elías, 'Alto, color de canela, pelo castaño, ojos verdes, dos colmillos de oro' (Tall, cinammon- coloured skin, reddish-brown hair, green eyes, two gold canines) (*C*.929). Julio Reyes is similarly described in a pleasant light, 'siempre se reía. Era un joven de color trigo. Sus ojos cafés eran amables, parecían de un hombre bueno' (he was always laughing. He was a young man the colour of wheat. His brown eyes were kind, they looked as though they belonged to a good man) (*C*.957); similarly Pablo Mares, 'Su cara era dorada, su frente bien hecha, sus ojos claros, nariz recta y manos cuadradas. Hermoso ejemplar' (He had a golden complexion, high forehead, light eyes, straight nose and broad hands. A beautiful specimen) (*C*.961). Elías Acosta is described as, 'el de los ojos verdes y las cejas negras, hombre hermoso, con su color de durazno maduro' (the one with green eyes, black eyebrows, a beautiful man, his skin like a ripe peach) (*C*.966). Among those that are favourable, what all of these men have in common is the golden skin tone of those of mixed blood. This connects with the notion of *mestizaje*, the racial hybridisation of the Mexican people with mixed indigenous and European ancestry, and therefore conforms to the government's programme of Mexicanisation with its idealisation of *mestizaje* and the national unity that this was intended to achieve. *Mestizaje* then, is a metaphor for the hybridisation of the text which, with its mixture of genres including confession, autobiography and multivocal 'novel of the Revolution' produces a multi-layered text.

The golden skin of the mestizo is favoured by Nellie who does not want to let her doll marry a man with dark skin; but neither does she favour the white, blue-eyed soldiers. (According to Clive Griffin (1993: 69) blue eyes and blond hair are traditionally sinister features in Mexican literature.) The descriptions of those who fall into the category of 'white' are favourable, unfavourable and neutral, such as the one of Rafaela's friend, Colonel Bustillos, 'tenía unos bigotes güeros [. . .] era blanco, con los ojos azules [. . .] portaba sombrero tejano blanco y vestido azul marino [. . .]' (he had a fair moustache [. . .] he was white, with blue eyes [. . .] he wore a Texan hat and navy blue clothing) (*C*.930). Some of the men, when they are not named and thereby given an identity, are simply described as 'a tall officer with blue

---

[34] Garro also uses the expression 'ojos de perro amarillo'. This, I suggest, may stem from indigenous accounts of the conquest where the conquerors are described as having dogs with 'burning yellow eyes'. See Miguel León-Portilla, *The Broken Spears: The Aztec Account of the Conquest of Mexico,* Boston: Beacon Press (1992: 30–31).

eyes', or (tall with green eyes) (*C*.952–53). Most of the men are distinguished by the colour of their eyes, skin and clothing. Catarino Acosta 'se vestía de negro' (*C*.933). General Urbina's dark clothing and skin has negative connotations, 'portaba su pantalón ajustado de trapo negro [. . .] los huesos forrados de piel morena [. . .] sus venas gordas palpitando bajo la piel prieta' (he was wearing his tight trousers made of black cloth [. . .] his bones covered in dark skin, his big veins throbbing beneath the the dusky skin). Often, many of the references to black, dark colours and dirt are associated with death. Julio, who looks like a child with his 'golden curls' wants to be small again to avoid fighting and ends up burnt and (ironically) shrunken; his body charred and blackened (*C*.948). Colours (and vision) are, then, for Nellie, as eloquent as sounds (and voices), and together help to form the pictures she presents of the Revolution.

WHAT NELLIE HEARD

References to sounds can basically be divided into four types. First come the *disparos* (shots), *balazos* (gunfire) and *cañonazos* (cannon-fire) characteristic of the machinery of war which are juxtaposed with the sound of Rafaela's sewing machine. Then there are the *gritos* of the children, the people in the courtroom, the fighting men, and *Mamá* calling her children. The *cantos* y *risas* and the sound of the chords of a guitar are associated with both the people fighting in the Revolution, who sing *corridos* about its heroes and events, and in a more peaceful vein, with Mamá, singing to her children, or while at her sewing-machine. The fourth reference to sound is in the context of its absence or 'lack' – silence – which often appears as 'ni una palabra' (not a word) (*MM*.977). Silence, as in *Los recuerdos del porvenir*, is used to suggest both subjection and resistance. The first three types of sound (including the sounds of the two kinds of machinery) appear in the section 'ELLA' Y LA MÁQUINA ('Her' and the machine):

> El ruido de la máquina, con su llanto de fierros, era en la noche la única verdad de los seres [. . .] Cuando funcionaba un cañón grande era un ruido que a mí me parecía como que se abría la boca del cielo del lado del camposanto. Me estremecía de tristeza; las casas me las imaginaba desmoronadas [. . .] ¿Qué era el pobre sonido de aquella máquina junto a las voces del cañón? (*MM*.983)

> (The sound of the sewing machine, with its iron cry, was at night the only human truth [. . .] When a large cannon went off it made a noise that to me was like the heavens opening up next to the graveyard. I shuddered with sadness, I imagined the collapsed houses [. . .] What was the little sound of that sewing machine next to the voice of the cannon?)

This passage also clearly belies Nellie's purported 'cold aloofness'. As with gunshots and cannon-fire, for Nellie loud voices suggest dominant personalities, oppression and a lack of rationality. She associates them with different generals, such as the man who insulted her mother, General Rueda: 'Hombre alto, tenía bigotes güeros, hablaba muy fuerte' (A tall man, with a fair moustache, he talked very loud) (C.940). She also remembers Villa's voice, but his shouts, though frightening, are clear and vibrant, suggesting a just call to arms (and Campobello's admiration), '[. . .] le pegó un grito a sus hombres. Un grito de aquellos que él usaba para los combates, vibrantes claros, que estremecían' (He shouted to his men. His voice like the one he uses in combat, ringing, clear, that sends a shiver through you) (C.958). Not surprisingly most such references to the loud noises of battle come in Section III: EN EL FUEGO:

A las diez de la noche la balacera fue más fuerte. Pasaron parvadas de villistas gritando: '¡Viva Villa!' Otro rato largo, los enemigos entraban. Parecía que la calle fuera a explotar. Por las banquetas pasaban a caballo, tirando balazos, gritando. Comenzó el saqueo. Mamá contaba que, al oír los culatazos de los rifles pegando en las puertas, les gritó que no tiraran, que ya iba a abrir. Decía que había sentido bastante miedo [. . .] Se fueron saliendo de la casa [. . .] Iban gritando que muriera Villa y tirando balazos al cielo. (C.953)

(At ten o'clock the exchange of fire was more intense. Groups of Villistas passed by shouting 'Long live Villa!' Another long pause, the enemy came in. It seemed as if the street were about to erupt. They rode along the pavements, firing and shouting. The plunder began. Mamma told us how, on hearing the rifle butts hitting the doors, she shouted to them not to shoot, that she was going to open up. She said she had been quite frightened [. . .] They started leaving the house [. . .] They were shouting death to Villa and firing bullets into the air.)

Even the songs of the revolutionaries are shouted. The section entitled ABELARDO PRIETO begins with the verse of a *corrido* about him and ends with 'Las gargantas de los soldados, más que cantarlas, gritaban las palabras' (The soldiers' hoarse voices shouted rather than sang the words) (C.963). When Nellie's older brother is about to be shot for helping Perfecto Ruacho to escape, his mother goes to prevent it (and succeeds) (C.955). Later Nellie makes the point that the Revolution is indeed a civil war, brother taking arms against brother and shouting his allegiance to a particular general, 'Los enemigos eran: los primos los hermanos y amigos. Unos gritaban que viviera un general y otros decían que viviera el contrario' (the enemy were cousins, brothers and friends. Some shouted long live one general and others shouted long live his opponent) (C.957). The child-narrator's assumed ingenuousness when she explains that it is this vociferous proclaiming of loyalty that explains the killing, only thinly disguises the author's irony here and shouting generally represents, for Nellie, the absence of rationality that characterises war.

Shouting also represents oppression and a lack of compassion and, above all, it inspires fear in the narrator and her mother. In the courtroom scene, in *Las manos de mamá*, Rafaela describes how, when the authorities are trying to take away her children, she keeps her voice low while others all around her are shouting:

> Volvieron las voces a gritar en mi contra. 'Habló la ley'. 'Son mis hijos' les volví a decir con miedo de sus gritos. Siguieron las voces grita y grita. 'Mis hijos, míos, de mi carne de mis ojos, de mi alma, solo míos' repetí *sin levantar la voz*. Las voces se elevaron. Me hacían sufrir.
>
> (*MM*.978 [my emphasis])

> (The voices started shouting against me again. 'The law has decided'. 'They are my children' I said again, afraid of their shouting. The voices went on shouting and shouting. 'My children, mine, of my flesh, of my eyes, of my soul, only mine' I repeated, *without raising my voice*. Their voices got louder. They made me suffer.)

This scene sustains the idea of the serene mother, forbidden to show anger, fighting for her children. There are occasions, however, when that image of serenity is transgressed and Rafaela is the one who shouts. Here, shouting is a transgression of acceptable behaviour. This happens when she believes her son is dying and is looking for a doctor: 'Ella enloquecida, iba y venía. Se le moría su hijo. Le gritaba a Dios, le pedía a la Virgen, lloraba' (She came and went, like a madwoman. She shouted to God, she begged the Virgin, she wept) (*MM*.980). Rafaela's lack of resignation to God's will is intrinsic to her freedom-loving and fiercely independent character and again she transgresses her role for, as Hirsch claims, 'The active, angry rebellious woman cannot be a mother; the mother can be neither active nor rebellious' (Hirsch 1989: 38). The mother should be silent.

Silence is usually juxtaposed with speech, whether this be as a result of self-control, emotional pain, fear or as in the case of Samuel Tamayo, shyness, 'Cuando hablaba, se ponía encendido, bajaba los ojos y se miraba los pies y las manos. No hablaba' (When he spoke, he went bright red, lowered his eyes and looked at his hands and feet. He didn't speak) (*C*.956). When Villa addresses the people of Pilar de Conchos to ask why they are afraid of him, '*Nadie se atrevió a hablar* – "Digan muchachos, hablen" – les decía Villa' (*No-one dared speak* – "Tell me me lads, speak up" – Villa said to them) (*C*.959 [my emphasis]). When Rafaela returns for her children to the aunt's house, 'Su cara expresiva, era imprecisable: ni risa, ni llanto, *ni una palabra*' (Her face was impassive: she did not laugh, or cry, *nor say a word*) (*MM*.977 [my emphasis]). When Nellie learns of the death of a soldier who was her friend she says, '*Me quedé sin voz*, con los ojos abiertos abiertos; sufrí tanto' (I lost my voice, my eyes were staring into space, I suffered so much) (*C*.933 [my emphasis]).

Occasionally silence signifies peace, or resignation. When Mamá sits the children at the table to feed them, 'No nos decía nada; se estaba allí, callada como una paloma herida, dócil y fina. Parecía una prisionera de nosotros – ahora sé que era nuestra cautiva' (She didn't say anything; she was just there, quiet as a wounded dove, gentle and refined. It was as if she were our prisoner – I know now that she was our captive) (*MM*.974). Alternatively, silence is related to the idea of absence or 'lack', as in this description of la Plaza de las Lilas: 'silenciosa y perfumada, sitio de amor, lugar donde la vida es un beso mal dado y un sueño que no se realiza' (Silent and perfumed, a place of love, a place where life is a misplaced kiss and a dream that does not come true) (*MM*.985).

Sometimes the shouting and the silence are juxtaposed, as when Nellie recounts how one November morning a handful of men 'con el grito de la revolución y la bandera tricolor, quebraban el silencio del pueblo, mandando balazos a todas las rendijas donde estaban los rurales' (with the cry of Revolution and the tricolour, broke the silence of the town, firing bullets into all the cracks where the *rurales* were hiding) (*C*.963). The breaking of the silence by shouts combined with gunshots becomes a characteristic of the Revolution.

Nellie (like the child-narrator in *Balún-Canán*) is often a silent observer. Silence allows children (especially girls – 'little girls should be seen and not heard') to observe and to listen to things which they might not normally be able to witness but for their discreet presence, 'Yo la oía, sin mover los ojos ni las manos. Muchas veces me acercaba a sus conversaciones, sin que ella me sintiera' (I listened to her, without moving my eyes or hands. Many times I got close to their conversations, without her hearing me) (*C*.944). Later, Nellie goes with her mother to see the revolutionary leader, Felipe Ángeles, who has been shot. Nellie's remarks about overhearing conversations is another way she gives verisimilitude to her version of events during the Revolution: Pepita Chacón 'estuvo platicando con mamá; *no le perdí palabra*' (was chatting with Mamma; *I didn't miss a word*) (*C*.946 [my emphasis]). Her words also disclose her feeling that she is merely an observer rather than a protagonist of the Revolution.

NELLIE'S NARRATORIAL DISTANCE

Nellie's aloofness with regard to the horrors of war that she was witness to and claimed were normal to her child's eyes has been much remarked upon. However, such sights were bound to have had some effect on her impressionable child's mind and, in effect, they remained in her unconscious until they emerged in the form of these multivocal texts. Early critics of Campobello's novellas (particularly *Cartucho*) criticised what they considered to be a cold-blooded and detached view of death, not what they would expect from a little girl.[35] More recently, however, the adult/child-narrator dichotomy has been explored and a more realistic view of the effect of the terrible scenes of war on the child psyche have been taken into consideration. One reaction was clearly detachment, as Dennis Parle points out: 'To her it was all a spectacle with excitement, color and drama'.[36] This appears to be supported by Nellie's own references to what her young eyes saw: 'Hombres fuertes tirados allí para regalo de mis ojos, apretando entre los dedos las bastillas que sus mamás les pusieron en la orilla de sus ropas deslavadas' (Strong men lying there for my eyes to enjoy, pressing between their fingers the hems that their mammas put on their washed out clothing) (*MM*.983). She emphasises the sewing repairs done to the soldiers' clothes by their mothers as it is something she can relate to personally. Furthermore, she says, 'Necesitaba tener en mi alma de niña aquellos cuadros llenos de terror' (I needed to have those scenes of terror in my child's soul) (*C*.943).[37] A morbid fascination for gory detail, is not uncommon in children (or indeed adults) provided its source has not affected them personally.

However, this apparent narratorial distance is contradicted on several occasions. Nellie evidently does feel great compassion for her mother, 'lo único que sentía era que hacían que los ojos de mamá, al contarlo, lloraran. Ella sufrió mucho presenciando estos horrores' (the only thing I felt was that they made Mamma's eyes cry as she talked about them. She suffered a lot witnessing those horrors) (*C*.943).[38] Nellie's own apparent detachment from the

---

[35] Dennis J. Parle writes, 'The child's point of view, which dominates throughout the novel, presents the Revolution from a coldly objective and emotionally aloof perspective' (Parle 1985: 201–10). However, he does reveal Nellie's emotional involvement and sensitivity to her mother's and other people's suffering. John Rutherford merely refers to 'the unconscious cruelty of her cold, detached, almost clinical attitude' (Rutherford 1971: 64).

[36] Parle writes, 'The key to the novel's narrative technique is the continuous shifting of perspective between the child's and the adult's contrasting views of reality [. . .] Shifting the narrative perspective to the present and recalling the past now as an adult, the narrator suggests the reasons for her emotional indifference. With phrases like "decía mi mente de niña", "decían mis ojos empañados de infancia", she insists she was only a child, and did not really understand the significance of brutality or the meaning of death' (Parle 1985: 202–3).

[37] ' "Los fusilados" de C. tienen mucha semejanza con los (grabados) de Posada [. . .] encierran una ingenuidad de observación natural a todo niño pero expresada muy rara vez en la literatura' ('Those shot' in *Cartucho* are very similar to those [engravings] by Posada [. . .] they encompass a freshness of observation natural to all children but very rarely expressed in literature) (Rand Morton 1949: 165).

[38] 'Nellie doesn't invent anything she tells; she saw, she lived, she recorded it all. Her vision was not that gentle contemplation of other normal little girls, but episodes of brutality, of monstrous atrocity. The only sweetness in her life comes from those two hands, her mother's hands [. . .] The only thing that moves her is the memory of her mother, a peaceful haven in the thick of the bullets' (Poniatowska 1988: xi).

suffering of people she did not know personally (plausible in a war situation where death is a common sight), contrasts with her mother's compassion for all the people from her region (her *paisanos*) – even for turncoats.

Rafaela, rather than being hard-hearted about what she sees attempts to hide her emotions from the outside world. After witnessing a hanging, in the section EL AHORCADO (The Hanged Man), when everyone is outside enjoying the treat of eating watermelon together, Nellie comments: 'Mamá no decía nada, pero ya no comió la sandía' (Mamma didn't say anything, but she didn't eat the watermelon) (*C*.942). She is unable to hide the emotion in her eyes from Nellie, however. In front of her children, recounting what had happened to some *villistas* who had changed sides (one of them, her friend Fidelina's brother) her sorrow shows: 'Muchos fueron los fusilamientos, todos eran mis paisanos – decía mamá con su voz triste y *sus ojos llenos de pena* [. . .] la voz de mamá temblaba al decir que aquel hombre, soldado de la revolución, era nativo de su tierra [. . .] mamá se secaba las lágrimas, sufría mucho' (There were many executions, they were all my countrymen – said Mamma with her voice sad and her eyes full of sadness [. . .] Mamma's voice trembled when she said that that man, soldier of the Revolution, was a native of her region [. . .] Mamma dried her tears, she suffered a lot) (*C*.943 [my emphasis]).

What appears to be a lack of compassion in Nellie, except where her mother and own friends are concerned, reveals two things. On the one hand, she sees herself as useless to her mother – merely a burden – and would like to be a man with what she sees as the necessary strength, emotional control and ability to act, to enable her to protect her mother from danger. Paradoxically, Campobello is here unwittingly reinforcing the masculine/feminine binary that attributes such qualities to men even though she repeatedly reveals that her mother possesses all of these characteristics herself. On the other hand, her child's imagination and senses seem to need the sights and sounds of war. Her 'spirit soar[s] to find images of dead men' and she enjoys hearing stories of tragedy. In retrospect, her adult authorial voice acknowledges how she became accustomed to awful sights: '¡Terrible cosa! Mis ojos estaban acostumbrados a ver morir con plomo caliente, hecho pedacitos dentro del cuerpo' (Terrible thing! My eyes were used to seeing people die from hot lead, broken into lots of little pieces inside their bodies) (*MM*.981). Yet Nellie's ostensible indifference to death is again belied when confronted with the sight of the dead woman with her dead companion at her side. She reveals that it is an effort to conceal how much these sights affect her when she later states: 'Íbamos a llegar. Allí había casas, tomaríamos café, olvidaríamos los ojos borrados con tierra y la mujer en sus enaguas' (We were about to arrive. There were houses there, we would drink coffee, we would forget those eyes obliterated by earth and the woman in her petticoats) (*MM*.981).

Most early criticism of *Cartucho* concentrated on the following passage in EL CENTINELA DEL MESÓN DEL ÁGUILA, to support claims that Nellie was a cold, indifferent child: 'Más de trescientos hombres fusilados en los mismos

momentos, dentro de un cuartel, es mucho muy impresionante – decían las
gentes, pero nuestros ojos infantiles lo encontraron bastante natural' (More
than three hundred men shot at the same time inside a barracks is absolutely
horrifying – people said, but our children's eyes found it quite natural)
(*C*.940). However, it is to be expected that constant exposure to scenes of
carnage would render them less horrifying, as the spectator's sensibilities are
hardened. This is clearly revealed in this passage which explains how General
Rueda and ten of his men enter the family house and treat them roughly.
Nellie describes her mother, 'Los ojos de mamá, hechos grandes de revolución, no lloraban; *se habían endurecido* recargados en el cañón de un rifle de
su recuerdo' (Mamma's eyes, were filled with the Revolution, they did not
cry, they had become hardened resting on the rifle barrel of her memory
(*C*.940 [my emphasis]). This quotation is important in my reading of
Cartucho, because it exposes Nellie's ambiguous attitude to male and female
roles. Rafaela is only once depicted as weak and submissive by Nellie (then it
is with her own children). Indeed, she stands up for herself here, and on
numerous other occasions, against all odds. As well as debunking the myth of
the *mujer sumisa y débil*, then, this vision of women reveals that a multivocal
account of the Revolution is the only authentic one possible.

NELLIE'S IDEAL MOTHER?

In *Las manos de mamá* there exists a tension between Nellie and her
mother as regards their role as protagonist. Is the novella about a mother idealised by her self-effacing child, or about a child and a mother-figure she idealises, but whom, she feels, neglects her? Nellie clearly admires her mother's
sacrifice for the men of the Revolution and her sons, but harbours resentment
that she herself does not occupy a more central role in Rafaela's life.

Nellie's ambivalent attitude to her mother is evident in a careful reading of
Cartucho and *Las manos de mamá*. Campobello emphasises the visual sense
in her loving descriptions of her mother; however, the importance of the other
senses is equal to that of sight and cannot be overstated. There is a link
between Nellie's reference to the senses, memories of her mother and the
early mother–child relationship. As Oyarzún affirms, '[. . .] el estadio pre-
verbal, imaginario, estaría localizado en la imagen materna y va asociado a
percepciones no tanto visuales sino táctiles, olfativas y degustativas, flujos
imaginarios no simbólicos' (The preverbal, Imaginary state would be located
in the maternal image and it is associated not so much with visual as with
tactile, olfactory and taste perceptions, the flow of the imaginary not the
symbolic) (Oyarzún 1996: 185).

Nellie exists both in the world of the senses (the preverbal Imaginary associated with the mother) as well as in the verbal (the Symbolic associated with

the father). In calling her work *Las manos de mamá* rather than *Los ojos de mamá,* Campobello gives prominence, according to the eyes/hands binary opposition, to her own and her mother's femaleness and thus, their position as women in Mexico; and also to her relationship with her mother. In both *Cartucho* and *Las manos de mamá* Nellie attaches great importance to her mother's hands, or to her mother holding her hand, and refers to the *lack* of physical contact between mother and daughter, as does Campobello. This confirms my view that although Nellie did greatly admire her mother, her idealisation of *Ella* is related to her own unfulfilled desire for love and affection. Irene Matthews writes:

> Throughout *Cartucho*, memory – the mother's 'truths' and observations – is combined with fantasy, the child's imaginative and ideological projections: an artifice of narrative psychology whose slippages ironize the association between the mother's history and the child's desire. *Cartucho* is structured as a projection of infantile desire – represented in the difference between the demand for love and the appetite for satisfaction.
>
> (Matthews 1993: 151)

This difference between demand and satisfaction is fundamental to the mother–child relationship and Chodorow's words (quoted earlier) that we can never receive enough love from our mother (whether this is good for us or not) must be borne in mind in a discussion of that relationship.

In *Cartucho*, when Rafaela is hurrying to try and save her son from being shot, Nellie describes how she herself witnessed the event: 'Yo iba detrás de ella y a veces podía trotar a su lado; *ella no me agarró ni una sola vez la mano*; a veces me agarraba de su falda; *pero ella*, en su nerviosidad, *me aventaba la mano*; parecía que yo le atrasaba el paso y *ni siquiera volteaba a verme*' (I went along behind her and sometimes I could trot by her side; *she didn't hold my hand even once*; sometimes I would grab hold of her skirt, but she, in her nervousness, *would push my hand away*, it seemed I was slowing her down and *she didn't even turn round to look at me*) (*C*.954 [my emphasis]). Again, here, the similarity with the relationship between the little girl-narrator and her mother in *Balún-Canán* is striking. Nellie attempts to excuse her mother's indifference toward her by saying it was because of her nervousness, but the inclusion of such tell-tale words and phrases as 'ni una sola vez' (not once), 'aventaba' (pushed away) and 'ni siquiera' (not even), reveal the concealed hurt and resentment Nellie feels towards her idolised and idealised mother. Later, however (only) when Rafaela is assured of her son's safety, she covers her eyes with her hand: 'me buscó con la otra mano y así salió jalándome' (reached out for me with the other hand and went out dragging me along behind her) (*C*.955). The importance of this incident is only revealed at the end of the novel when Ismael Máynez is relating one of the major victories over the *carrancistas*. Nellie adds, 'Los ojos de mamá tenían una luz muy

bonita, yo creo que estaba contenta. Las gentes de nuestros pueblos habían
ganado a los salvajes' (Mamma's eyes had a lovely light in them, I think she
was happy. The people of our towns had beaten the savages). She then
changes tense in the last two sentences of the novel, to describe an ideal
version of the future in which, 'Volverían a oírse las pezuñas de los caballos.
Se alegraría otra vez nuestra calle; *mamá me agarraría de la mano* hasta
llegar al templo donde la Virgen la recibía' (The sound of horses' hooves
would be heard again. Our street would be happy once more; Mamma would
take me by the hand until we reached the temple where the Virgin would
receive her) (*C*.968 [my emphasis]). In other words she rewrites the story with
her desire fulfilled. In 'reality', however, her desire for more mother love
remains unfulfilled and her own feelings towards her mother ambivalent.

  Nellie's adoration of her mother is disguised by comments that reveal her
feeling that she is neglected by her also. Nellie insists that she is a burden to
her mother and avoids criticising her directly. She praises her for cooking for
them, bathing them and making their clothes: ordinary tasks for a mother; but
not, it would seem, for a woman of Rafaela's social class, for Nellie reiterates,
'[. . .] todo, con sus manos, lo hacía para nosotros' (she did everything for us,
with her own hands) (*MM*.976). Nellie *appears* to believe that they do not
deserve so much attention and belittles herself and her siblings, 'nosotros, los
que no éramos nada' (we, who were nothing) (*MM*.976). Nancy Friday
explains the reasons for such self-denigration:

> Children think their parents are perfect, and if anything is wrong it is their
> fault. We have to think our parents are perfect because as children we are
> so totally dependent. We can't afford to hate mother, so what we do is turn
> our anger against ourselves. Instead of saying she is hateful, we say, 'I am
> hateful'. Mother has to be all wise and kind. (Friday 1977; 1988: 26)

Similarly, her statement that they are preventing their mother from being elsewhere, or with someone else, does not come across as entirely sincere as this
is revealed to be untrue when Rafaela leaves the children with her sister for a
long period and goes off on her own.

  By hinting that she feels that she was sacrificed to the cause of the Revolution, Nellie undermines the stereotype of the Mexican mother who sacrifices
all, including her own needs, for the sake of her children. She pays tribute to
her mother's tireless tending of the wounded in the section HERIDOS DE
PANCHO VILLA (Pancho Villa's Wounded Men), but there is a hint of her own
envy at the privileged position as receivers of Mamá's attention of those
suffering physically: 'Curó catorce; yo le detuve la bandeja. Mamá era muy
conocida de la gente que sufría' (She cured fourteen of them, I held the tray
for her. Mamma was very well known by people who were suffering) (*C*.952)
– well known by people who were suffering, but less well known by those
who were not – is the implication here. Conversely, she describes the joy she

and her brothers feel when *mamá* returns to the aunt's house to collect them, 'Se abría la gloria cuando lográbamos verla venir: volvía Mamá, estaba con nosotros, tornábamos a la vida' (We were in heaven when we finally saw her coming: Mamma was back, she was with us, we were alive again) (*MM*.974). However, even then, Rafaela only touches them and does not kiss them as Nellie affirms: 'No nos hacía cariños, no nos besaba' (She didn't caress us, she didn't kiss us) (*MM*.974). Indeed, after paying scant attention to them, she automatically brushes them aside: 'se desanudaba el pelo, cantaba, iba y venía; casi sin fijarse nos hacía a un lado' (she let down her hair, she sang, she came and went, almost without realising it she pushed us to one side) (*MM*.974). Although Rafaela is an emotional person when it comes to her *paisanos* killed by the Revolution, she is undemonstrative as regards affection for her children. No wonder then, that Nellie places so much emphasis on *mamá*'s hands and eyes: these were the means by which she measured her mother's affection. In spite of her long absence Rafaela sits in the doorway, smoking a cigarette and looking out, 'entonces nosotros no le hacíamos ruido' (then we tried not to make any noise) (*MM*.974). Finally, there are hints of resentment in Nellie's tone beneath her regret at her mother's having left them behind, alone and unprotected, at the mercy of the elements, when she allowed herself to die: 'Hoy la veo a usted como entonces; pero los pliegues de su falda se mueven muy rápido y se la llevan lejos, lejos, donde la vida no alcanza y donde usted ya no puede protegernos de los relámpagos ni de las nubes de polvo, ni del agua que azota nuestros ojos' (Today, I see you as then; but the folds of your skirt move very quickly and they carry you far far away, where life can't go and where you can no longer protect us from the lightning, the clouds of dust, or the water that whips our eyes) (*MM*.976).

There is a great deal of evidence to suggest that Rafaela is a very independent woman who does what she wants and what she feels she has to do, regardless of anyone else, to such an extreme as to die leaving behind her children as orphans. After Nellie's little brother dies and her mother follows him, no longer wanting to live, the narrator expresses her understanding of her mother's decision not to remain with them; but there is also a hint of resentment that she would abandon all of them for the sake of the youngest, '[. . .] a pesar de que, como dueña de nuestras vidas, las ofrecía en montón a cambio de aquel niño que borró la alegría de nuestra casa, pidió morir. Sus manos en ademán enérgico, rechazaban la vida' (in spite of the fact that, as mistress of our lives, she offered them all up as a sacrifice for that boy who erased the joy from our household, when she asked to die. Her hands, in a determined gesture, rejected life) (*MM*.988). Nellie attempts (somewhat unconvincingly) to justify, to herself as much as to anyone else, her mother's rationale for leaving the rest of the children without a mother: 'Ella, como siempre, apresuró el paso para ir junto al que más la necesitara' (As usual, she hurried to be with the one who needed her most) (*MM*.988). However, her address to her mother suggests ambivalence in the way Nellie views Rafaela's sacrifice for the youngest sibling and the notion that they should follow her rather than her remaining with them: 'No le escribo nada que tenga sombras: Usted quiere que vayamos alegremente rimando nuestros pasos hasta el lugar donde usted espera' (I won't write anything for you that has a cloud. You want us to go joyfully keeping in step to the place where you are waiting) (*MM*.988). There is more than a little compromise in these words. Nellie is not saying what she really feels about her mother leaving them behind, as she does not want to be the one to reproach her.

The explanation for this is again found in feminist psychoanalysis: 'Our efforts to see mother clearly are frustrated by a kind of denial. It is one of our most primitive mechanisms of defence. Early on, children begin to avoid knowledge that mother is anything less than the "good mother" she pretends to be' (Friday 1977; 1988: 26). Nellie's mother's aloofness no doubt helped Nellie to establish her own sense of self; but in the atmosphere of early twentieth-century Mexico, the notion of the 'good enough' mother had not yet been enunciated. Nellie reveals herself to be a lonely child, in spite of her brothers and sisters. Even her initial friendship with them is destroyed by their conformity and enjoyment of school: 'Ahí fue donde comencé a separarme de su amistad; dudé de su rebeldía, me habían hecho una gran traición. Mi soledad era absoluta' (That was when I began to leave their friendship behind; I doubted their rebellion, they had betrayed me terribly. I was absolutely alone) (*MM*.986). She feels different from the others and takes refuge in nature, refusing to go to school. Her mother, realising she is exceptional, does not oblige her to attend but instead allows Nellie's aunt, Isabel, to teach her. Neither does she oblige her to make her First Communion: 'Mi carácter necesitaba la libertad y como lo sabía ella, me dejó' (My character needed freedom and as she knew that, she let me be) (*MM*.987).

Nellie's loyalty to her mother in spite of the affective neglect she suffered, reveals the ambivalent nature of the mother–daughter relationship. Rafaela undoubtedly loves Nellie, but at the same time Nellie resents the fact that her mother could be separated from her without suffering the same feelings of loss that she herself experienced. This would appear to be a clear example of incomplete individuation. Yet, although Nellie's mother transgresses her role as the *madre abnegada* by being less than affectionate and loving towards her children, she does fulfil the role of 'good enough' mother as she obliges Nellie to experience the disillusionment necessary for her individuation to take place. If it appears that Nellie has failed to individuate successfully, this may be because the traditional patriarchal model for individuation 'is defined as the separation of the self from all others' (Stanford Friedman 1988: 56). 'Individualistic paradigms' affirms Stanford Friedman, 'do not recognize the significance of interpersonal relationships and community in women's self-definition, nor do they explain the ongoing identification of the daughter with her mother' (Stanford Friedman 1988: 56). Thus Nellie's close identification with her mother and representation of hers and other women's voices in her 'autobiography', is normal from the point of view of critics of women's auto-biography.

While traditional psychoanalysts, then, would view Nellie's/Campobello's obsession with her mother as unnatural and resulting from the child's incomplete individuation, Nellie does, in fact, recognise her mother's separateness but not without a certain resentment. The achievement of differentiation of self by an infant comes about, to quote Nancy Chodorow, only 'insofar as its expectations of primary love are frustrated'. Without this frustration and the ensuing anxiety and ambiguity felt by the child, the development of ego capacities which would help to ward off these anxieties, would not be initiated (Chodorow 1978: 69–70).

I referred earlier to the purported greater closeness between mothers and daughters than between mothers and sons, which may lead to incomplete differentiation or individuation in daughters.[39] Such incomplete differentiation would explain Nellie's (and Mariana's in *La 'Flor de Lis'*) obsessive love of her mother. Even at seven years of age she still wants to be part of her: 'Ella cantando al ritmo de la máquina; la máquina, una niña de acero entre sus manos, dejándose llevar por ella y por sus cantos. Yo estaba a su lado. Si ella no tenía sueño, yo no lo tenía; si cantaba, cantaba yo' (She, singing in time to the sewing machine, the machine a steel child in her hands, letting itself be carried along by her and her songs. I was by her side. If she wasn't sleepy, neither was I; if she sang, I sang) (*MM*.983). Feminist revisions (such as that of Hirsch) of Freud's theory claim, however, that such close affiliation between mother and daughter is natural and is deliberately destroyed by patriarchy to ensure women's powerlessness.[40]

At the very beginning of the novella, when Nellie returns as an adult to the place where she grew up, her feelings of loss and powerlessness are made evident when she imagines she sees her mother, and in a moment of great poignancy, cries out for her:

Y estaba allí, la vieron mis ojos, míos de niña. *Usted* hizo el milagro y fui derecho: corriendo. Era yo niña, usted me quería así. Me arrimé al postigo. Ella no está; crujiendo las maderas, y yo, hecha mujer, vestida de blanco y sin rímel en los ojos, grité sobre la puerta: ¡Mamá, mamá, mamá! (*MM*.972)

[39] Freudian psychoanalysis centres on the nuclear family and cites the importance of the father in the child's process of differentiation of self, as it is easier for the child to compare mother and father than mother and self. However, Minsky explains that Lacan, unlike Freud, stresses that the father may only be a symbolic rather than an actual father, and that separation from the mother followed by attachment to the father occurs whether or not the father is present as 'the child experiences the place of the father and the Oedipal crisis through cultural substitutions' (Minsky 1989: 149).

[40] Hirsch writes: 'For Freud, anger between child and mother, anger directed specifically at the mother, fundamentally underlies the sequence of individual maturation; it makes that linear narrative possible. The repression of the initial fusion with the mother is the condition of the construction of the subject' (Hirsch 1989: 168).

(And there she was, I saw her with my own eyes, my little girl's eyes. You performed a miracle and I went straight to you, running. I was a little girl, you loved me like that. I went up close to the outer door. She isn't there; the wood creaking, and I, a woman now, dressed in white and with no eye make-up, shout through the door: Mamma! Mamma! Mamma!)

3

SENSIBILITY AND SUBALTERNITY:
MEMORY AND MOTHER-FIGURES
IN ROSARIO CASTELLANOS' *BALÚN-CANÁN*

> If [. . .] the subaltern has no history and cannot
> speak, the subaltern as female is even more
> deeply in shadow.[1]

INTRODUCTION

Balún-Canán, Rosario Castellanos' first novel, published in 1957, is the
story of a seven-year-old girl's impressions of life in the state of Chiapas, in
south-western Mexico. The socio-economic status of women in rural Chiapas
society in the 1930s, when the author herself was growing up there, placed
them at the lower end of a political (that is, power holding) hierarchy, where
only the Indians have less say in their own destiny.[2] The position held by the
girl-narrator, therefore, places her in the category of Other. Castellanos' feminist agenda comprised a denunciation – often through humour – of the
marginalisation of women, but also of the indigenous people.[3] Her fiction was

---

[1] Gayatri Chakravorty Spivak (1993: 66–111).

[2] I shall use the term 'Indians' (as a translation of *indios*) when the cultural inferiority
associated with this group is implied in the text and 'indigenous (people)' otherwise. In her
essay 'Teoría y práctica del indigenismo' (Dec. 1964) Castellanos writes, with regard to
the work of the Instituto Nacional Indigenista (established in 1948) that, 'Ya ni la palabra
"indio" va cargada forzosamente de desprecio ni la palabra "ladino" de esa ambigüedad
que oscila entre el elogio y el insulto' (Castellanos 1988: 126). However, I am respecting
current usage whereby many indigenous people themselves refuse to accept the term
'indio'.

[3] Paul Julian Smith considers Castellanos has been unsuccessful in attempting to
combine the 'dominant narrative form of the realist novel and the subaltern experience of
Indians, women and children' (Smith 1992: 135). However, his interpretation of Castellanos' allusions to the closeness to nature of the indigenous people as essentialising and
stereotyping and therefore flawed, overlooks the fact that Castellanos sought to avoid the
idealisation of the 'noble savage' employed by the *indianista* writers of the nineteenth
century, and also to produce a mythical representation of them rather than a realist one.
According to Renate von Hauffstengel, the *indianistas* wrote stories which were totally
distanced from reality and which gave an idealised picture of the indigenous people (von
Hauffstengel 1966).

usually written from the focal point of these two groups, though in the third person. *Balún-Canán*, has such a third-person narrator in the second part of the novel, but the first and third parts are narrated in the first-person by a seven-year-old girl.

Like the other works discussed in this book, *Balún-Canán* clearly has certain autobiographical elements as Elena Poniatowska affirms in her Prologue to *Meditación en el umbral* (Poniatowska 1995*b*: 14); and Cynthia Steele confirms in her article in INTI (Steele 1994–5: 321–322). A brief biography of Castellanos reveals the similarities between parts of her life and *Balún-Canán*.

Born in Mexico City on 25 May 1925, Rosario Castellanos was taken by her parents to their native Chiapas the following year, where she grew up on the family ranch near the Jataté River, and in the town of Comitán. Rosario was looked after as a child by her *cargadora* María Escandón,[4] and by an indigenous wet-nurse, Rufina, a *tojolabal* from San Bartolo (a farm near Ocosingo) whom the Castellanos family took to Comitán from their ranch, Chapatengo (Chactajal in *Balún-Canán*). According to Cynthia Steele, this ranch had previously belonged to three of Rosario's aunts and they became the model for the three aunts in the novel. The family remained in Chiapas until the Lázaro Cárdenas land reforms deprived them of their property in 1941, when they returned to Mexico City.[5] Rosario studied Philosophy at the UNAM (Universidad Autónoma de México) and became part of a group of young writers who later became known as the Generation of 1950. She received grants which enabled her to research the contribution of women to Mexican culture and to write *Balún-Canán*, for which she received the Mexican Critics' Award for the best novel of 1957. She returned to Chiapas where she lived and worked for the *Instituto Indigenista* in direct contact with the indigenous cultures of the region, thereby expanding her experience of indigenous culture. She wrote poetry, essays, novels and short stories and became a diplomat until her untimely death in Israel in 1974 (Ahern 1990: 140–149).

One of the inevitable consequences of exploring the use of first-person narrative by women is to examine gendered memory. I do this by looking at how childhood experience or events from the writer's past are remembered and depicted by the writer as an adult. Also, by exploring the relation between Castellanos' gender and her writing, I attempt to show how, having been denied participation in other activities due to her gender, the need for Castel-

---

[4]   Although referred to by Poniatowska (1995*b*: 15) as 'indígena', María Escandón was, according to Steele, Castellanos' aunt and considered herself white, but as she was illegitimate the family connection went largely unrecognised (Steele 1994–95: 320).

[5]   Cárdenas' presidency ended in 1940. Presumably the reforms continued to be implemented under Ávila Camacho. (Castellanos was born in 1925 so clearly, historical accuracy is not a priority in the novel.)

lanos to express herself is manifested in her writing.[6] Incorporated in the notion of 'gendered memory' is the importance placed on the senses in descriptions and how reference to the senses produces images. According to some psychoanalysts, the particular nature of the mother–daughter relationship, whereby the usual separation that occurs between mother and son is not so rigorously enforced by society, allows for a *potential* continued intimacy that is not necessarily present in the mother–son relationship (where too much intimacy may be considered unhealthy for the child's psyche). Hence, the importance of the senses associated with the pre-Oedipal phase may continue into childhood and beyond. In *Balún-Canán*, where such mother–daughter intimacy does not take place between the narrator and her biological mother, the child seeks it elsewhere and finds it with her *nana*. Castellanos' writing is very much related to gender; what it means to be female and the multivocal nature of her work expresses many different ways of being female. In *Balún-Canán* there are as many female voices or perspectives as there are female characters. Each one is different from the other; not one conforms to the stereotypes demanded by Mexican patriarchy (see Chapter One). The narrator's mother, Zoraida, appears far from self-sacrificing. She leaves most of the care of her children to *nanas* and *cargadoras*. Yet her monologue in the second part of the novel, reveals that society left her no alternative other than to marry and have children.[7] Zoraida's unmarried sister-in-law, Matilde, loses her virginity. She is not given to study and appears weak and dependent. Yet she refuses to accept the fate that society would impose on her and chooses oblivion instead. Her older sister, Francisca, is strong, but she is eventually killed by the Indians who work for her. Thus Castellanos reveals both the future options available for the girl-narrator as a female, and the ways women can refuse to conform to them. Clearly, she wished to present more than a mere story about childhood.

The story starts with the indigenous Tzeltal *nana* telling the little girl a story derived from a Mayan creation myth from *El libro de consejo*. This sets the tone for the first part of the novel which concentrates on the girl's view of life in Comitán, in a remote part of Chiapas, and her relationship with her *nana* and the other people in her world. These are mostly her family members: her father, César Argüello, her mother Zoraida, and her younger brother, Mario. The *nana*, like the narrator, is never named.[8] The family, who have been landowners for generations, experience for the first time the changes

---

6 See Chapter One, p. 17, 'Autobiography'.

7 Although Castellanos' own mother was different from Zoraida in many ways, her remarks about her mother's lack of education and self-esteem indicate that they profoundly influenced her own determination to escape such a life; see Castellanos (1975).

8 Also, the *nana* is the only other person in the household who has the same low status as the little girl, in the hierarchical society of rural Chiapas. It is significant, therefore, that neither the little girl nor the *nana* has a name. This is part of the reason for their affinity, both being nameless, therefore voiceless and marginalised beings.

affecting the social hierarchy produced by the Revolution. While such changes were less strongly felt in the remote south-west of the country than in the north, by the time of President Lázaro Cárdenas' land reform, the absolute superiority of the *cashlanes*[9] was beginning to crumble even there. *Balún-Canán* traces the effects of this erosion of power on the landowning Argüello family.

News of Cárdenas' land reform policy is brought to the Argüello ranch by 'Tío' David, a friend of the family. This is followed by the closing of the Catholic school attended by the narrator, and the demand by the Cárdenas administration – committed to secular education – that César Argüello set up a school to provide an education for the children of the Indians who work for him. Violence against the family manifests itself first in the form of a machete attack on one of the *peones* loyal to the Argüellos; then by the fire set in the sugar refinery; and finally, in the murder of César's illegitimate nephew, Ernesto, who has come to work for him.[10] The first part of the novel also sees the emotive leave-taking of the narrator and her *nana* who remains behind (because she is afraid of the *brujos*) when César decides to take his family to Chactajal, where the Argüello country estate lies, to sort out the problems there. It ends with the arrival of the family at Chactajal, after a difficult journey full of bad omens and encounters with hostile Indians. Sensual emphasis in this part is on touch (the *nana*'s lap), as well as (to a lesser extent) on smell and hearing – all associated with the pre-Oedipal phase of development.

The second part of the novel, with its omniscient narrator, has its emphasis on sight, as the anonymous observer relates all that it sees regarding the action of the novel. This contrast found in the binary sight/touch is similar to that in Campobello's *Cartucho* and *Las manos de mamá*. That the second part makes scant reference to the little girl and contains most of the 'action' of the novel, reinforces the notion of the 'active' (omniscient) male narrator and the passive first-person female who only writes memoirs.[11] In fact, the apparently 'omniscient' narrator of this part of the novel, turns out to be a collection of the many voices of the different marginalised peoples – Indians, women and César Argüello's white but 'bastard' nephew, Ernesto. It contains the stories of the women characters; the increasing hostility of the Indians who work for César and the reasons for such hostility. Also, it relates the succession of failures of Ernesto: in setting up a school, in fitting in with the family, in forming

---

9   This is the term used in the novel by the indigenous people to refer to those of European descent (a derivation of *castellanos*). The term *ladinos* is used elsewhere, though this also refers to indigenous people who have absorbed some aspect of European culture.

10   According to the *nana* the illness and subsequent death of the narrator's brother is also the result of an act of violence, but brought about by the *brujos* of Chactajal.

11   Castellanos writes with irony about her presumed female passivity and mediocrity in her poem 'Autorretrato' (Castellanos 1985; 1995a: 185–187).

a relationship with Matilde; and finally, in getting himself murdered when he is acting as messenger for César.[12]

The third part of *Balún-Canán* sees the return of the family to Comitán and César's departure for Tuxtla to try and obtain help from the state governor. Mario falls ill, according to the *nana,* bewitched by the *brujos* of Chactajal who are 'eating' him. Zoraida, terrified by her own superstition and the doctor's inability to save her son, beats the *nana* for telling her what she dreads hearing and sends her away for good. The narrator is at once deprived of her *nana*'s love and made to realise that her mother would rather it was she who were dying than Mario. Zoraida sends the children to Catechism classes with her friend Amalia, in an attempt to make sure Mario takes Holy Communion before he dies. But Mario, terrified by the new childminder's stories of demons who take children away just as they are about to commune, does not want to take Communion. His sister, having decided that she must also protect herself from the demons (since no-one else will as she is not the male child) hides the key to the sacristy so that the First Communion cannot take place. Mario dies without making his First Communion and the narrator is overcome by guilt and wants her brother's forgiveness. After visiting his tomb in the family mausoleum and seeing that his name has not yet been etched in stone with those of the other late members of the Argüello family, she writes his name all over the walls to atone for her misdeed.

It would appear that Castellanos' motives for writing through a child-narrator, on the one hand, and the many voices of the marginalised on the other, was to avoid the label of 'Autobiography' being placed on her work, the reasons for which I discussed in Chapter One. However, while it is clearly possible that the child-narrator is indeed Castellanos herself, she is above all creating a work of fiction, with a child as narrator.[13] One of the problems of child-narration according to Henry James is that 'small children have many more perceptions than they have terms to translate them' (cited in Dorrit Cohn 1978: 45–46). Castellanos gets around this problem by using various devices, such as the use of sense-perceptions, to give verisimilitude to her child-narrator.

It is worthy of note in the case of *Balún-Canán* that the subjective first-person narrator of the first part of the novel disappears when separated from

---

12 This is a deliberate statement about the inadequacy of Ernesto who due to his illegitimacy occupies a low status and has low self-esteem both of which contribute to his feelings of inferiority and position him in a parallel, though dissimilar, subordinate role to the female characters in the novel. From the point of view of gender, therefore, he fails to live up to the male, *ladino,* ideal of superiority and dominance. Consider, for example, how he exacerbates his inferior status when he 'even' makes himself ridiculous in the eyes of the indigenous children by being unable to teach them, getting drunk in the classroom and striking one of them.

13 See Rhoda Dybvig (1965) and Catherine Grant (1991) for an exploration of the autobiographical nature of *Balún-Canán* and the child-narrator.

her *nana* during the second part, where she is replaced by the third-person 'omniscient' narrator. In other words she is textually lost, which is analogous to her own feelings of loss when deprived of her *nana*. The little girl is mentioned only occasionally in the second part, and on one of these occasions it is merely to describe how she is literally lost and then found by her Aunt Matilde when both are attempting to run away from Chactajal and their female destiny. The first-person narrator returns in the third part when *niña* and *nana* are reunited. After Mario's illness and the *nana*'s banishment, the narrator finds a new significance and subject position as she becomes the protective older sister against the danger of the dreaded *Catashaná* – until Mario dies.[14] She then assumes yet another role of importance as the only surviving Argüello child who must be pampered and kept from harm if the line is to continue. Heteroglossia is thus also present in these various roles adopted by one individual as he or she consequently assumes a different 'language' appropriate to that role. It is only when she finally begins to write that the narrator reasserts herself as a subject in her own right.[15] In other words, until she finds herself through writing she is insignificant (both in her own eyes and as a woman in Chiapas society) and 'lost' inasmuch as she lacks a sense of self.

GENDER AND STATUS IN CHIAPAS

Claudia Schaefer rightly states that Castellanos, unlike earlier *indigenista* writers, subverts the victim/victimiser dichotomy in her treatment of the Indians: 'while their interpersonal relationships tend to fall into patterns of dominator and dominated, all are victims of one sort or another – of a suffocating environment, a tyrannical *patrón*, an inherited mythology, a decadent society, an unresponsive spouse, or an unresolvable psychological conflict within the characters themselves' (Schaefer 1992: xxvii). The child-narrator is also a victim of emotional neglect by her parents.

Laura Lee Crumley de Pérez and Luz Elena Zamudio Rodríguez have both written about the *niña*'s lack of confidence with regard to her relationship with her biological mother and her subsequent emotional dependence on her *nana*, but neither has addressed the ambivalent feelings of the little girl for her mother.[16] Crumley de Pérez writes, with regard to the psychology of the child-narrator in *Balún-Canán*, how the little girl, because of the *desamor* she experiences with her mother and the loving relationship she experiences with

[14] *Catashaná* is a demon from indigenous mythology combined with Catholicism who carries children off as they are about to take their First Communion.

[15] See Monique Wittig's 'The Mark of Gender' for a discussion on women's asserting themselves as subjects (Wittig 1986: 66; 68)

[16] Crumley de Pérez (1984: 491–503). Zamudio Rodríguez (1996).

her *nana*, identifies the indigenous world as wholly benevolent and the *ladino* world as hostile and cold. This seems to me a simplification of the child's feelings and Crumley de Pérez's description of the little girl's view of 'la madre ausente' as 'cruel, indiferente y arbitraria' overlooks the confusion in the child's feelings for her mother. (I shall discuss this in more depth in the following section: *Gente menuda: niña* and *nana*.) The subordination of women and Indians and discourses on patriarchy and power are ideas that have been explored by critics of *Balún-Canán* who have also addressed the child's relationship with her mother.[17] However, no critic has really addressed the rationale underlying Castellanos' motives for choosing to narrate the first and third parts of her story *through the eyes* of a child.[18] According to Castellanos, the child's world is very similar to the mythical world of the Indian where the action of the novel is set. Her argument that only children are able to participate in the world of the indigenous people due to their inno-cence, imagination and innate goodness, appears to apply in the case of *Balún-Canán*, at least as far as the narrator is concerned.[19] Mario, on the other hand, has no close connection with the world of the indigenous people even though he too might have been breast-fed by the *nana* to whom the narrator is so attached. According to Object–Relations theory the explanation for this lies in the more lasting bond that normally exists between mothers and daughters than between mothers and sons, due to the 'fact' that girls do not have to reject their mother (as do boys in order to pass beyond the Oedipal stage of develop-ment) because the 'sexual' attraction they feel towards the mother is not (unlike in the case of the sons) a threat to the father.[20] However, the rejection of the girl-narrator by both her father and mother, both of whom favour their male child, leads the narrator to find comfort and security with the *nana*, whom she is therefore naturally reluctant to give up. Mario, in contrast to his sister, is already incorporated into the world of the ruling élite merely by virtue of his sex. Mario is considered by his parents as the only inheritor of Chactajal and the only one worth fighting for to retain the old privileges of the landowners, and to halt the encroaching land reform. The *niña* is made aware

---

17 For example Donald Frischmann (1985: 665–678), cites Phyllis Rodríguez Peralta (1977: 68–69): 'In this closed society of the Chiapas region, isolated from the mainstream of Mexican life, all women seem to be marginal figures, alienated from society and from each other. They encompass not only the expected victims of man's brutality, but the brutality of women to women. There are no tender relationships, not even between mothers and daughters.'

18 The explanation for writing the memoirs given by Poniatowska (1987: 90), that Emilio Carballido advised Castellanos to recuperate her childhood memories – and *Balún-Canán* appeared, does not explain her reasons for choosing a child-narrator.

19 Castellanos/Carballo (1965: 418–419). The concept of the child's innate goodness is a legacy of Romanticism and is reminiscent of Rousseau's idealistic concept of the 'noble savage'.

20 For an explanation of this theory see Chodorow (1978: 92–95).

of this when Don Jaime Rovelo comments on the time César has spent in Tuxtla trying to see the state governor, saying: 'No pelea únicamente para él, sino para Mario' (He is not just fighting for himself, but for Mario too) (235).[21] After Mario dies, he tells the little girl: 'Ahora tu padre no tiene por quién seguir luchando' (Now your father has no-one to carry on fighting for) (281). Mario too realises his superior status and position in the eyes of his parents and society as a whole. It is the feeling of rejection by her parents, as a direct result of her gender, therefore, that leads the little girl to identify with the indigenous world of her *nana*.

Castellanos makes clear the narrator's inferior status (as a girl) in several ways in *Balún-Canán*. First, she has no name in the novel (unlike her brother) either in the first or third parts – where she is narrating in the first person and would not naturally use her own name – or in the second part, which is related in the third person. (She is nowhere called by her name by anyone – her *nana* calls her 'niña'.) Secondly, her mother makes no attempt to conceal from her daughter the fact that she hopes it will not be Mario (the male child) who dies if, as augured by a local *bruja*, God is to vent his rage and she is to lose one of her children (256).[22] When the prophecy comes true and Mario dies, César and Zoraida do not hide their regret that it was he who died and not their daughter.[23] The *niña*'s inferior status and lack of privilege is also revealed when she is discovered reading a manuscript relating the history of the Argüello family (60). The manuscript contains the story told by the *Tzeltal* of the Chactajal region about how their lands were possessed and how they were colonised by the Argüello family many generations earlier. It is written in a style similar to that of the three 'indigenous' texts, quoted at the beginning of each part of the novel: *El libro de consejo*, the *Chilam Balam de Chumayel* and the *Anales de los Xahil*. The little girl is scolded and told that it is her brother's birthright as he is the male and that she must not 'play' with it. This in itself is significant since it is assumed she is playing with the text rather than reading it because she is a girl. This signifies how the world of literature (i.e. knowledge and power) is reserved for males.

[21] From here onwards all references to the text will consist of the page number in parentheses of the 20th edition of *Balún-Canán*, published by Fondo de Cultura Económica (FCE), Mexico 1995.

[22] Castellanos recalls the real life incident in 'Vida ¡Nada te debo!', which she remembered very well in spite of being only eight years old, of how a friend of her mother's in a spiritist session with her, had a revelation: '[. . .] dijo a mi mamá que acababa de aparecérsele un espíritu que le avisó que uno de sus hijos iba a morir. Entonces mi mamá se levantó como resorte y gritó "Pero, ¿no el varón, verdad?" ' (she told my mother that a spirit had just appeared to her and told her that one of her children was going to die. Then my mother sprang up and shouted: 'But it won't be the boy, will it?') (Poniatowska 1987: 113–14).

[23] Compare this with the comment made by Castellanos' own mother to her 'mira, tu papá y yo porque tenemos la obligación te queremos' (Look, your father and I love you because we are obliged to) (Poniatowska 1987: 118).

Elena Poniatowska has suggested that it is often lonely or solitary children who grow up to become writers. This is certainly the case with Rosario Castellanos who constantly refers to her loneliness in her articles, poems and essays:

> Para sentirme acompañada yo no necesité prácticamente nunca de la presencia física de otro. Cuando era niña hablaba sola, porque soy Geminis. Antes de dejar de ser niña ya había comenzado a escribir versos [. . .] (Castellanos 1995: 17–18).[24]

> (In order not to feel alone I almost never needed the physical presence of another person. When I was a little girl I used to talk to myself, because I am a Geminian. Before I became an adolescent I had already begun to write poems.)

In *Balun-Canan* the narrator's loneliness is exacerbated by the fact that as a girl she is excluded from many activities which are the prerogative of male children and therefore only enjoyed by Mario. One such activity is kite-flying. However, the little girl, disallowed from utilising the wind for her own diversion, comes to consider it as an ally. In so doing she again enters the world of the indigenous people, which, in gendered terms, was traditionally a passive female world where the relationship with nature was one of respect and reciprocity, unlike the exploitative one of patriarchal society which tends/needs to harness and use nature for its own profit and pleasure.[25] Her awareness of the segregation between male and female activities appears in the statement 'Nosotras miramos, apartadas de los varones, desde nuestro lugar' (We watched, separate from the males, from our place) (22).

The rigidity in male and female roles is again in evidence when 'Tío' David first comes to visit. He sings to the children about how things are beginning to change in the social context and they are all going to become poor. Mario's response is to say he wants to be a hunter of quetzals like 'Tío' David, while the little girl says she wants to be the owner of the house that invites those who arrive at mealtimes to eat. Castellanos thus points out the provider/nurturer binary.

The narrator's attitude to Mario, at this stage, is largely one of detachment and almost rivalry. She refers to him as *mi hermano*, whom she looks up and down 'Porque nació después de mí, y cuando nació, yo ya sabía muchas cosas' (Because he was born after me, and when he was born, I already knew lots of things) (9).[26] However, Mario's greater importance in his parents' eyes

---

[24] This appears in an article sent by Castellanos from Tel Aviv on 19 July 1973.

[25] See Castellanos' essay 'El desplazamiento hacia otro mundo' (July 1965), for her ideas on the relationship between humans and nature (Castellanos 1988: 67).

[26] The term *hermano* when used by the indigenous people has quite different implications as usually *el hermano menor* is under the care of *el hermano mayor* who is a kind of

does not go unnoticed by Mario nor by his sister. In spite of her being older and more knowledgeable, he still behaves in a superior manner as no secret is made of the fact that as the male, he is the heir and the most important child. When she tries to teach him something the narrator observes how Mario just looks at her as though she was undeserving of merit, then shrugs his shoulders with indifference (10). The *niña* is outraged by such indifference for she has not yet learned to accept her inferior role as is revealed by her reaction to this: 'La rabia me sofoca. *Una vez más* cae sobre mí todo el peso de la injusticia' (I am suffocated by rage. *Once more* all the weight of injustice falls on me) (10 [my emphasis]). Her outrage puts her in a bad mood which is later transferred to her *nana*, the only person in the household below her in the social hierarchy, and upon whom she can therefore vent her anger with impunity.

As with the Indians, the narrator as both a child and – more importantly – a *female* child, has little voice and hardly any control over her own destiny. Poniatowska writes that Castellanos identifies with the indigenous people because they too are victims, and if it had not been for her limited and indifferent parents, she quite possibly would not have become a writer. The failure of her marriage later on, further consolidated her literary vocation (Poniatowska 1985: 131). The little girl comes from what 'Tío' David refers to as *gente menuda*, a category of 'others', which includes women of lower social class, female children, Indians, the poor and people like himself. 'Tío' David, who is old and has to make his living hunting quetzal birds for their valuable tail feathers, is also denied a place in the category which he contrasts with *gente menuda*: that of *gente de respeto* (24). He scolds the narrator for asking about the Nine Guardians: 'Niña, no seas curiosa. Los mayores lo saben y por eso dan a esa región el nombre de Balún-Canán. La llaman así cuando conversan entre ellos. *Pero nosotros, la gente menuda* más vale que nos callemos' (Child, don't be so curious. The wise ones know and that is why they give that region the name Balún-Canán. *But we, the nobodies*, should just keep quiet) (26 [my emphasis]). However, Mario is not included in the category of *gente menuda* as 'Tío' David volunteers information to Mario when he says he wants to be a hunter too. The little girl again reveals her awareness of the gender bias when she relates how she is told to remain silent and ignorant while he is encouraged with the words 'pregunta, indágate' (ask, find things out). She responds by breaking the silence that has been imposed on her with a small act of rebellion: 'Yo rasgo el silencio con un acorde brusco de guitarra' (I break the silence with a brusque chord on the guitar) (26). Later on, when Mario is ill and she feels responsible for his illness, which she imagines to be a punishment for stealing the key to the sacristy, she is unable to tell the truth because she feels defenceless: 'Porque me comerían los brujos a mí;

guardian (see *Balún-Canán* 28, 60 and 63). Here it is used to show the lack of unity between the narrator and her brother. Later on, when they become accomplices in the theft of the sacristy key, she refers to him more often as 'Mario'.

a mí me castigaría Dios, a mí me cargaría *Catashaná*. ¿Quién iba a defenderme? Mi madre no. Ella sólo defiende a Mario porque él es el hijo varón' (Because it would be me the sorcerers would eat, me that God would punish, me that Catashaná would carry off. Who would defend me? Not my mother. She only defends Mario because he's the boy) (278). Again the blatant favouritism shown towards the male child is manifested, as well as the vulnerability experienced by the female child.

NIÑA AND *NANA*

The world of literature: reading and, by implication, learning, knowledge and the power of the word are denied to the girl-child (when she is forbidden to read the family history and her school is closed by an inspector). She will have no need of any of those things in a world in which her role has already been assigned to her. (Given the nature of mothering, and Chiapas society, she, as with her mother, will have little say in the choice of the husband she is destined to serve, if, indeed, she is lucky enough to find, or be found, a husband.) Thus, having been denied the usual source of knowledge that is available to males in a patriarchal westernised society (literature), the *niña* turns to the only source available to her – the unwritten and orally transmitted folkloric knowledge of indigenous culture – her *nana*: 'Entonces, como de costumbre cuando quiero saber algo, voy a preguntárselo a la *nana*' (Then, as usual when I want to know something, I go and ask my *nana*) (27). It is through the relationship with her *nana*, and the absorption of this knowledge that she is able to participate in both the *ladino* and the indigenous worlds. Her participation in the latter introduces her to another world and the idea of cyclical time as presented in the stories told to her by her *nana*, derived from indigenous myths. Her relationship with her *nana*, though, is ambiguous. She is aware of the social division between them yet she recognises her *nana* as the only source of love and warmth available to her.

There are several reasons for the closeness that exists between the little girl and her *nana*. The first of these is that the *nana* is a mother substitute: indeed she is the 'good enough mother' *par excellence*. Not only was she the child's wet-nurse, but she is the one who deals with the day-to-day care of the little girl, feeding and dressing her, taking her out (11) and teaching her good manners (12). Secondly, and more importantly, the *nana* is also the little girl's spiritual mentor and guide. She teaches her how to behave with respect for all things and shows her a different – indigenous – version of events and way of seeing the world. Finally, it is clear throughout the first part of the novel, and up until the *nana* is sent away, that she is also the child's source of warmth and love and that it is she who really cares about the little girl. This is revealed in several ways.

The *nana* tells the little girl how she is breaking the (indigenous) law by loving those who have the power and give the orders. The *niña* identifies with the Indians when she hears this (and at other points in the narration), for she says for the first time she sees her father as he really is. At the same time she becomes aware of her own position as one of 'los que mandan':

> 'Es malo querer a los que mandan, a los que poseen. Así dice la ley.' [. . .] Yo salgo, triste por lo que acabo de saber. Mi padre despide a los indios con un ademán y se queda recostado en la hamaca, leyendo. Ahora lo miro por primera vez. Es el que manda, el que posee.[27] Y no puedo soportar su rostro y corro a refugiarme en la cocina. Los indios están sentados junto al fogón [. . .] Hablan y es como si cerraran un círculo a su alrededor. Yo lo rompo angustiada. 'Nana, tengo frío.' Ella, como siempre desde que nací, me arrima a su regazo. Es caliente y amoroso. Pero tendrá una llaga. Una llaga que *nosotros* le habremos enconado. (16–17 [my emphasis])[28]

> ('It's wrong to love those who are in charge, who own everything. That is what the law says'. [. . .] I leave, sad about what I have just learned. My father dismisses the Indians with a gesture and stays lying in the hammock, reading. Now I see him for the first time. He is the one in charge, who owns things. And I cannot bear his face and I run to take refuge in the kitchen. The Indians are sitting by the hearth [. . .] They talk and it is as if they were closing the circle that surrounded them. I break it in anguish. 'Nana, I'm cold.' As always, from the time I was born, she pulls me on to her lap. It is warm and loving. But she will have a sore. A sore that we will have provoked.)

Here the *nana*'s lap is a metaphor for belonging, home, hearth or motherland.[29] *Regazo* is one of the many significant words that recurs in the text. I shall discuss some of the others in more detail presently, but limit myself here to making the rather obvious connection between 'lap' and warmth and maternal love. When frightened, upset, or just cold, it is to her *nana* that the

---

[27] Compare this with the previous reference to her father, where he is again a distant, imperious figure: 'Mi padre recibe a los indios, recostado en la hamaca del corredor. Ellos se aproximan, uno por uno, y le ofrecen la frente para que la toque con los tres dedos mayores de la mano derecha' (My father receives the Indians, lying in his hammock on the porch. They approach one by one and offer him their foreheads so that he can touch them with the first three fingers of his right hand) (15). Here is a picture of colonial life, of *personas de respeto* and *gente menuda* as 'Tío' David calls them (24). This custom is also described in Ricardo Pozas' *Juan Pérez Jolote* (1996: 74 and 115).

[28] This extract also reiterates the point made earlier about the male privilege of reading. This is not the only time the narrator describes her father lying in his hammock engaged in a pursuit that implies privilege in both the educational and the economic sense. It even occurs in the narrator's dream (32).

[29] Later on, when the girl-narrator buries her head in the lap of Amalia's aged mother, the latter meaning takes on greater importance (280). Crumley de Pérez identifies it with the lap of Mother Earth herself, endowing the word *regazo* with mythical proportions (Crumley de Pérez 1984: 498–99).

little girl runs to bury her face in the blue *tzec*, not to her biological mother's more elegant but infinitely colder lap.

In the final encounter between the little girl and her *nana*, when the family leaves Comitán to go to the ranch in Chactajal and the *nana* stays behind because she is afraid of the *brujos*, there is an emotive leave-taking scene. In it is revealed the mutual love felt by the little girl-narrator and the *nana*, as well as the latter's concern for the spiritual welfare of the child. The strength of this bond is evidently not of a lasting nature as far as the little girl is concerned, given that only a short time (by adult standards) after this parting, the narrator mistakenly believes an indigenous woman in the street to be her *nana*. She justifies her error with the remark that 'todos los indios se ven iguales'.[30] I have omitted the long invocation to God to take care of the little girl, made by her *nana* in the following quotation, and included only the part showing the maternal tenderness which is at no point shown towards the little girl by her own mother:

> Mi *nana* me lleva aparte para despedirnos [. . .] Luego mi *nana* me persigna y dice: 'Vengo a entregarte a mi criatura. Señor tú eres testigo de que no puedo velar sobre ella ahora que nos va a dividir la distancia' [. . .] La *nana* se pone de pie. Y luego se vuelve a mí, diciendo: 'Es hora de separarnos niña'. Pero yo sigo en el suelo, cogido de su *tzec*, llorando por que no quiero irme. Ella me aparta delicadamente y me alza hasta su rostro. Besa mis mejillas y hace una cruz sobre mi boca. 'Mira que con lo que he rezado es como si hubiera yo vuelto, otra vez, a amamantarte'. (64)

> (My nana takes me to one side to say good-bye [. . .] Then my nana makes the sign of the cross on me and says: 'I come to deliver my child to you. Lord you are witness that I can not watch over her now that distance is going to divide us' [. . .] Nana stands up. And then she turns to me, saying: 'It is time for us to part, child.' But I stay on the floor, clinging on to her *tzec*, crying because I don't want to go. She gently pushes me away and lifts me up to her face. She kisses my cheeks and makes the sign of the cross on my mouth. 'Look, with all that I have prayed it is as if I had breast fed you again.')

I have mentioned both the ambiguity and the spiritual nature of the relationship between the little girl and her *nana*. These are revealed in the opening chapter of the novel. The first words of the novel are spoken by the *nana* and

---

30 Far from revealing the narrator's racism, I believe this to be an ironic, self-critical comment on the part of Castellanos (one of many), for her own guilt at failing to recognise that her Indian *cargadora*, who remained as her companion for many years, was also a woman whose life she might have improved by teaching her to read (see '¡*Vida, nada te debo!*'). It is also a more general comment on what is a common failing among people of any race, but more particularly the dominant one in a given situation, to recognise the individuality of members of the 'other' race subordinate to them. This is then, an early example of post-colonial discourse; see Anderson (1991).

are from the indigenous myth (or version) of the Conquest, but she is told by the *niña* not to tell her that story. The narrator knows, through her own experience of injustice, that the domination of the Indians by the whites cannot be right; yet she herself attempts to dominate her *nana*, thus revealing further ambiguity in their relationship.[31] Telling the story repeatedly is her *nana*'s only way of expressing her feelings about the humiliation of her people by the *ladinos*. (Though later, in the incident at the fairground when the Indian nearly falls from the Ferris wheel, she shows them through her tears.)

Part of the ambiguity observed in the relationship between *niña* and *nana*, lies in the narrator's awareness of their difference. The *nana* herself reminds the child that they are different and that therefore their eventual separation is inevitable. The little girl is further reminded of it by two incidents. The first takes place in the kitchen, when the *nana* convinces her not to spill her milk deliberately, as if she drinks only coffee she will turn into an Indian: 'Su amenaza me sobrecoge. Desde mañana la leche no se derramará' (Her threat scares me. From tomorrow the milk won't be spilt) (10).[32] It is also significant of course that the white children drink (white) milk while the Indians – even the children – drink (black) coffee. The second incident precedes the one with the milk and occurs while the narrator is having her hair combed. Here, her words are those of a small child reflecting on what she knows about her *nana* and what she has been told is 'proper' by an adult in authority (her mother) and who believes that therefore it must be true '¿Sabe mi nana que la odio cuando me peina? *No sabe nada. Es india,* está descalza y no usa ninguna ropa debajo de la tela azul de su tzec. No le da vergüenza. Dice que la tierra no tiene ojos' (Does my nana know that I hate her when she combs my hair? *She doesn't know anything. She's an Indian*, she goes barefoot and doesn't wear any clothes under the blue cloth of her tzec. She's not embarrassed. She says the earth doesn't have eyes) (10 [my emphasis]). In spite of her love for her *nana*, the narrator's prejudice is already ingrained. The aforementioned ambiguity in the relationship between *niña* and *nana* is a result of the child's awareness of the fact that there is someone even lower than herself in the social hierarchy.

This statement by the little girl has been used as an indication that the *niña*'s relationship with her *nana* is one of love/hate (Castillo 1992). However, such ambivalence is clearly common in the mother–daughter relationship. Also, prejudice is learnt by children from adults and is not something

[31] It should also be borne in mind, notes Renée Scott, that the narrator is educated entirely by her wet-nurse at the age that, according to Piaget, the child acquires a notion of justice (Scott 1992: 22–30).

[32] This has also been taken as an expression of the narrator's racism towards the Indians. However since I do not believe that young children are racist, I see it more as the expression of the insecurity of one who, as a white girl and a child, is on the very borderline of the social hierarchy between *gente de respeto* and *gente menuda*.

innate to them. Castellanos has made observations on the purity and inno-
cence of children and their subsequent suitability as 'vehicles for the transmis-
sion of unadulterated ideological viewpoints' (Poniatowska 1987: 131). There
is considerable disagreement over whether this purity and innocence actually
exists. Nuala Finnegan points out that the child-narrator, from the beginning
of the novel is 'very much a cultural receptacle of the racist and sexist ideolo-
gies of her environment' (Finnegan 2000: 21). This is indeed the case, as the
'ambiguous' nature of the little girl's relationship with her *nana* surely indicates. What appear to be rascist and sexist attitudes are imitated rather than
reasoned behaviour.

However, the following quotation does indicate her feeling that, in spite of
their both being marginalised by patriarchy, the child-narrator sees the indigenous women as Other: 'Tropezamos con las indias que tejen pichulej, senta-
das en el suelo. Conversan entre ellas, en su *curioso* idioma, acezante *como
ciervo perseguido*. Y de pronto echan a volar sollozos altos y sin lágrimas *que
me espantan*, a pesar de que los he escuchado tantas veces' (We come upon
the Indian women who are weaving with *pichulej* grass, seated on the ground.
They talk among themselves, in their *curious* language, panting *like a hunted
deer*. And suddenly they let fly high, tearless sobs *which frighten me*, even
though I've heard them so many times before) (11–12 [my emphasis]). The
fact that the child-narrator associates the indigenous people with deer, as do
they themselves, suggests that the relationship between the *niña* her *nana*, like
the one between the little girl and her mother, is ambivalent (rather than
ambiguous), comprising a sense of affinity as well as of separateness. A true
idea of her relationship with her *nana*, is revealed in the moment she feels
excluded from the circle of Indians in the kitchen (17).

A further indication of the closeness that exists between *niña* and *nana* is
the way the child enters into the indigenous world and shares spiritual communion with her *nana* who educates the little girl into her ways and beliefs.[33]
The fact that Castellanos (as narrator) has a more privileged access to the

---

[33] On account of her close association with the indigenous people and her attempts to
penetrate their psyche and to represent something of their cosmology, Castellanos has been
labelled an 'indigenista' writer by some critics. However, Castellanos herself refutes this
idea, claiming that these writers present a stereotypical view of the Indians as exotic, poetic
and intrinsically good while she recognises their weakness and capacity for violence,
betrayal and hypocrisy, magnified by the atrocious misery in which they live. She adds,
'Otro detalle que los autores indigenistas descuidan – y hacen muy mal – es la forma [. . .]
descuidan el lenguaje, no pulen el estilo [. . .] por pretender mis libros objetivos muy
distintos no se me puede incluir en este corriente' (Another detail that indigenista authors
overlook – and they do wrong to do so – is form [. . .] they pay little attention to language,
their style is unpolished [. . .] as my books have quite different objectives I cannot be
included in that trend) (Poniatowska 1987: 111–12). The approach of Mexican Indianist
writers before Castellanos included the simple documentary style of the conditions and
inhumane treatment experienced by indigenous people, such as that of Gregorio López y
Fuentes (*El indio*) and the anthropological study by Pozas (*Juan Pérez Jolote*).

indigenous world as a child, does not necessarily equate that world with the
world of white children and thereby, infantilising the Indians. Rather, it is
because as a *female* child, the narrator, like the Indians, is a marginalised
being: even though an outsider she poses less of a threat, so they are able to
'be themselves' in front of her (as when they are sitting together around the
fire in the kitchen). It would be more accurate to say she is an observer but
from within the circle (she is curled up on her *nana*'s lap) listening to them,
not excluded. The following quotation not only shows the influence her
nana's stories and pieces of indigenous folklore have on the narrator, but also
indicates the child's attempt to seek adult approval, ' "¿Sabes? Hoy he conocido al viento." Ella no interrumpe su labor. Continúa desgranando el maíz,
pensativa y sin sonrisa. Pero yo sé que está contenta. "Eso es bueno niña.
Porque el viento es uno de los nueve guardianes de tu pueblo" ' ('You know
what? Today I met the wind.' She doesn't interrupt her work. She continues
stripping the grain off the corn cobs, thoughtful and unsmiling. But I know she
is pleased. 'That is good child. Because the wind is one of the nine guardians
of your town') (23).

Various episodes reveal that the *nana* cares as much for the little girl's spiritual, as for her physical well-being. The little girl reciprocates such feelings
on at least two occasions. First, when her mother makes insulting remarks
about the Indians (on learning of the decree promulgated by Cárdenas that
landowners must teach the Indians to read), the little girl and Mario discreetly
leave the room, closing the door as they go, in case their *nana* should walk by
and happen to overhear and be hurt by what Zoraida says:

> ¿Dónde se ha visto semejante cosa? ¡Enseñarles a leer cuando ni siquiera
> son capaces de aprender a hablar español! [. . .] Es que no los conoce; es
> que nunca se ha acercado a ellos ni ha sentido como apestan a suciedad y a
> trago. Es que nunca les ha hecho un favor para que le devolvieran
> ingratitud. No les ha encargado una tarea para que mida su haraganería. ¡Y
> son tan hipócritas, y tan solapados y tan falsos! [. . .] Y yo hubiera pre-
> ferido mil veces no nacer antes que haber nacido entre esta raza de víboras.
> (46–47)

> (Whoever heard of such a thing? Teach them to read when they are not
> even capable of learning to speak Spanish! [. . .] He doesn't know what
> they're like, he's never been close to them or smelled how they stink of
> filth and drink. He's never done them a favour only to have them show
> ingratitude in return. He hasn't given them a task to measure their idleness
> by. And they are such hypocrites, so sly and so false! [. . .] And I would
> have preferred a thousand times never to have been born than to be born
> amongst this race of vipers.)

Such a vituperative outburst on the part of Zoraida could only be the result of
her own frustration and feeling of lack of self-worth. This low self-esteem is

passed on to the little girl because of her mother's rejection of her.[34] As far as
the little girl narrator of *Balún-Canán* is concerned, it is her *nana*'s influence,
or as María Estela Franco puts it, her 'sensibilidad y amor a la naturaleza'
(sensitivity and love of nature) that is more in evidence in the novel than her
mother's character (Franco 1984: 156). The second occasion on which the little
girl's sensitivity and empathy with her *nana* is revealed is when she notices that
her *nana* is crying tears of bitterness at the humiliation of the Indian who hangs
from the revolving Ferris Wheel at the fair, then asks for another ticket:

> El indio palpa a su alrededor el desprecio y la burla. Sostiene su desafío.
> 'Quiero otro boleto.' [. . .] Los curiosos se divierten con el acontecimiento
> que se prepara [. . .] Se hacen guiños [. . .] Mi nana atraviesa entre ellos y, a
> rastros, me lleva [. . .] Quiero preguntarle por qué. Pero la interrogación se
> me quiebra cuando miro sus ojos arrasados en lágrimas. (40)

> (The Indian feels the disdain and mockery around him. He keeps up his
> challenge. 'I want another ticket.' [. . .] The onlookers are amused by what
> is about to take place [. . .] They wink at each other [. . .] My nana crosses
> between them and drags me away [. . .] I want to ask her why. But my curi-
> osity is shattered when I see her eyes awash with tears.)

It is usually her *nana* who takes the little girl out to see interesting things
that will nourish her spirit and stimulate her curiosity – a trip to the fair, or to
the circus, when the *nana* dresses in her best *tzec* and patiently waits with the
children for the show to start until, finally, their ticket money is returned to her
because no-one else has turned up to watch. The *nana* has managed to instil
some of her patience into the little girl. Unlike Mario who merely cries until
he gets what he wants, the *niña,* like the Indians, has learnt to wait in silence.
When she questions her *nana* about why her mother goes to visit *La Tullida*
and fails to understand the brief explanation she is given, she is resigned to the
fact that there is no point in imitating her brother's behaviour: 'Todavía no es
suficiente lo que ha dicho, todavía no alcanzo a comprenderlo. Pero ya
aprendí a no impacientarme y me acurruco junto a la *nana* y aguardo. A su
tiempo son pronunciadas las palabras' (What she says is not yet enough, I
don't yet manage to understand it. But I have already learnt not to get impatient and I cuddle up next to my nana and wait. She will tell me when the time
comes) (28). Patience is the strength of those who have no power.

The *nana* also teaches the little girl not to be arrogant and take advantage of
her position as one of the ruling class but to remember that rich and poor are

---

[34] María Estela Franco claims that such remarks reveal the complicity of the oppressed
in their own oppression, due to their belief in their own inferiority, and supports this view
with a statement about the effect of the two maternal influences on Rosario as a child: one,
her mother, was governed by the dissatisfaction of being a woman and unloved and the
other, the *nana*, who, due to her class and her situation as a woman, found herself powerless in a devalued world (Franco 1984: 156).

mutually dependent. She explains that, according to the indigenous law, established before the arrival of Christianity, when the world was ruled by four gods, it was decided that the rich should look after and help the poor because of the benefit they receive from them. The law also states that no rich person can enter heaven unless they are led by the hand by a poor person (30). When the child then asks her, '¿Quién es mi pobre nana?' (Who is my poor person nana?), her *nana* does not try to dupe the child with her reply by making her think she knows everything, nor to sermonise like her mother's friend, Amalia, who teaches Mario and her the catechism, but merely instils further the virtues of patience, wisdom and humility: 'Ella se detiene y mientras me ayuda a levantarme dice: "Todavía no lo sabes. Pero si miras con atención, cuando tengas más edad y mayor entendimiento, lo reconocerás" ' (She stops and while helping me to get up says, 'You don't know yet. But if you pay attention, when you are older and have greater understanding, you will recognise them') (31).

An Unwilling Mother

Chapter X of the novel begins with the narrator describing herself ill in bed in a darkened room. It is her *nana*, even under these circumstances, and not her mother who is at her bedside (31). The child has been so deeply affected by the sight of the wounded Indian brought in on a stretcher, bleeding from multiple machete wounds and one hand almost severed, that she becomes delirious. Even in her fever she is concerned that no-one is looking after the unfortunate Indian. When she drifts off into a dream she sees very disturbing images of her mother – who is nowhere near her bedside – dropping the bloody entrails of an ox at the feet of *la Tullida*; and of her father, lying in his hammock, reading (once again), surrounded by skeletons, laughing silently. She flees and runs to her *nana* (of course) who is washing clothes on the stones of a turbulent red river (33).[35] Her deeply disturbed state is revealed again later when she sees a figure of Christ in the hermitage which her mother and the indigenous women are cleaning in preparation for the coming festival. Terrified, she tries to escape but is unable to open the door. Her mother's way of dealing with her terror is to slap her. In her mother's eyes the little girl sees alarm and anger rather than concern.

In this way the little girl experiences the contrasting indigenous and *ladino* worlds; the first associated with her *nana* and the other Indians, whom she

[35] Water carries well-known maternal symbolism which I address in Chapter Five of this book. The colour red has obvious symbolic connotations including that of blood and puberty, that is, the leaving behind of the state of childhood (and dependence on the mother) and the initiation into womanhood. In *Balún-Canán* it is also associated with the indigenous people as I explain in the section on the senses later in this chapter.

perceives with sympathy but yet as Other, the second with her parents and their friends and relations, from whom she is detached. It is significant that the first chapter, narrated by the little girl, starts with the voice of the *nana*. It is she who is the centre of the little girl's world. The narrator then goes on to describe her parents, but they are enormous, distant almost mythical figures:

> Y cuando me yergo puedo mirar de frente las rodillas de mi padre. Más arriba no. Me imagino que sigue creciendo como un gran árbol y que en su rama más alta está agazapado un tigre diminuto. Mi madre es diferente. Sobre su pelo – tan negro, tan espeso, tan crespo – pasan los pájaros y les gusta y se quedan. Me lo imagino nada más. Nunca lo he visto. (9)

> (And when I stand up straight I can see my father's knees. No higher. I imagine that he keeps growing like a great big tree and that in his highest branch a tiny tiger is crouched. My mother is different. Over her hair – so black, thick and curly – birds fly and stop and stay because they like it. I only imagine it. I've never seen it.)

The exaggeration here is clearly tongue-in-cheek, as a seven-year-old child would be at least as tall as her father's waist and well aware of the fact that birds do not nest in people's hair. The distance between child and adults is mythologised as are the size and awesomeness of her parents.[36] However the little girl's admission that this image of her parents is only in her imagination gives her a self-awareness and maturity for her years that is not recognised by her parents who seem oblivious to her individual qualities. Her imagination has been nurtured by stories about giants and mythological creatures with semi-human characteristics, such as the *dzulúm*, told to her, not by her parents, but by her *nana*. Thus the great size attributed by the little girl to her parents reflects their inaccessibility in her eyes, as well as her consciousness of her own 'smallness' in their eyes.

Zoraida's reaction to her daughter's behaviour in the hermitage is representative of the relationship that exists between the little girl and her mother. She is impatient and at times violent with those she considers her inferiors, such as her daughter and the *nana*. According to María Estela Franco, this type of angry outburst appears to have its origins in the feelings of impotence arising from not feeling free or valued, of a person feeling themself obliged to occupy the space that has been designated them (Franco 1984: 35). The result of Zoraida's unwillingness to mother is that she rarely takes her daughter anywhere, nor plays with her, nor talks to her, nor even tells her anything. The little girl recounts how, whenever she asks her mother to take her along when she goes to see 'la Tullida' (the Cripple), she is confronted with a negative 'siempre me rechaza' (she always rejects me) and told she is too small to

---

[36] This detracts somewhat from Paul Julian Smith's view that this is simply a 'realist' novel written in the traditional mould (Smith 1992: 128–160).

understand things (27). The use of the verb *rechazar* (reject) – rather than *negar* (refuse) here is very revealing of the emotional state of the child and is evidence of the rejection and insecurity she feels. The solidarity that one might expect between mother and daughter is absent from women in this social milieu. As Castellanos describes to Poniatowska in '¡Vida, nada te debo!' (Life, I owe you nothing!): 'la mujer mexicana no sólo está dispuesta a anularse totalmente sino a anular a su hija. Que no le vaya a ir mejor que a ella. Si ella no pudo aprender a leer o no pudo escoger al marido ¿por qué rayos la hija sí va a poder?' (the Mexican woman is not only totally prepared to lose her own identity but to deprive her daughter of an identity too. Her daughter is not going to have a better time of it than she did. If she couldn't learn to read or choose a husband, why on earth should her daughter be able to do so?) (Poniatowska 1987: 116). The fact that the *niña* always goes to ask her *nana* when she wants to know something emphasises the point that her mother has little time for her.

The mother is not mentioned again until the end of Chapter II, and then only in the third person by the *nana* (12).[37] The first interaction between the narrator and her mother does not appear until Chapter V, and then it is in the form of negation of the child's desire. The narrator's request to go to the circus does not express an unreasonable desire for a child with few playmates or diversions, who wishes to satisfy the illusion produced by 'esos libros de estampas iluminadas' (those books of coloured prints) that she and Mario look through before going to sleep. (The word *iluminada* suggests both the light and illusion of another world beyond the reactionary, provincial one inhabited by the little girl and her family).[38] Yet it is met with derision by her mother who makes no attempt to conceal her cynicism about the quality of the show, ' "Pero ¿cuál circo? Son unos pobres muertos de hambre que no saben cómo regresar a su pueblo y se ponen a hacer maromas" ' (What circus? They're just starving down-and-outs who have no means to get home and start doing somersaults) (17). The delights of the circus are advertised over a loudspeaker 'para solaz del culto público comiteco' (for the recreation of the cultured Comitán public). However the children (accompanied by their *nana* not by

[37] Her father is even more distant than her mother and seen by the little girl merely as a figure of authority. With Mario, her younger brother, the relationship develops from one where they live as separate entities to a true fraternal closeness. Mario and she are rivals in the first part of the novel, due to the narrator's knowledge that he is the favourite, then they become allies – united in their mutual terror of hell – after the start of the Catechism classes with Amalia, in the third part.

[38] There is a glimpse here of Castellanos' belief that reality is often deficient and its place must be taken by fiction. This has led her (and also Campobello and Garro) to explore what she refers to in one essay as, 'that abyss between the project and the carrying out of it (that distance between feeling and the way it is expressed)' (Castellanos 1975: 12). In *Balún-Canán* she does this by idealising or denigrating the characters and dramatising certain events from her childhood while excluding or playing down others.

their parents) are the only ones in the audience. The 'cultured people' of Comitán, if they exist at all, are either too concerned with the more pressing realities of the deteriorating social situation or, like Zoraida, lacking any sense of fun or magic.

I have already referred to the dual nature of the child's feelings for her mother; she experiences both unrequited love and awed admiration in her mother's presence and is clearly grateful for any attention she receives from her. The following quotation suggests an almost awed admiration and a desire for her mother's love:

> Yo voy detrás de ella, porque me gusta verla arreglarse [. . .] Yo miro extasiada [. . .] Para colmarme el corazón llega el momento final [. . .] La ayudo a elegir [. . .] Sé que no habla conmigo; que si yo le respondiera se disgustaría [. . .] Por eso yo apenas me muevo para que no advierta que estoy aquí y me destierre. (227–28)[39]

> (I follow her around, because I like to watch her smarten herself up [. . .] I watch in ecstasy [. . .] My heart overflows as the final moment comes [. . .] I help her choose [. . .] I know she's not talking to me, that if I answered her she would be cross [. . .] That's why I hardly move, so she won't notice I'm here and send me away.)

The narrator's words indicate that Zoraida clearly does not fulfil the requirements needed to be a 'good-enough mother' but it is pertinent here to remember the words of Rich that 'we can never have enough of our mother's love'. Furthermore, the descriptions of moments spent with her mother are often overshadowed by some external object or incident that creates fear in the little girl. For example, it is not until the third part, when the *nana* has been dismissed and not yet replaced by the new *cargadora*, that Zoraida takes her children to visit *La Tullida*. Even then, the 'charitable' visit is in exchange for a reading of her cards so that she will know what fate lies in store for Mario. The negative results of the reading cause Zoraida to lose her temper with the old woman and reveal that she has only been visiting her so that God will reward her by protecting Mario.

The only time the children are seen to laugh is in the second part when they go to the river to bathe together and Zoraida tries to make the old mule she is riding speed up – cutting a somewhat ludicrous figure, however, so that the narrator seems to be laughing *at* her rather than *with* her. It is also only on this occasion that Zoraida is seen to pay attention to the *niña* – teaching her to swim. It is significant that this incident appears in the omniscient third-person

---

[39] The association of the *madre-patria*, the mother/land, is present here in the use of the verb *desterrar* and there is a clear correlation between *Balún-Canán* and *La 'Flor de Lis'*, both in this respect and in the awed admiration felt by the daughter for her glamorous mother. I will broach this subject in more detail in Chapter Five of this book.

narrative of the second part, rather than in the childhood 'memories' of the first and third parts. No emotion is attached to it, which suggests that the *niña* is being deliberately selective in what she chooses to remember about her mother, possibly to strengthen her feelings of neglect. According to Aminatta Forna, however, an exclusive mother–child bond, where only the biological mother cares for her children is peculiar to Anglo/European culture in the last few decades only (Forna 1998). Zoraida's explanation, in the second part, of how she felt obliged to marry César and produce a male heir, contributes to the multivocal nature of the novel by giving mothers a voice and counteracting what would otherwise be exclusively a child's point of view.

Be that as it may, the perceived or actual lack of closeness between the little girl and her real family, particularly her mother (in Chapter IV, the narrator finally mentions her father again but still not in relation to herself), lead the child to associate more closely with her *nana* and the indigenous world, their concept of (circular) time and memory, associated with nature, the elements and the senses.[40] All these elements represent for the *niña* (in a psychoanalytical reading) a substitute for the unconsciously longed for pre-Oedipal phase of closeness with the mother that has been denied her by Zoraida.

MULTIVOCALITY AND MEMORY: *LA SOMBRA DEL VENADO*

Elena Poniatowska writes in *¡Ay vida, no me mereces!* that *Balún-Canán* emerges from three visions: those of a dead deer, a defenceless child and a journey through the highland rain forest. 'Alrededor suyo surgen innumerables imágenes, evocaciones de olores, de colores, de formas que van hallando una estructura' (Around them numerous images, evocations of smells, colours and forms arise which gradually find a structure) (Poniatowska 1987: 123). This quotation pinpoints the three interrelated concepts in the novel of nature (and the senses); multivocality (and alternative discourse); time (and memory). These ideas are, in turn, epitomised by three elements: the deer (nature/the senses); the defenceless child (alternative discourse/memory); the journey (memory/the senses). With regard to time and memory Castellanos writes:

---

[40] Cynthia Steele refers to the negative effects of this 'essentialising' of the indigenous people when she discusses Jesus Morales' *Memorial del tiempo*. Steele explains that his background is similar to that of Castellanos – a long-established family from Chiapas – and, using post-colonial discourse, refers to the way he insists, in his work, on relating the indigenous peasants to the land and to harmony with nature, with a similar effect (Steele 1993: 255).

[. . .] algo que a mi modo de ver es esencial, como fuente de nuestras impotencias y de nuestras incertidumbres, de nuestras dificultades para ubicarnos (cuando nos ubicamos), de nuestras frustraciones, del limbo en que nos movemos: nuestra idea o sensación del tiempo [. . .] ¿Qué nos falta para alcanzar la plenitud, para tener acceso al mundo de lo propiamente humano? Aparentemente, voluntad, tesón, constancia. *Pero en verdad, de lo que carecemos es de memoria.*

(Castellanos 1975: 122–23 [my emphasis])

(Something which, to my mind is essential as a source of our incertitude, our difficulty in finding out where we are (when we do find out where we are), of our frustrations, of the limbo in which we move about: our idea or sensation of time [. . .] What do we need to attain plenitude, to have access to the world of what is really human? Apparently, will power, persistence, steadfastness. *But in fact, what we lack is memory.*)

Memory, a major concern in Castellanos' writing, is present in *Balún-Canán*, firstly transformed by the adult process of writing as the textual author draws on recollections of childhood and transcribes them into literature; and, secondly, as a more immediate experience for the child-narrator. The latter incorporates the depiction of experiences in the child's present, in the form of sense–related (sensual) images, which appear as part of the narrative and which will later be transformed into memories by the adult (textual) author. In order to understand this concept it is necessary to think of time in terms of a cycle in which the past, present and future exist simultaneously and may therefore be repeated.[41] This recalls the Mayan concept of time found in the quotation (at the beginning of Part II) from the *Chilam-Balam*, which suggests that everything waxes and wanes, like the moon, including the power of different peoples (75).

The narrator's memories, then, are usually awakened by external stimuli – sounds, smells, tastes, colours and other strong visual images. On their way to market, sounds predominate: 'Ahora empezamos a bajar la cuesta del mercado. Adentro suena el hacha de los carniceros y las moscas zumban torpes y saciadas. [. . .] Se oyen los granos de arroz deslizándose contra el metal de la balanza' (Now we start down the hill to the market. Inside, you can hear the thud of the butchers' cleavers and the flies buzz heavy and sated [. . .] You can

---

41 However, Carlos Monsiváis associates circular time with underdevelopment because, 'El tiempo del subdesarrollo suele ser, en cuanto a forma, circular [. . .] porque los hallazgos son los mismos, porque la imitación se suple con la imitación, porque los procesos históricos jamás concluyen, jamás la rebelión da paso a la independencia, jamás la insurgencia culmina en autonomía [. . .] Todo cambia, todo se transforma, todo sigue igual' (The time of underdevelopment is usually, as far as form is concerned, circular [. . .], because the same discoveries are made, because imitation is replaced by imitation, because historical processes are never over, rebellion never leads to independence, insurgence never culminates in autonomy [. . .]. Everything changes, everything is transformed, everything remains the same) (Monsiváis 1986: 152).

hear the grains of rice sliding against the metal of the scales) (11–12). Later, when Doña Pastora arrives peddling her wares, smell, sound (contrasted with silence) and colour are evident:

> Es mediodía. El viento duerme, cargado de su propia fragancia en el jardín. De lejos llegan los rumores: la loza chocando con el agua en la cocina; la canción monótona de la molendera. ¡Qué silenciosas las nubes allá arriba! La mujer deshace los nudos del envoltorio y bajo la tela parda brota una cascada de colores. (47–48)

> (It's midday. The wind sleeps, heavy with its own fragrance in the garden. From afar the sounds reach us: water splashing against china pots in the kitchen, the monotonous song of a woman grinding maize. How quiet the clouds are up there! The woman undoes the knots of her bundle and from under the grey cloth springs a cascade of colours.)

In *Balún-Canán*, the prominence given to the senses is related to the greater proximity to the indigenous world (with its emphasis on the sensory) of the child-narrrator than the other members of her family.[42] The indigenous people's closeness to nature and the elements has its roots in a tradition of respect for the natural world on which the people's survival had always depended. It is as a result of their greater dependence on nature, exacerbated by their poverty and the fact that they live in mostly rural areas. They have been largely excluded – sometimes by choice – from the consumer-orientated, technological world and its related commodities and comforts, all of which serve to distance people from nature (for better or worse) and to dull the senses on which survival depends. This means that they are bound to appear closer to nature. In the novel, such continued closeness to nature is reflected in the references to the wind and the other 'guardians' of the area inhabited by the narrator and her family; and to other elements such as fire, used both as a source of comfort, around which they sit and commune, and later, as a weapon of resistance against *ladino* oppression when they set fire to the Argüello's mill.

Where references to bright colours are made by the *niña*, it is almost invariably in relation to the indigenous people; while the colours black, grey and white are those associated with the *ladinos*. This can be read as another binary opposition; and Castellanos can be accused of perpetuating yet again the binary system by linking the serious 'adult' sombre colours (and culture) with the *ladinos*, and the exotic bright colours (and nature) with the indigenous people. Thus, descriptions of the indigenous people by the child-observer, where the visual sense is stimulated, can be seen in two ways. They represent

---

[42] While it is true that César Argüello talks to the Indians and speaks their language, this has nothing to do with having empathy with them as people or an interest in their culture, but rather with the rule established by the landowners that forbids Indians from speaking Spanish.

an example of the whites viewing the 'natives' as exotic, and also the child's attraction to bright colours which parallels the indigenous people's own aesthetic sense. The former positions the indigenous as Other and the latter positions both child and indigenous as Other, giving them a shared alternative discourse but, arguably, also infantilising the indigenous people.

Allusions to the senses are marked in the text by the repetition of the words *olor, sabor, sonido, colores* (smell, taste, sound, colours) and by words related to or derived from these, such as *huele, aroma*; *sabe a, gusto, suena(n), sonando, son, ruido, rumor*; and by the reference to different colours. The repetition of words (related to the senses, to memory and to Kristeva's semiotic *chora* as opposed to the symbolic *system* of language) in a text is one example of Kristeva's idea of the semiotic disrupting the symbolic (Kristeva 1984: 70, 102). The colours associated in particular with the indigenous are *rojo* (red) and *amarillo* (yellow); while *negro* (black), *gris* (grey) and *blanco* (white), as I suggested earlier, are often found in relation to the whites or *cashlanes*. There is significant repetition of other words also, which assumes importance in the narrative because these words are often related to the indigenous world and hence to their collective memory. They are as follows: *memoria* (memory), *viento* (wind), *palabra* (word), *silencio* (silence), *ciervo/venado* (deer), *sangre* (blood), *sombra* (shadow), *hermano* (brother), *frío/calor* (hot/cold), *regazo* (lap), *mejilla* (cheek), *río/agua/corriente* (river/water/current) *and fuego* (fire) (as well as all the words related to this one, such as *ceniza* (ash), *brasa* (hot coal), *rescoldo* (embers), *llama* (flame), *arde* (burn) etcetera). The actual smells, sights, tastes and sounds themselves reveal the sensual harmony between the little girl and the indigenous people. However, the sensual references serve a further purpose, which is to represent the consciousness of the narrator without the need for elaborate language or thought processes, both of which would detract from the verisimilitude of the child-narrator. Castellanos was evidently concerned about verisimilitude as where the child is narrating, the chapters and sentences are both shorter and the vocabulary, while lyrical, is not very difficult. Feelings and psychic states, impressions and thoughts are conveyed largely through the use of a select vocabulary relating to the senses. The task of creating verisimilitude is usually accomplished through what Dorrit Cohn calls 'psycho-narration' – a way of writing that 'renders consciousness' and which claims many advantages over other methods of doing so. One of the most important advantages of psycho-narration, claims Cohn, is its 'verbal independence from self-articulation':

> Not only can it (psycho-narration) order and explain a character's conscious thoughts better than the character himself (or herself) it can also effectively articulate a psychic life that remains universalized, penumbral, or obscure. Accordingly psycho-narration often renders, in a narrator's knowing words, what a character 'knows' without knowing how to put it into words. (Cohn 1978: 46)

This is not to suggest that the lyrical and poetic language of *Balún-Canán* could conceivably have been written by a seven-year old, but rather, that the references to the senses in *Balún-Canán*, are not mere scenic description.[43]

The verisimilitude of the child-narrator as observer (for example) is sustained when, from time to time, she describes how she is able to witness all the events she relates, such as when Mario is ill and the doctor comes to visit him, 'Entraron juntos a la recámara y yo aproveché *que no reparaban en mí para entrar detrás de ellos*' (They entred the bedroom together and I took advantage of the fact *that they didn't notice me going in after them*) (267 [my emphasis]). Also when 'Tío' David is talking to Amalia, 'Cuando Amalia salió de la cocina tío David se volvió hacia mí, que *había permanecido quieta en un rincón*' (When Amalia left the kitchen Uncle David turned to me, who *had been standing quietly in a corner*) (273 [my emphasis]). It is precisely due to her insignificance that the narrator is able to witness certain events.

Sense-related descriptions, then, do more than simply describe physical reality. In the text, various smells and aromas are remarked on by the narrator. This, significantly (in view of the point made above about the relation between the indigenous and the senses) usually happens when she is with her *nana*. When her *nana* takes her by the hand to the town, the *niña* is aware of the different smells in the shops, streets and market, 'Pasamos frente a las tiendas que huelen a telas recién teñidas' (We pass in front of the shops that smell of recently dyed fabric) (12). Later, during the morning break at the girls' school, she describes the sound and smell of the servants who arrive with the pupils' lunch, 'sonando el almidón de sus fustanes, olorosas a brillantina' (the rustle of their starched petticoats, smelling of brilliantine) (15).[44] There are also references to colour, such as the way the indigenous women adorn their hair with coloured ribbons or wear their best and most colourful clothes for fiestas. These images described by the narrator produce a positive picture of the indigenous people which contrasts with the one given by Zoraida. Other smells which also elicit memories in the child-narrator's mind are to do with familiarity and association. When the children go with their *nana* to see the circus performance, the narrator comments on the smell of fresh manure which would have been familiar to her, living on a ranch and surrounded by animals (18). Another smell which suggests nostalgia for a lost

---

[43] Although, according to Cohn, 'where the narration of external reality is intimately related to subjective perception, there is no clear borderline between the external and internal scene. When they are introduced by perception verbs, the sights a character sees and the sounds he (or she) hears link psyche and scene, and psycho-narration can no longer be clearly differentiated from scenic description' (Cohn 1978: 49).

[44] This is before the school is closed by a government inspector on the pretext of its not being up to the standard of state education required by the Lázaro Cárdenas administration literacy programme. (In reality it was to do with the religious instruction imparted which was against the law at that time.) The programme evidently took into account the needs of the rural proletariat rather than the underclass that includes women.

time is that of clean sheets (61). Other smells may be bitter but equally evocative of a lost youth, 'Entre las rocas crece una flor azul y tiesa que difunde un agrio aroma de polen entre el que zumba, embriagada, la abeja' (Between the rocks a stiff blue flower grows releasing a bitter aroma of pollen among which bees buzz, drunkenly) (65).[45] Others again produce a clearly negative reaction in the narrator which corresponds to her feelings, such as the smell of wine coming from the mouth of 'Tío' David (not a real uncle) whom the children have been told by their parents they must be kind to and respect, but whose age and dirty, unkempt appearance they find repellent, 'De su boca vacía sale un olor a fruta demasiado madura que marea y repugna' (From his empty mouth a smell of overripe fruit emerges which is repugnant and makes you feel sick) (24). Associated with the *nana*, smells take on extra significance. When she takes the children to the circus and the little girl asks why no-one has come, her *nana*'s reply reflects the closeness to nature and the elements of (the indigenous) country people: 'No es tiempo de diversiones, niña. Siente: en el aire se huele la tempestad' (This is not the time for having fun, child. Smell the air, a storm is brewing) (19). The smell of the storm augurs the tempestuous times ahead. In stark contrast to the association by the *niña* of smells with (relatively) happier times and memories, is the airless, odourless quality of the days that she experiences after Mario's death:

> La luz regresa y vuelve a irse [. . .] Pero yo no llevo la cuenta del tiempo que ha transcurrido desde que estoy recorriendo la casa, abriendo y cerrando las puertas, llorando. Camino torpemente, con lentitud. Doy un paso y después, mucho después, otro. Avanzo así en esta atmósfera irrespirable de estrella recién derribada. El día se esparce, desmelenado y sin olor, en el jardín. (283)

> (The light returns then fades again [. . .] But I don't keep track of the time that has gone by since I began wandering through the house, opening and closing the doors, crying. I walk awkwardly, slowly. I take a step and then, much later, another. That's how I move about in this suffocating atmosphere of a recently fallen star. The day spreads out before me, empty and joyless in the garden.)

Thus, the narrator's existence after Mario's death takes on a colourless as well as an odourless quality. Colours are used in a similar way to smells but they have, in addition and not unusually, a symbolic significance. The association between the indigenous and bright colours referred to earlier, is reiterated on several occasions. The itinerant salesmen who come to Chactajal with

---

[45] Castellanos remarked in various interviews about how she spent much of her girlhood shut indoors and overprotected, especially after the death of her brother. These images, evoked through the senses, suggest moments of freedom and happiness that were grasped by a rather lonely and unhappy child.

their mules carry dolls with brightly painted cheeks (36); and the *nana*, sitting on a deerskin stool, mending clothes, has before her on the floor 'el tol con los hilos de colores' (the gourd full of coloured threads) (27). Then there is a reference to indigenous mythology, as when 'Tio' David tells the children about going to Tziscao, where the nine guardians live and the lakes are of different colours (26). The colours red, yellow and black also appear frequently in association with the indigenous world. This stems from their appearance in the creation myth as recounted by the *nana* to the narrator:

> Entonces uno de los cuatro señores, el que se viste de amarillo, dijo: 'Vamos a hacer al hombre para que nos conozca y su corazón arda de gratitud como un grano de incienso' [. . .]. 'Hagamos un hombre de madera', dijo el que se vestía de rojo [. . .] el que se vestía de negro dijo: 'mi consejo es que hagamos un hombre de oro.' (28)

> (Then one of the four lords, the one who dresses in yellow, said 'Let's make man so that he knows who we are and his heart burns with gratitude, like a grain of incense' [. . .] 'Let's make a man of wood', said the one who dresses in red [. . .] the one who wore black said: 'my advice is that we make a man of gold.')

Black, here, has the symbolic significance that links it with death and foreboding as well as with superstition. The man of gold represents the rich man (*cashlán*) who came to enslave the poor (Indians). Similarly, when the *custitaleros* come to Chactajal, the *nana* says: 'Trajeron malas noticias como las mariposas negras' (They brought bad tidings, like black butterflies) (15).

More often, however, black is associated with the world of the whites or *ladinos.* In Chapter XVI, when the government inspector comes to Miss Silvina's school, his sombre appearance is redolent of officialdom and authority: 'El desconocido estaba allí, ante nosotras. Alto, serio, vestido de casimir negro' (The stranger was there, before us, tall, serious, dressed in a black cashmere suit) (50). Señorita Silvina is also dressed in black but for a different reason and with quite a different effect, '[. . .] con su vestido negro, con su azoro, con su pequeñez, parecía un ratón cogido en una trampa. Los ojos implacables del inspector se separaron despectivamente de ella y volvieron a la libreta' (small, flustered in her black dress, she was like a mouse caught in a trap. The implacable eyes of the inspector disdainfully looked away from her and back at the notebook) (51). She has never had to speak to a man before, or feel his disdain. How different an image from the earlier picture of her, surrounded only by the servants and the girls, where she does not feel threatened by the male presence. Still small but like a little saint rather than a mouse, she appears in an idyllic setting of gently falling leaves, 'La maestra nos vigila con mirada benévola, sentada bajo los árboles de bambú. El viento arranca de ellos un rumor incesante y hace llover hojitas amarillas y verdes. Y la maestra está allí, dentro de su vestido negro, tan pequeña y tan sola como un santo dentro de su nicho' (The teacher watches over us benevolently, sitting beneath the bamboo trees. The wind rustles them ceaselessly and makes their little white and green leaves rain down. And the teacher is there, in her black dress, as small and solitary as a saint in his niche) (14). The fact that her black dress is mentioned twice underlines the importance of the way Castellanos uses colour to lyrical and psychological effect.

When used in association with the *ladinos*, black is juxtaposed with faded colours, grey and white as in the description of the colourless quality of Amalia the spinster's existence. She is too old to marry or go into a convent, having dedicated her youth to looking after her aged and infirm mother. Castellanos presents the metaphors of a withering flower, and the image of printed matter that has become illegible, to suggest Amalia's lost youth and the fact that the third possibility for a life of her own, through learning and literature, has also been denied her.

> Cuando nos abren la puerta es como si destaparan una caja de cedro, olorosa, donde se guardan listones desteñidos y papeles ilegibles. Amalia sale a recibirnos. Lleva un chal de lana gris, tibio, sobre la espalda. Y su rostro es el de los pétalos que se han puesto a marchitar entre las páginas de los libros. Sonríe con dulzura pero todos sabemos que está triste porque su pelo comienza a encanecer. (33)

> (When they open the door to us it is as if they had taken the lid of a fragrant cedarwood box where faded ribbons and illegible papers are kept. Amalia comes out to greet us. She is wearing a shawl of colourless, grey wool over her shoulders. Her face is like petals that have faded between the pages of a book. She smiles sweetly but we all know she is sad because her hair is beginning to turn grey.)

Amalia's life has revolved around her mother to such an extent that she has prepared every detail for her approaching death: 'Y la soltera saca de un cestillo de mimbre un pedazo de lino blanquísimo. "Es para taparle la cara cuando muera"' (The spinster takes out of a wicker basket a perfectly white piece of linen. 'It's for covering her face when she dies') (34). The sadness of Amalia's existence, and her resignation, is spelled out in this second reference to her greying (and thus the prospect of growing old alone): 'Nos acaricia afablemente con la mano izquierda mientras con la derecha se arregla el pelo, que se le está volviendo blanco' (She caresses us affably with her left hand while with the right one she pats her hair, which is turning white) (36). Reference to the sad, ageing, lonely Amalia has already appeared earlier in the novel (12). Such images evidently have a profound effect on the little girl – the narrator and would-be author – who is determined to escape the loneliness fate often holds in store for women. That such a fate was not reserved only for

spinsters is revealed later on by Castellanos when she writes of life in the
remote provincial town:

> Mi experiencia más remota radicó en la soledad individual; muy pronto
> descubrí que en la misma condición se encontraban todas las otras mujeres
> a las que conocía: solas solteras, solas casadas, solas madres. Solas en un
> pueblo que no mantenía contacto con los demás. Solas, soportando unas
> costumbres muy rígidas que condenaban el amor y la entrega como un
> pecado sin redención [. . .]. Retratar esas vidas, delinear esas figuras, forma
> un proceso que conserva una trayectoría autobiográfica. Me evadí de la
> soledad por el trabajo [. . .]. (Castellanos 1995a: 17)

> (My earliest experience was of individual loneliness, very soon I discov-
> ered that all the other women that I knew were in the same state: lonely
> spinsters, lonely wives, lonely mothers. Lonely in a town that had no
> contact with the outside world. Lonely, putting up with rigid customs that
> considered love and passion unpardonable sins [. . .]. To paint a picture of
> those lives, draw those figures, is part of a process of autobiographical
> development. I evaded loneliness through work.)

Castellanos makes a clear association here between the feeling of solitude
of the individual, exacerbated in the case of girl-children who are rejected by
(or absent from) their mothers, and the need to purge the feelings of solitude
or lack of identity produced by such rejection, through writing. Autobiographical writing may contribute more to establishing a sense of self than other
kinds of writing as the writer must create a fictional identity for the narrator/
protagonist. The fact that colour is used to represent memories and sentiments
in Castellanos' fiction is consistent with the words she uses in the quotation
above – *retratar* (to portray) and *delinear* (to draw) – the vocabulary of art.

The third sense which is given importance in the text is that of hearing.
Given the lowly status of the little girl (due to her age, and more particularly to
her gender), and because of the fact that she is expected to remain silent, she is
able to take up the traditional passive (female) position of observer and
listener. Her own silence has ensured that she become a good listener, and this
in turn guarantees her receptivity to sounds that would go unnoticed to a
(generally male) speaker. In this way the silence imposed on the marginalised
has been inverted to become a source of strength. Many of the other references to sound are associated with the wind – an oft-repeated word of particular significance in the discourse of the indigenous people.

Even before the narrator tells her *nana* that she has met the wind, she is
aware of its presence and force (9, 14, 20). She personifies it with both positive and negative characteristics. In winter, it arrives 'armado de largos y
agudos cuchillos' (armed with long, sharp knives) which penetrate their flesh
anguished by the cold. In summer it comes 'perezoso, amarillo de polen [. . .]
con un gusto de miel silvestre entre los labios' (lazy, yellow with pollen [. . .]

with the taste of wildflower honey on its lips) (23). It is associated with scenes of peace and tranquillity such as this and, by contrast, with ones of anguish. When the narrator describes her terrible memory of their Indian worker bleeding silently to death as the *nana* wipes her fevered brow, the wind howls (in sympathy or anger) on the plains (31). The final reference to the wind comes when the little girl is going to the crypt to visit her dead brother. It is the Day of the Dead in November and the wind is 'Un largo viento fúnebre que recorre ululando la llanura' (A long mournful wind that traverses the plain, howling) (286) that echoes her own sadness.

Other sounds produce feelings of unease and foreboding, in particular during the journey from Comitán to Chactajal. As they make their way through the mist and rain, the way for the travellers is slippery and dangerous and the narrator remarks on the sounds the horses and mules make: '[. . .] sus cascos rayan la superficie de las lajas produciendo un sonido desagradable y áspero' (their hooves scrape the surface of the rocks producing a harsh, disagreeable sound) (66). Being subjected to the vicissitudes of nature but separated from her *nana*, causes the sounds to be amplified so that each one becomes signifi-cantly distinctive and threatening to the *niña*. She then describes how one sound takes over and fills the space around them. It is the swollen Jataté river dragging broken branches and dead cattle (67). Finally, before the incident – Ernesto's killing the deer – which, for the indigenous people is full of fore-boding, she asks: '¿En qué momento empezamos a oír ese ruido de hojarasca pisada?' (At what point did we start to hear that noise of leaves being trodden underfoot?) (68). There is a suggestion here that she and the Indians began to hear the noise before her parents. The following quotation shows the way the senses are used to transmit the psychic state of the narrator:

> Nos dejan solos. Cierro los ojos porque no quiero ver las sombras que la llama de la veladora proyecta sobre la pared. Amortiguados por la nube de tul que me envuelve, llegan los sonidos: el jadeo intranquilo de Mario. Las pisadas, las voces lejanas, en la casa, en la calle. El tsisquirín de los grillos. Sube y baja la respiración, acompasada, igual. El sueño me va llenando de arenilla los párpados. (265)

> (They leave us alone. I close my eyes because I don't want to see the shadows projected by the candlelight onto the wall. Cushioned by the cloud of [mosquito] net that surrounds me, the sounds reach me: Mario's agitated breathing. The footfalls, the distant voices, in the house, in the street. The chirp of the crickets. My breathing rises and falls, rhythmic, even. Sleepi-ness makes my eyelids feel gritty inside.)

It is the loneliness of the narrator, and her knowledge that as the girl-child she is worth less to her mother than Mario is, that augment her sense of isola-tion and, in turn, her sensitivity to sights and sounds. Thus she is the one who is awakened by the almost imperceptible noise of her mother entering the room at night to check on Mario. The figure of her mother is 'medio borrosa a través de los pliegues de tul del pabellón, impreciso a contraluz de la trémula llama de la veladora' (somewhat blurred through the folds of the mosquito net, unclear against the light of the flickering candle flame) (265). She leans over Mario's bed as if to scrutinise his sleep while Mario, in the deep sleep of the secure, does not stir.

There is another incident in which the little girl's mother appears as a shadow; when the narrator is reading the text about the Argüello family in the garden: 'Una sombra, más espesa que la de las hojas de la higuera, cae sobre mí. Alzo los ojos. Es mi madre' (A shadow, deeper than that made by the fig tree leaves, falls over me. I look up. It's my mother) (60). Here, the mother preventing the little girl from reading, casts a shadow across her life as well as across the pages of the book.

The *sombra* also appears to be symbolic of the hierarchical nature of Chiapas society, first appearing in the description of the patriarchal relationship between the landowning families and the Indians, 'Unos quieren seguir, como hasta ahora, a la sombra de la casa grande. Otros ya no quieren tener patrón' (Some want to carry on as they have up until now, in the shadow of the big house. Others no longer want to have a master) (32). Thereafter the shadow is usually related to indigenous myth and superstition, such as the spectre *el sombrerón*, who wanders the countryside at night leaving his sign of ill-omen on the heads of the animals (60). The idea of *sombra* as spectre or part of the inner being, or conscience, of the indigenous people is reiterated during the journey to Chactajal (when Ernesto kills the deer), 'Los otros indios se inclinan también hacia ese ojo desnudo y algo ven en su fondo porque cuando se yerguen tienen el rostro demudado. [. . .] Desde entonces los indios llaman a aquel lugar "Donde se pudre nuestra sombra" ' (The other Indians also lean over that naked eye and see something deep within it because when they stand up their faces have changed. [. . .] From then on the Indians call that place 'where our shadow rots') (69).[46]

Another group of words I wish to discuss are those related to fire: *brasero* (stove), *ceniza* (ash), *rescoldo* (embers), *fogón* (hearth), and *arde* (burn) and the connection that exists between one and the other. The opening paragraph of the novel, which contains the story of the defeat of the indigenous people by the European colonisers, describes how the latter tried to deprive the Indians of even their language, as this would facilitate the loss of their collective (cultural) memory:

> Y entonces, coléricos, nos desposeyeron, nos arrebataron lo que habíamos atesorado: la palabra, que es el arca de la memoria. Desde aquellos días

---

[46] I believe this extract illustrates perfectly what is meant by the term 'closeness to nature' used with reference to the indigenous people. It is a closeness related to myth rather than, as some would have it, a 'mythical closeness'.

arden y se consumen con el leño en la hoguera. Sube el humo en el viento y se deshace. Queda la ceniza sin rostro. Para que puedas venir tú y el que es menor que tú y les baste un soplo. (9)

(And then, angrily, they dispossessed us, they snatched away from us what we had treasured: the word, which is the ark of memory. Since those days they burn and are consumed along with the wood in the fire. The smoke rises in the wind and dissipates. The ash is left without a face. So that you and the one who is younger than you, can come and just by blowing.)

However, it is not only the words of the indigenous people that are consumed by fire; the Argüello cane mill is also burnt down in the second part of the novel. Also (in Chapter XIII) the narrator remembers when the anti-Cristero government soldiers came to burn the contents of the Church, destroying the altar with their rifle butts then setting fire to the wooden figures of the saints, which are described as if they were real people: 'Ardían, retorciéndose, los mutilados cuerpos de los santos' (The mutilated bodies of the saints writhing as they burned) (41).

In most of the other references to fire, however, there is the idea of the warmth and comfort it can provide, 'La *nana* coge las tenazas y atiza el fogón. Afuera el aguacero está golpeando las tejas desde hace rato' (Nana picks up the tongs and stirs the fire. Outside, the heavy rain has been beating down on the roof-tiles for some time) (21). The narrator associates fire with the kitchen and her *nana*, and with the Indians who come and sit around it and talk (16). This idea of the closeness of the indigenous people to the elements is reinforced by the following references, which also suggest how the narrator attempts to associate herself with the former, 'Estamos en la cocina. El rescoldo late apenas bajo el copo de ceniza. La llama de la vela *nos* dice por dónde anda volando el viento' (We are in the kitchen. The embers are barely live under the flakes of ash. The candle flame tells *us* which way the wind blows) (20 [my emphasis]). The idea of the oral tradition, and of stories being told around the fire also appears: 'Encendimos la vela al entrar a la cocina. Y cuando estuvimos todos sentados alrededor del fogón, Vicenta dio principio a su relato' (We lit the candle as we went into the kitchen. And when we were all sitting around the fire, Vicenta began her story) (257).[47] The concepts of fire, the hearth, warmth and nurture reflected in this scene have obvious gender connotations as the hearth is traditionally associated with the maternal figure and her role as nurturer. Even Zoraida (the only time she is seen in a sympathetic light) is engaged in the task of keeping a fire going, something she knows how to do because of the poor circumstances she lived in before

---

[47] The oral tradition is associated with the indigenous, the marginalised, the Other, as opposed to the written tradition associated with patriarchy. The question of the transition from the oral tradition to that of the written word which the narrator (and Castellanos) strives after and finally achieves, will be addressed later.

she married. When the *niña* is finally taken by her mother to visit *La Tullida*, she describes the following scene: '[. . .] mi madre va al rincón en el que está el brasero de barro blanqueado. Sopla la ceniza, la avienta y el pulso del rescoldo empieza a latir otra vez. Apenas. Y luego más, más rojo' (my mother goes into the corner where the whitewashed clay stove is. She blows on the ash, revives it and the pulse of the embers begins to beat once more. Only just. Then more, and more red) (241–42). Here, unusually, it is her mother who is associated with warmth and the hearth, rather than the *nana*. But this is not the case in her own house. After Mario has died and the *nana* has been sent away, the narrator finds the house cold and devoid of love, 'Voy a la cocina. En el fogón el copo enfriado de ceniza' (I go to the kitchen. In the hearth the ashes are cold) (284), where hitherto there had always been warmth and the comforting lap of her *nana*.

Finally, the frequent appearance of the word *sangre* needs to be considered briefly. Several feminist writers have used this as a metaphor for woman's condition. The appearance of blood at puberty and on the sheet of the marriage bed has been seen, in traditional societies, as a sign of initiation into different states, or stages, of development. [48] In *Balún-Canán*, one such stage of development is the inevitable separation of the little girl from her *nana*. The parting is not only a physical one, but an emotional and spiritual separation too. (The difference in their social status would assume greater importance once the narrator grew out of childhood, as would her knowledge that the *nana* is not her real mother.) The frequent repetition of the word *sangre* (and its derivatives) signifies the painful process of maturation. In the incident in which the wounded *peon* lies bleeding to death (31–32), the *niña*'s fixation on the blood reveals the emotional turmoil she is suffering as a result of her straddling the two worlds – the white and the indigenous; see reference to Crumley de Pérez (1984: 494) at the end of this section.

How does the narrator's experience in the world of the indigenous people differ, if at all, from what she would experience in the world of the *ladinos*? The mythical tales and stories told to her by her *nana*, have a profound effect on the child. They are told by the *nana* in the ambiguous third person plural *Ustedes*. The little girl does not want to hear how 'nos desposeyeron, nos arrebataron lo que habíamos atesorado' (9) as she feels guilty about her position, as one of the oppressors. Either she must be an accomplice to the exploitation of the Indians or she must feel guilty. Later on she will feel guilty about Mario's death. This is in part related to her condition as woman.

---

[48] Isak Dinesen's story 'The Blank Page' was a watershed in feminist writing and her story, about blood as a metaphor, was taken up by feminist writers including Susan Gubar whose essay, ' "The Blank Page" and the Issues of Creativity' treats this theme. Gubar makes the comparison of the ink on the blank page with the initiation into the writing process; see Gubar (1986: 292–30).

Her *nana* also teaches her about nature. The wind is 'un animal que trisca' (an animal that gambols) (22), as well as a voice that speaks to her and keeps her company in her lonely and isolated existence (23). Her being aware of the wind as a life force also allies her to the indigenous people. When she tells her *nana*: '¿Sabes? Hoy he conocido al viento', the personal 'a' is used to indicate the wind's status as an animate being.

The little girl's participation in the indigenous world is precipitated by what Crumley de Pérez refers to as 'deep psychic conflicts' (Crumley de Pérez 1984: 494). Such conflicts, she affirms, may lead to some children from ruling class/white families being able to enter into such a world; in *Balún-Canán* it is the seven-year-old girl but not her brother who does so. The fact that this participation, where she is accepted because of her child status, does not last is due to some extent to the death of Mario. The increased amount of attention she receives thereafter from her biological mother makes it easier for the little girl to be weaned from the emotional dependence on her *nana*, as the latter's role as mother figure is taken over by its 'rightful' owner. This decreased emotional dependence also explains how the narrator fails to recognise that the indigenous woman she sees in the street is not her *nana*.

POLYPHONY AND THE OMNISCIENT NARRATOR

Castellanos has been criticised for the imperfection of *Balún-Canán* due to the change in narrator.[49] The effect of this change, however, with the first and third parts of the novel narrated in the first-person by the child, and the second part by a seemingly omniscient narrator, is to produce a multivocal novel which presents different focalisations without detracting from the primacy of the little girl's story in the first person. In the second part of the novel, multivocality is reinforced by the appearance of various subaltern voices in Chiapas society.

Parting from the premise established by deconstructionists that identity is necessarily fragmented, the second part may be read as representative of such fragmentation in Castellanos' identity. The death of Mario means that the traditional role to be assumed by Castellanos in Chiapas society is subverted, as she is encouraged to study and becomes an academic and a writer. The many voices present in the second part represent the various possible existences that might have been hers had it not been for the 'accident' of her birth as a woman in a landowning family. There is clearly a correlation between Castellanos' own fear of spinsterhood expressed in her writings and interviews, and the figure of Matilde, César's spinster sister. But what of the male characters represented in the second part? Ernesto is the character who is

---

[49] For a discussion of style in *Balún-Canán* see Grant (1991).

portrayed in the most detail. He is a blood relative of César's but because he is illegitimate he is, as are women and Indians, a second-class citizen. Chapter I of the second part begins with an apparently objective description of César showing Ernesto around his ranch. In fact it reveals Ernesto's story, César's power and the relationship between the two.

Ernesto is marginalised because although white he is poor (and, worse, illegitimate). It soon becomes clear that he is insecure and thus grateful to César for accepting him into the family and helping him. His admiration for César is equalled only by his envy and desire for upward mobility. This is thwarted by the discovery that he was not the only child engendered out of wedlock by his father who – to add insult to injury – had committed suicide because of his unpayable debts. Further, Ernesto's machismo is put to the test when César takes him to watch a calf being treated for a maggot-filled wound; seeing this commonplace ranching sight turns his stomach, and he is reminded that he is not made of the same material as his uncle after all. His final humiliation comes when, absorbed in his thoughts, he does not think to dismount and open a gate for César who, treating him like any other of his workers, asks what he is waiting for (88). Ernesto's lack of a voice, contrasted with César's power, is reiterated in Chapter III. His feelings of humiliation with regard to César are compounded by the fact that his uncle considers him unfit for ranch work, so he is given unimportant minor tasks to do and has no specific job. Worse yet, he finds himself relegated to the house, the private space associated with women, at Zoraida's beck and call, and is even asked to look after the children – clearly women's work in Chiapas in the 1930s. Not only does he consider the work degrading but, also, his self-esteem is so low that he distrusts children and thinks they spy on adults, knowing much more than their innocent faces reveal: 'Esos ojos tan grandes, tan nuevos, son implacables para descubrir los secretos vergonzosos, las debilidades ridículas de los mayores' (Those eyes, so big and new, are implacable when it comes to discovering the shameful secrets and the ridiculous weaknesses of adults) (93). Ernesto's lack of confidence is further revealed in his refusal (because he does not know how) to teach the indigenous children in the school that César is obliged to provide for the families that work on his land.

Ernesto's insecurity is contrasted with another subaltern's secure sense of self, that of Felipe, one of the Indians who works for César. Felipe is very much a product of Lázaro Cárdenas' Mexico as he has been indoctrinated at political rallies, has learnt to read and knows that, before the law, the indigenous people and the whites are equal. Also, he goes against the traditions of his own people, including that of collective decision-making by the elders, on matters affecting the indigenous community.[50] Thus he begins to assume a *ladino* style patriarchal and paternalistic attitude (as opposed to that of his

[50] For further clarification see Ricardo Pozas' explanation of the Chamula system of government and the patriarchal nature of their society (Pozas 1996: 78–86).

own people which is also a deeply patriarchal society), as he assumes authority over the other Indians and demands their loyalty. He represents modern Mexico, a paternalistic secular state where man is god and the centre of all things. His political awakening is likened to a revelation, and Cárdenas to Christ: 'Él había conocido a un hombre, a Cárdenas; lo había oído hablar. (Había estrechado su mano, pero éste era su secreto, su fuerza.) Y supo que Cárdenas pronunciaba justicia y que el tiempo había madurado para que la justicia se cumpliera' (He had met a man, Cárdenas and had heard him speak. (He had shaken his hand but that was his secret, his strength.) And he knew that Cárdenas proclaimed justice and that the time was right for justice to be done) (105). Felipe's strength, in fact, is that unlike the other Indians he is not afraid of César, as he believes in the law and thinks it will protect him. His self-assurance is revealed when César gets angry at his insistence that their legal right should be granted and that he should provide them with a school building as well as a teacher:

> '¿Cuál escuela quieren que se abra? Yo ya cumplí con mi parte trayendo al maestro. Lo demás es cosa de ustedes.' *César espera una respuesta balbuciente, una humildad repentina, una proposición de tregua. Pero el semblante de Felipe no se altera. Y su acento no se ha modificado* cuando dice: 'Voy a hablar con mis camaradas para que entre todos resolvamos lo que es necesario hacer'. (99 [my emphasis])

> ('What is this school that you want opened? I already did my bit by getting the teacher. The rest is up to you.' *César expects a stammering reply, a sudden humility, the calling of a truce. But Felipe's face does not change. And his voice has not altered* when he says 'I'm going to speak to my comrades so that between us we can do whatever needs to be done.')

Felipe pays lip-service only to the indigenous tradition of collective decision-making, because he knows that his fellow Indians, who speak only Tzeltal, have no voice in the *ladino* world. His voice is heard again in Chapter VII when he describes the construction of the school, undertaken by the indigenous people themselves. Significantly, his description is written in a style that resembles two other pieces of 'indigenous' text: the *Chilam-Balam* and the account of the ownership history of Chactajal.

The other Tzeltal (apart from Felipe) think they need the white man's spirit to build the school. This suggests that they, like the women in Castellanos' Mexico, contribute to the perpetuation of their own oppression.[51] The fact that

---

51 According to Gerda Lerner, 'Women have for millenia participated in the process of their own subordination because they have been psychologically shaped so as to internalize the idea of their own inferiority. The unawareness of their own history of struggle and achievement has been one of the major means of keeping women subordinate' (Lerner 1986: 218). Castellanos also berated women for precisely this in her essay 'La liberación de la mujer' (Castellanos: 1988).

Felipe can read, speak Spanish and write about the building of the school indicates his participation in the *ladino* world from which César attempts to exclude 'his' Indians. This, like the end of the novel where the little girl writes Mario's name, suggests that Castellanos sees literacy as a possible way out of marginalisation and a means for allowing the voices of the marginalised to be heard.[52]

The other marginalised beings whose voices are represented in the multi-vocality of the novel are all women. Chapter V describes the arrival of Matilde, César's sister, by mule with the *custitaleros*, and goes on to recount her and her sisters' stories. Francisca, the eldest sister is a strong, independent woman who single-handedly runs the ranch where the three orphaned women live and Romelia, the next eldest, is a sickly hypochondriac who escapes her sister's domineering ways by going to Mexico City for treatment. Matilde, the youngest, was orphaned young and has been brought up by Francisca but eventually she too flees from her sister (who continues to treat her like a child) hoping that she will come to find her, but she is disappointed when Francisca makes no attempt to do so. Matilde feels unwelcome at Chactajal and tries to be useful and unobtrusive. She represents the feelings of obligation and super-fluity felt by dependent spinsters with no means of support other than the goodwill of relations. Matilde might well be Castellanos' alter ego, given her feelings of worthlessness, and is the type of figure that would have impelled Castellanos to become educated in order to be able to support herself and avoid the spinster's fate.

Matilde's story is combined with that of Ernesto in Chapter VI, when she enters his room and the inevitable seduction takes place. However, due to her own lack of self-worth, Matilde despises and rejects Ernesto following this incident. Their story continues in Chapter X when he saves her from drowning, unaware that it is a suicide attempt because she is pregnant with his child. Even though Ernesto is prepared to do the honourable thing and marry Matilde, she refuses him because he is illegitimate. In doing so, she seals her own fate: to become a single mother condemned to a life of either poverty or prostitution, in accordance with the social dictates of the time. This fate, in Matilde's eyes, is preferable to a life in a loveless marriage and her courageous decision not to marry Ernesto may have been prompted by Castellanos' observation of her own parents' mutual lack of affection. However, the unfortunate Matilde's future is altered in Chapter XIII, when Doña Amantina, the *curandera*, arrives to perform an abortion on her. Even without the burden of an illegitimate child, Matilde must leave Chactajal to go to an unknown fate, ordered to do so by César. She clearly accepts the fact that her life is in her brother's hands, as she asks him: '¿No me vas a matar?' (Aren't you going to

---

[52] This is comparable with the use of the internet to disseminate information by the indigenous people of Chiapas during and after the 1994 uprising by the EZLN (Ejército Zapatista de Liberación Nacional).

kill me?), thereby revealing further criticism of the patriarchal nature of society in Chiapas, where either husband, father or brother holds the power of life or death over a woman. Matilde is not mentioned again and the reader can only speculate as to her future. However, her very absence from the text describes her lack of future more eloquently than any words could do.

Ernesto, meanwhile, has made a fool of himself by getting drunk and hitting one of his pupils. He is asked by César to deliver a letter to the *Presidente Municipal* asking for help and, during his journey, fantasises about the way he will be treated as an equal by the President and taken into his confidence. However, on his way to Ocosingo he is shot between the eyes by an Indian (Felipe) who destroys the letter and sends the horse, with Ernesto's body tied on, back to Chactajal. The rebellion of the Indians has reached the stage where César and Zoraida have to carry Ernesto's body to the hermitage themselves as the Indians refuse to help.

In Castellanos' pessimistic vision, then, both Ernesto's and Matilde's voices are silenced, punished for their transgression. The other subaltern voices that appear through the multivocality of the second part of the novel, are those of the other indigenous people who live on Argüello land, including Felipe's wife, Juana. Felipe urges the other men to make a pact to build the school together and to do as he tells them, but finds he is unable to trust them. However, this expectation of obedience also reveals his participation in the patriarchal *ladino* world, as he eschews the tradition of collective decision-making by the men of his community.

Felipe's relations with Juana are also influenced by his contact with the *ladino* world. Juana has not had any children (she believes it is because a *brujo* has dried up her womb), and she acknowledges that Felipe has stayed with her even though that alone would be just cause for separation according to indigenous law. Yet, this is a mixed blessing in her eyes as, since his last trip to Tapachula, she finds him changed, 'Traía la boca llena de palabras irrespetuosas, de opiniones audaces' (He came back with his mouth full of disrespectful words, of daring opinions) (108). She has become afraid of him and secretly desires him to leave and not return. She too compounds her own position of subordination, since, as she is childless she could support Felipe in his struggle for justice without risking her children's lives, but she chooses to remain within her subaltern role and indigenous culture.[53] In the years of 'Progress' during the Presidencies of Ávila Camacho and Miguel Alemán in the 1940s and 1950s, it was considered necessary to incorporate the indigenous people into the capitalist economy. As far as the INI was concerned at that time, this was seen as the only way they could achieve progress and equality. By the late 1950s many intellectuals were aware of the damage caused to the indigenous communities by acculturation, and some writers, like

---

[53] Compare this with the active role taken by the women of the EZLN; see Calmus (1995).

Castellanos, sceptical of the possibilities of social change, reflected this in their work (Steele 1985: 22–23). Juana's refusal to participate in Felipe's struggle, and her idea that she might return to work in the Argüello household, is largely due to the fact that Felipe no longer fulfils his traditional role of provider for her and only refrains from abandoning her altogether out of charity, but it also reveals her subaltern mentality. The negative effects of Felipe's acculturation illustrate the growing awareness of intellectuals, during the late 1950s, that it might not be the answer to improving the situation of the indigenous people; but he also represents the paternalistic attitude that was current at the time.

I conclude this chapter with a final word about the autobiographical nature of *Balún-Canán* and the correlation betwen the *niña*'s and Castellanos' experience. The relationship of the child-narrator with her *nana* and her subsequent participation in the indigenous world; the separation from her *nana* (the principal maternal figure in her life), along with the death of her younger brother, together produced a schism in her life which separated the eras/ cultures of oral and written tradition. The determination of the child, whose acutely sharp observation of the sort of life that she could expect as a woman in rural Chiapas, to become an independent person able to support herself rather than depend on a man in a loveless marriage like her mother, was augmented by her experiences as an Other alongside her *nana*. The limited possibilities open to women at the time Castellanos was growing up in Chiapas, as well as the circumstances of her brother's death, which led her parents to encourage her education and intellectual development in his place, contributed to her becoming a writer. In addition, the responsibility and guilt felt by the little girl for the death of her brother conduce to the fact that the character, at the end of the novel, becomes 'a writer' when she finally takes up the pen, or at least a pencil, to write the memory of her brother:

Y con mi letra inhábil, torpe, fui escribiendo el nombre de Mario. Mario, en los ladrillos del jardín. Mario en las paredes del corredor. Mario en las páginas de mis cuadernos. Porque Mario está lejos. Y yo quisiera pedirle perdón. (291)

(And in my inexpert, clumsy handwriting, I started writing Mario's name. Mario, on the bricks in the garden, Mario on the dining-room walls, Mario on the pages of my exercise book. Because Mario is a long way away. And I would like to tell him I'm sorry.)

4

MULTIVOCALITY AND GENDERED TIME
IN ELENA GARRO'S
LOS RECUERDOS DEL PORVENIR

> No hay un sólo tiempo: todos los tiempos están
> vivos, todos los pasados son presentes.[1]

INTRODUCTION

Elena Garro was born in Puebla on 15 December 1920 of a Spanish father and mestiza mother but grew up in Iguala, Guerrero.[2] While *Los recuerdos del porvenir* makes no claim to being autobiographical, nevertheless it does have autobiographical elements and refers to a type of landscape and a small provincial town in Mexico, which were familiar to Garro. Furthermore, the exploration of memory such as that undertaken in *Los recuerdos del porvenir*, cannot exclude references to autobiography.

Immersed in literature from an early age, Garro and her siblings were encouraged to read the books in their father's extensive library; her mother's words when the children complained of being bored were, 'tengan virtud' (be virtuous) (Muncy 1986: 67).[3] Garro studied Spanish literature at the UNAM (Universidad Autónoma de México) then became a reporter, writing for magazines and newspapers, after she married Octavio Paz in 1937. They travelled extensively because of his studies and diplomatic appointments and Garro wrote *Los recuerdos del porvenir* in Switzerland during the 1950s, although it was not published until 1963. The novel was awarded the Xavier Villaurrutia prize that year and was translated in 1969 as *Recollections of Things to Come*. After separating from Paz, Garro spent many years in Paris, Spain and New York before returning to Mexico to live in Cuernavaca, Morelos, with her daughter Helena Paz, where she died on 22 August, 1998.

The story is set in an arid province of Mexico. Ixtepec, the town, is also the first-person plural collective narrator. It is the 1920s and the town is governed by a military *cacique*, Francisco Rosas, whose ruthlessness the townspeople

---

[1] Carlos Fuentes (1997).
[2] Other sources give 5 December, 11 December and 12 December as her date of birth.
[3] These words are almost repeated in *Los recuerdos del porvenir* when Ana Moncada tells Isabel, the protagonist, '¡Reza, ten virtud!' (Garro, 1994: 31).

attribute to his unrequited love for Julia Andrade, his concubine. They live together in Ixtepec's only hotel, the Hotel Jardín, along with the other officers and their lovers. The other protagonists of the story are the Moncadas whose sons, Juan and Nicolás, will be killed by the General and whose daughter, Isabel, will become his lover; Julia, and a stranger, Felipe Hurtado, who arrives one day on the train from Mexico City and with whom Julia 'disappears'. The magical disappearance of the couple concludes the first part of the book. Part Two describes a plot to rescue the town's priest, Father Beltrán, from the military, after religious ceremonies are banned by the Mexican Church authorities and the churches closed by the government of Plutarco Elías Calles. This legislation, and resistance to it by those faithful to Roman Catholicism, sparks off the Cristero War (1926–29) between government troops and the *cristeros* (so named because of their battle cry of *¡Viva Cristo Rey!*) Finally, Isabel Moncada fails to prevent the execution by Rosas' troops of her brother, Nicolás (for his involvement in the plot) and is allegedly turned to stone. The plot is circular, beginning and ending with the image of the aforementioned stone. The novel contains frequent references to the corruptness of Calles' regime, described by Garro as a dictatorship, and to the dichotomy between the official policy of modernisation and the reality of the backwardness and apathy of provincial towns like Ixtepec, whose inhabitants fail to benefit from post-revolutionary 'progress'; and between the allegedly democratically elected government and the brutality it employs to keep itself in power.

NATIONALITY, IDENTITY AND MULTIVOCALITY

In *Los recuerdos del porvenir*, Garro offers, through the heteroglossia discernible in her writing, a criticism of the idea of a national identity and a fixed, official reality as propounded by the status quo. Though not published until 1963, *Los recuerdos del porvenir* was written in the 1950s when nation-building was at its peak in Mexico (Stoll, 1990: 200). Garro's use of the first person plural 'we' suggests an ironic detachment from the idea of nationhood that was propagated throughout the post-revolutionary era. This concept of a homogeneous nation remained unchallenged to any serious degree until the student demonstrations and the massacre at Tlatelolco in 1968 led an establishment figure – Octavio Paz, no less (then ambassador to India) – to resign his post in protest at the Government's action, thus marking what has been described as, 'the exit from consensus politics of important parts of the urban population' (Rowe and Schelling 1994: 160). Paz affirms in his *Posdata* to *El laberinto de la soledad*, that, 'Lo que ocurrió el 2 de octubre de 1968 fue, simultáneamente, la negación de aquello que hemos querido ser desde la Revolución y la afirmación de lo que somos desde la Conquista y aún antes'

(What happened on 2 of October 1968 was, simultaneously, the negation of what we have wanted to be since the Revolution and the affirmation of what we are since the Conquest and even before then) (Paz 1970: 113). Garro pre-empts Paz's realisation that Mexican national identity is a myth when, in *Los recuerdos del porvenir*, she reveals her belief that even as early as the time of the Cristero War, the Revolution could no longer be deployed as a symbol of that identity (Rowe and Schelling 1994: 163).

Multivocality, often present in the text tinged with irony, exposes the injustices of the post-revolutionary government. Lola Goríbar, a wealthy landowner, expresses her limitless admiration for her son Rodolfo. It was thanks to him that her land had been returned to her and the Government had paid for the damage caused by the followers of Zapata. '¡Es tan bueno Elvira!' (He's so good, Elvira!) (67) she exclaims, fingering the diamond brooch obtained with her son's ill-gotten gains. Similarly, her son's own thoughts and actions expose the corruption that exists in post-revolutionary Mexico: '[. . .] después de cada viaje, Rodolfo, ayudado por sus pistoleros traídos de Tabasco, movía las mojoneras que limitaban sus haciendas y ganaba peones, chozas y tierras gratuitas' (after every trip, Rodolfo, helped by his henchmen brought from Tabasco, would move the boundary stones which marked the limits of his estates and obtain free farmhands, huts and lands) (68). Not only is the continuing existence of the semi-feudalistic system of landholding, which the Revolution had pledged to destroy, revealed here, but so is the Government's complicity with such criminal acts. When Rodolfo is warned by Ignacio, the baker's brother, that he risks his life by moving the boundary stones, as the *agraristas* have threatened to kill him if he does so, Rodolfo snubs Ignacio and smiles:

> ¿Cuántas veces lo habían amenazado? Se sentía seguro. El menor rasguño a su persona costaría la vida a docenas de agraristas. *El gobierno se lo había prometido y lo había autorizado para apropiarse de las tierras que le vinieran en gana.* El general Francisco Rosas lo apoyaba. Cada vez que ensanchaba sus haciendas, el general Francisco Rosas recibía de manos de Rodolfo Goríbar una fuerte suma de dinero que se convertía en alhajas para Julia. (68 [my emphasis])

> (How many times had he been threatened? He felt safe. The slightest scratch to his person would cost the lives of dozens of agrarian reformers. *The government had promised him and had authorised him to take over whichever lands he wanted.* General Francisco Rosas supported him. Every time he expanded his ranches, General Francisco Rosas received from Rodolfo Goríbar a tidy sum of money which became jewellery for Julia.)

Ignacio is later found hanged one morning from a tree on the outskirts of Ixtepec, with four other Indians.

Another of the young men of Ixtepec, Tomás Segovia, secretly admires

Rosas, whom he equates with the Roman patrician, ruling without the 'least notion of piety' (71) over a nation of slaves. His cynical attitude and the existence of an official discourse which is manipulated to hide the truth is nowhere more clearly revealed than in the following extract:

> 'Nos hubiera ido mejor con Zapata. Cuando menos era del sur' suspiró doña Matilde [. . .] 'Matilde habla como un general del Gobierno' dijo Segovia con aire divertido, y pensó en el nuevo idioma oficial en el que las palabras 'justicia', 'Zapata', 'indio', y 'agrarismo' servían para facilitar el despojo de tierras y el asesinato de los campesinos. (73)

> ('It would have gone better for us with Zapata. At least he was from the south' sighed Dona Matilde [. . .] 'Matilde talks like a general from the Government' said Segovia amused, and he thought of the new official language in which the words 'justice', 'Zapata', 'Indian', and 'agrarianism' were used to facilitate the plundering of lands and the murder of peasants.)

Segovia's racism and the cynicism of the Government that assassinated Zapata, are also exposed in the following passage:

> '¡Es verdad! ¿Sabes que el Gobierno le va a hacer una estatua?' preguntó doña Elvira con alegría. '¡Para que no digan que no son revolucionarios! ¡No tiene remedio, el mejor indio es el indio muerto!', exclamó el boticario recordando la frase que había guiado la dictadura porfirista y aplicándola ahora con malicia al uso que se pretendía hacer con el nombre del indio asesinado Emiliano Zapata. (73)

> ('It's true! Did you know that the government is going to make another statue of him?' asked Dona Elvira gaily. 'Who says they aren't revolutionaries! 'There's no doubt about it, the best Indian is a dead Indian!' exclaimed the pharmacist remembering the phrase that had guided the Porfirian dictatorship and maliciously applying it now to the use that was being made of the name of the murdered Indian Emiliano Zapata.)

Such dialogues are one way in which the heteroglossia in the novel becomes apparent. Multivocality takes other forms, however, one of which is the polyphony found in the voice of the collective narrator.

THE COLLECTIVE NARRATOR

Garro's choice of a first-person plural collective narrator – the voice of the people of Ixtepec (though not all of them) is unusual. Bertil Romberg defines the novel in the first person as, 'when the author has his [sic] point of view located within the fiction, and talks through the mouth of a spokesman, the narrator, who is made to assume the formal authority for the story' (Romberg

1962: 23). This quotation (in spite of Romberg's – or his translator's – disregard for gender), supports my view that Garro wrote *Los recuerdos del porvenir* with a collective narrative voice in order to distance the work from her own autobiographical voice, but also to represent the diverse nature of any marginalised group such as women, or even – as here – the old aristocracy in Mexico. Thus, although the so-called 'collectivity' of Ixtepec, the *nosotros* and *mi* used by the narrator is restricted to the privileged class to which she herself belonged, Garro succeeds in producing a multivocal version of the Cristero era, by allowing various marginalised beings to express their points of view. These include the Moncadas' indigenous servant, Félix; the old and penniless women of the town; the town's brothel owner; the town 'loco', Juan Cariño and above all, the young rebel, Isabel Moncada. Garro's novel is clearly subversive in the way it criticises the status quo and this is one reason Garro felt it necessary to disguise her own voice in that of the collective narrator. The independent attitude of the protagonist, Isabel Moncada, establishes that this is so very early on in the text, when she refuses to accept the role prescribed for her by society:

> 'A mí me gustaría que Isabel se casara' intervino la madre. 'No me voy a casar' contestó la hija. A Isabel le disgustaba que establecieran diferencias entre ella y sus hermanos. Le humillaba la idea de que el único futuro para las mujeres fuera el matrimonio. Hablar del matrimonio como de una solución la dejaba reducida a una mercancía a la que había que dar salida a cualquier precio. (23–24)

> ('I would like Isabel to get married' interrupted her mother. 'I am not going to marry' replied her daughter. Isabel disliked differences being established between her and her brothers. She found the idea that the only future for women was marriage humiliating. To speak of marriage as a solution reduced her to a commodity which had to be moved on at any price.)

This reveals a decidedly feminist thought process, although in other ways the novel seems very traditional in its conception. It appears to conform to Felski's definition of the pattern of the nineteenth-century novel of self-discovery, in which the choices for the female protagonist are limited to 'a stifling and repressive marriage or a form of withdrawal into inwardness which frequently concludes in self-destruction' (Felski 1989: 124). Indeed, Isabel's rejection of the idea of marriage leads her to end up turned to stone, or 'lost'. Her conscious decision to reject marriage and the antiquated social mores of Ixtepec by becoming the General's lover and attempting to participate in history, places her in a twentieth-century context, but her ultimate removal from Ixtepec society would be seen by Felski as the price she must pay for such transgression.

Although she set the novel at the time of the Cristero rebellion, it is obvious that Garro was criticising not only the political betrayals, assassinations and

corruption that took place in the aftermath of the Revolution but also the
legacy of such misdeeds. The cycle of violence was initiated, according to
Martín Moncada, by the bourgeoisie, and its legacy must be atoned for by
them too. Given the harsh criticism of the Revolution's failure to fulfil its
ideals, expressed by Garro in the novel, it comes as no surprise that the subsequent pressure on her led her to opt for self-imposed exile in Paris for several
years (Toruño 1995: 28).[4]

Although on the whole the novel has a linear plot, this is fragmented into
sections that do not follow one upon the other with any particular logic. Carol
Clark d'Lugo writes that such fragmentation of the novel in Mexico during
the twentieth century, 'evokes the social and political realities of the country'
(Clark d'Lugo 1997: xi). *Los recuerdos del porvenir* has also been classified
as an historical novel: a genre which also claims to evoke social and political
realities. Jean Franco calls the historical novel 'the genre privileged as the
allegory of national formation' but adds that women writers such as Garro
(and Castellanos) 'who attempted to plot women as protagonists in this allegory could not but confront the fact that national identity was essentially
masculine identity' (Franco 1989: xxi). Fragmentation in women's writing
would also therefore reflect the fragmentation of the self experienced by
women in a society where their identity is proscribed by a male establishment.
Although not all those who challenge the status quo in *Los recuerdos del
porvenir* are female characters, Garro's multivocal discourse is an attempt to
disrupt that idea of national identity. Isabel refuses to conform to the role of
the *sufrida y abnegada mujercita*, though in doing so she ends up a traitor to
Ixtepec and to her family. Ana Moncada, wife of Martín Moncada, is a
'woman with a past'. Julia, the General's mistress, prefers an unknown future
(or death) with Felipe Hurtado, rather than allow herself to be bought by
power and gifts and remain as mistress to a man she clearly does not love.
Even the town's prostitutes disrupt the idea of the *mala mujer* (and also
conform to certain stereotypical representations of prostitutes with hearts of
gold) when they show solidarity with other marginalised beings by protecting
the priest, befriending Juan Cariño and being the only inhabitants brave
enough to support him in protesting to Rosas when more Indians are hanged.
Similarly, the officers' *queridas*, including Julia, are described as devout and
regularly attend Mass (77). So when Lieutenant-Colonel Cruz's twin lovers,
Rafaela and Rosa, learn that the priest is to be executed, they refuse Cruz's
caresses and sleep apart from him in a separate bed (274). One male character
who challenges the status quo is Martín Moncada, who refuses to live in linear
time or to concern himself with material pursuits. Felipe Hurtado is another,
as he is more interested in imagination than in material progress.

---

4   Thus the castigation or elimination of Isabel from Mexican society mirrors, to some
extent, Garro's own circumstances, whereby she was obliged to live in exile due to problems regarding citizenship and political involvement.

The collective voice in *Los recuerdos del porvenir*, then, does not seem to represent a true cross-section of the town's inhabitants. Ixtepec's multitude of subjects, made up of rich and poor, Indian, *mestizo* and *criollo*, appear not to be equally represented in the 'we' used by the narrator. However, a careful reading reveals that the narration is not omniscient and that there are indeed representative voices for all the sectors of Ixtepec society. Representing women's voices are, among others, Doña Elvira, the widow who equates her widowhood with liberation; her daughter Conchita; Lola Goríbar, the wealthy mother of the man responsible for hanging the Indians and stealing their land; Dorotea, the elderly spinster who spends her days making altar cloths; Luchi, the owner of the brothel; Julia Andrade and the other officers' concubines; Ana Moncada and her daughter Isabel, both of whom are sexually transgressive women. The diversity of these voices reveal how it is as inappropriate to speak of a single 'female' voice as of a 'male' voice. The indigenous population is represented through the voices of Félix, the Moncadas' faithful servant; Ignacio, the baker's brother and the female servant who betrays the plot to save the priest. The old aristocracy is typified by the gentle Don Joaquín, whose vast house and garden is a refuge to abandoned and orphaned animals; while the new rich is represented by the ruthless Rodolfo Goríbar with his hired assassins. A destitute upper middle class is represented by Martín Moncada, Isabel's father, and by his sons, Juan and Nicolás. (Martín is unwilling to participate in modernisation – and chronological time – and attempts to stop time passing by stopping the clock from ticking. Juan and Nicolás are obliged to work in the mines so the family can survive and are willing to die for their beliefs when they side with the *cristeros*.) The military is represented by Francisco Rosas, more interested in Julia than in supressing rebellion and by the other officers (each of very different character), who live with their lovers in Ixtepec's only hotel.

Félix may be Martín Moncada's Indian servant, but among the people of his own class he is listened to and known with respect as *don Félix* (25). Furthermore, Félix's voice does not, because he is an Indian, remain unheard outside his own class. Martín depends on him as a source of knowledge and for good counsel: '¿Qué sería de él sin Félix? Félix era su memoria de todos los días' (What would become of him without Felix? Felix was his everyday memory) (22 23). More than that, the close association Martín feels between himself and Félix – 'su segundo yo' (his second self) – and the only person he does not feel strange with, transgresses the norm for a master/servant relationship (and, moreover, of another binary opposition) (23). The idea of a 'second self' may be read as a reference to the hybrid nature of the Mexican race and the fact that the majority of the population are of mixed indigenous and Spanish blood. Thus, the authorial voice emerges through the collective narrator, revealing the racial prejudice shown towards the indigenous people in Mexico and the antipathy felt by many towards indigenous culture, as well as a deep-seated feeling of sameness. Félix also transgresss his indigenous role by being the voice of reason – the domain of white Europeans only according to the traditional (colonial) view (Tritten 1979). He advises Martín to let Juan and Nicolás work in the mines at Tetela to help the family's economic situation and, when tempers are frayed by what is said at the gathering in the Moncada household one evening, Félix calms the situation in a practical way, by bringing a cool drink to cool tempers (24). Martín is grateful that he is not the one who has to produce practical solutions.

At the same time, the 'we' of Ixtepec also represents a society divided by race and class that does not conform to the official discourse of the, by then, institutionalised governing party of the 1950s: that Mexico is one people and one nation – *mexicano*. Jean Franco suggests that all those included in the collective voice are victims of marginalisation by the 'new' Mexico:

> [. . .] the old aristocracy, the peasantry (and former supporters of the assassinated revolutionary leader Zapata) the indigenous, and women, in sum, all those left behind by modernization and the new nation. Excluded from this collective memory is the official history propagated by the 'new men' who have forged post-revolutionary nationalism [. . .].
>
> (Franco 1989: 134)

But this does not take into account Lola Goríbar and her son whose vast amount of land and wealth has been accumulated through greed and extortion. The use of a collective voice also deliberately exposes the irony in the statements made by the narrator suggesting indifference to the indigenous population, when the authorial voice again comes through the narrative. Garro, as well as criticising the official discourse, is criticising the hypocrisy of those Mexicans who refuse to acknowledge their own *mestizaje*. Thus when Nicolás Moncada, ashamed by their attitude, reminds them, '¡Todos somos medio indios!' (We are all half Indian), Elvira is indignant, ' "¡Yo no tengo nada de india!" – exclamó sofocada la viuda' ('There's nothing Indian about me' – exclaimed the widow, in a choked voice) (27). Outright indignation is often tempered into mere indifference, as when Ignacio is found hanged one morning and the narrator comments: 'No volvimos a mentarlo. Después de todo, era sólo un indio menos. De sus cuatro amigos ni siquiera recordábamos los nombres. Sabíamos que dentro de poco otros indios anónimos ocuparían sus lugares en las ramas' (We didn't mention him again. After all, it was just one less Indian. We didn't even remember the names of his four friends. We knew that soon more anonymous Indians would occupy their places among the branches) (92–93). However, this can also be read as a reflection of the Indians' own attitude of resignation after hundreds of years of being marginalised as well as a reflection of the attitude of many of the *ladino* inhabitants of Ixtepec, including both those of the landowning class (Goríbar) and the middle class with pretensions to upward mobility (Tomás Segovia). For some (the widow Montúfar), prejudice towards the Indians is the result of fear and ignorance. '¡Son tan traidores!'⁵ (They are such traitors!) she says. Garro's mockery of her attitude is revealed when the widow, on learning of the death of Ignacio, the brother of Justina the baker, is upset not so much at his demise as because there will be no fresh bread that day for her breakfast. Her daughter Conchita, however, remembers Ignacio with compassion, and the gulf between the two generations – the young and idealistic girl and the middle-aged woman embittered by her unhappy life – is made patent. Yet there is hope, as Elvira is influenced by her daughter's sorrow and for the first time thinks, '¡Pobres indios! ¡Tal vez no son tan malos como creemos!' (Poor Indians, perhaps they are not so bad as we think) (83). This sympathy for the Indians becomes a nascent solidarity when the Roman Catholic Church comes under threat from the authorities: 'Llegaron las señoras y los señores de Ixtepec y se mezclaron con los indios, como si por primera vez el mismo mal los aquejara' (The ladies and gentlemen of Ixtepec arrived and mingled with the Indians, as if, for the first time, they were afflicted by the same grievance) (158). However, it is religion (a metaphor for spirituality), and not political ideology, that unites them.

Earlier comments by the narrator clearly reflect Garro's well-known concern for the oppressed and marginalised, at the same time as it describes the effect the violence has on the lives of the people and their sense of time. I am including this rather long quotation as it is central to the idea of the novel:

> En esos días era yo tan tan desdichado que mis horas se acumulaban informes y mi memoria se había convertido en sensaciones. La desdicha como el dolor físico iguala los minutos. Los días se convierten en el mismo día, los actos en el mismo acto, y las personas en un sólo personaje inútil. El mundo pierde su variedad, la luz se aniquila y los milagros quedan abolidos. La inercia de esos días repetidos me guardaba quieto, contem-plando la fuga inútil de mis horas y esperando el milagro que se obstinaba en no producirse. El porvenir era la repetición del pasado. Inmóvil, me dejaba devorar por la sed que roía mis esquinas. Para romper los días petrificados sólo me quedaba el espejismo ineficaz de la violencia, *y la crueldad se ejercía con furor sobre las mujeres, los perros callejeros y los indios*. Como en las tragedias, vivíamos dentro de un tiempo quieto y los personajes sucumbían presos en ese instante detenido. Era en vano que hicieran gestos cada vez más sangrientos. Habíamos abolido el tiempo. (64–65 [my emphasis]).

> (At that time I was so unhappy that my hours gathered together formlessly and my memory had become mere sensations. Unhappiness, like physical pain, evens out the minutes. Days become the same day, acts the same act, and people a single useless person. The world loses its variety, light is

---

⁵ Notice the similarity with the words used by Zoraida in *Balún-Canán*: '¡Y son tan hipócritas, y tan solapados y tan falsos!'

annihilated and miracles are abolished. The inertia of those repetitious days kept me quiet, contemplating the useless flight of my hours and waiting for the miracle that obstinately refused to happen. The future was the repetition of the past. Immobile, it let me be devoured by the thirst that gnawed away at my edges. To break up the petrified days, all that was left was the inefficient mirage of violence, and cruelty was inflicted with furore upon women, stray dogs and Indians. As if in a tragedy we lived in arrested time and the characters became prisoners in that time. It was in vain that they carried out increasingly bloody acts. We had abolished time.)

Clearly the last two sentences also imply a criticism of authoritarian regimes or states. The attempts by Calles' government to outlaw the Roman Catholic Church and replace it with a Mexican Orthodox Church, more closely connected and therefore answerable to the Government, was done in the name of the Mexican people, particularly the peasantry and the proletariat who, allegedly, were oppressed by the Roman Catholic Church. However, those who fought on the side of the *cristeros* were the very peasantry that allegedly wanted a secular state. The Government's 'doublespeak' is exposed in the following extract in *Los recuerdos del porvenir*, as is the inconformity of the townspeople. Following celebrations by the people of Ixtepec at the assassination of the tyrannical revolutionary general Álvaro Obregón, the news arrives that the government has banned acts of worship. It is not only the traditional defenders of religion – the landed gentry and the middle classes – who have come to protest:

> La gente salió a la calle, formó grupos y se dirigió al atrio de la iglesia. '¡A ver si nos dejan sin santos!' Bajo la luz violeta de la tarde, la muchedumbre fue creciendo. '¡Vamos a ver quién desmadra a quién!' Encerrados en una ira en voz baja, los pies descalzos curtidos por las piedras y las cabezas descubiertas, los pobres se agruparon bajo las ramas de los almendros. '¡Virgen de Guadalupe, ayúdanos a chingar a estos cabrones!' (157)

> (People came out on to the street, formed groups and set off towards the porch of the church. 'We'll soon see if you take away our saints!' Under the violet evening light, the crowd began to grow. 'Let's see who gets the better of whom'. Enclosed in a low-voiced anger, their unshod feet made leathery by the stones, their heads bare, the poor gathered together under the branches of the almond trees.'Virgin of Guadalupe, help us screw these bastards!')

According to Jean Franco, *Los recuerdos del porvenir* is not a historical novel in spite of the historical references but rather, 'it challenges the state's appropriation of meaning by evoking more ancient loyalties – to family, religion, and "imagined communities" which do not coincide with the nation' (Franco 1989: 134). However, while not a historical novel in the traditional sense, that is, a work characterised by what Daniel Balderston terms 'a heightened realism' and the 'ostentatious use of detail', its 'uncharacteristic use of

the fantastic calls into question the historical record of the revolution'
(Balderston 1989: 41). *Los recuerdos del porvenir* suggests that Garro aligns
herself with the marginalised, whatever their race, class or gender; the many
references to historical and political events and the heteroglossia in the voices
of the narrator and the people of Ixtepec reveal her disillusion with the
government. Martín Moncada's suggestion that they (the landowning class)
are receiving their just desserts at the hands of Rosas for betraying Madero,
comes as a surprise to his peers. They see the anarchy in the country as
resulting from the revolt of the Indians initiated by Madero, rather than as a
result of the wave of political assassinations that had taken place, beginning
with that of Madero. The feeling of security experienced by the better-off
(supporters of Porfirio Díaz) when Venustiano Carranza 'betrayed the Revolution' and took power, dissolved when they found themselves under 'un
gobierno tiránico y voraz que sólo compartía las riquezas y los privilegios con
sus antiguos enemigos y cómplices en la traición: los grandes terratenientes
del porfirismo' (a tyrannical and voracious government which only shared
wealth and privileges with its former enemies and accomplices in treason: the
great landowners who supported Porfirio Díaz) (72). In other words,
according to the textual author, the social injustice that led to Revolution had
been replaced by a similar, if not worse, tyranny: 'En verdad estaban asom-
brados de la amistad sangrienta entre los porfiristas católicos y los revolucionarios ateos. Los unía la voracidad y el origen vergonzoso del mestizo. Entre
los dos habían inaugurado una era bárbara y sin precedente en mi memoria'
(In truth they were surprised by the bloody friendship between the Catholic
supporters of Díaz and the atheistic revolutionaries. They were united by
voraciousness and their shameful *mestizo* origins. Between them they had
inaugurated a barbarous era without precedent in my memory) (72). Don
Joaquín's pessimistic prediction voices Garro's own beliefs about the treatment of the Indians:

> 'Tiene razón, Martín, y todavía veremos cosas peores, ¿Para qué creen que
> Rodolfito trajo a esos pistoleros de Tabasco? ¿Para cazar perros calle-
> jeros?' Don Joaquín al decir esto se estremecía pensando en los innume-
> rables perros famélicos y sarnosos que trotaban por mis calles empedradas,
> perseguidos por la sed, iguales en la miseria y en su condición de parias a
> los millones de indios despojados y brutalizados por el Gobierno. (72)

> ('Martín is right, and worse is yet to come. Why do you think that Rodol-
> fito brought those gunslingers from Tabasco? To shoot stray dogs?' Don
> Joaquín, on saying this, shuddered to think of the innumerable starving,
> mangy dogs that trotted around my cobbled streets, always thirsty, pariahs
> in a similar state of misery as the millions of Indians dispossessed and
> brutalised by the government.)

Garro clearly feels that dogs, having been domesticated by humans should therefore be the latter's responsibility.[6]

Another character in the novel who is marginalised is *el señor presidente* Juan Cariño, for two reasons: that he is considered by the townspeople to be crazy and he chooses to live in Ixtepec's brothel. His voice, in keeping with his marginalised position, goes unheard. Yet his role in the events that take place is significant, as is that of the prostitutes he lives with, though their efforts too, go largely unrecognised. The marginalisation of the prostitutes by the townspeople is revealed in the following lines when they are recruited by Juan Cariño to protest to Rosas about the hanging of Ignacio and the other Indians:

> 'Ustedes lo único que deben hacer es repetir a coro las palabras que yo diga al general.' 'Muy bien, pero acuérdese señor presidente que no tenemos permiso para caminar por el centro de Ixtepec.' '¡Bah! Tonterías.' A eso de las cinco de la tarde Juan Cariño desfiló por mis calles seguido de las 'cuscas' que *caminaban cabizbajas. Avergonzadas, trataban de ocultarse el rostro con las chalinas negras.* (87 [my emphasis])

> ('The only thing you have to do is repeat in chorus what I say to the general.' 'Fine, but remember Mr President that we are not allowed to walk around the centre of Ixtepec.' 'Bah! Nonsense.' At about five o'clock in the afternoon Juan Cariño paraded through my streets followed by the 'tarts' who *walked with bowed heads. In their shame, they were trying to hide their faces with black shawls.*)

Here, as well as commenting on the hypocrisy of the townspeople, Garro is alluding to the double standards of a government which officially bans prostitution as part of the revolutionary cleansing of a corrupt society, yet unofficially sanctions it by condoning its own officials' (represented by Rosas and his men) frequenting of the brothels.[7]

The voice of the marginalised is, indeed, represented then; but it does not form part of the collective voice of the first-person narrator, the 'nosotros' of Ixtepec. For the most part, it is to Ixtepec's élite that a voice is given. However, it is a diverse élite and one with a range of political sympathies and

---

6   This comparison with dogs that views Indians as dependants may not be considered politically correct now when marginalised peoples are finding their own voice, and discourses have changed drastically, but during the 1950s this was not the case. Those who wrote on behalf of the underdog such as Garro and the *indigenista* writers were well-intentioned; there was a genuine desire to help the Indians by speaking on their behalf.

7   María R. González (1996) writes: 'Desde la época de Plutarco Elías Calles (1924–1934) se hacen intentos por erradicar la prostitución, más sin ningún éxito. Los prostíbulos legales o clandestinos siguen proliferando y operando por toda la república, existiendo siempre en los márgenes sociales.' Debra Castillo also writes on prostitutes in Mexican society and fiction (Castillo 1998).

varying degree of social conscience. The women among this élite, with the exception of Matilde and Ana Moncada, are not represented in a sympathetic light. Other women, such as Luchi and Dorotea are viewed favourably but do not form part of the élite.

Luchi and Juan Cariño are two marginalised voices that add to the multi-vocality of *Los recuerdos del porvenir*. I shall discuss these two in conjunction as their relationship is particularly significant, representing as they do, the opposite poles of the mind/body binary. The view Luchi (the owner of the brothel) has of Juan Cariño shows her inconformity with official discourse about the nature of reality, including her own as a prostitute. Juan Cariño is considered by the townspeople to be alienated from reality. To them, it appears that he merely has an obsession with dictionaries (enough to classify him as a madman in some eyes). But he has given himself the task of patrolling the streets, picking up all the words denoting wickedness uttered that day, and keeping them hidden from evildoers to prevent further mischief being wrought. In spite of his 'madness' he shows lucidity when talking about words and insight into the power not only of words, but also of silence:

> Pues si era cierto lo que había dicho, lo importante era lo que no había dicho: que las palabras eran peligrosas porque existían por ellas mismas y la defensa de los diccionarios evitaba catástrofes inimaginables. [. . .] Ya eran demasiadas las que conocían los ignorantes y se valían de ellas para provocar sufrimientos. (60–61)

> (Well if it were true what he had said, the important thing was what he had not said: that words were dangerous because they existed for themselves and the defence of dictionaries prevented unimaginable catastrophes. [. . .] There were already too many known by ignorant people who used them to cause suffering.)

Juan Cariño's 'madness' protects him from danger and allows him to speak with impunity where other marginalised beings would have to be silent in order to survive. He is the only person in the town who dares to describe Rosas as a murderer to the soldiers at the General's headquarters: '¡Díganle a ese asesino que no vuelva a presentarse nunca más en la Presidencia!' (Tell that murderer never to set foot in the Presidential residence again!) (89). At the same time, his speaking the truth out loud initiates a change in the attitude of the people of Ixtepec. The variable nature of the meaning of words is communicated through Juan Cariño. He is the character most associated with the power of words to distort meaning and truth, because he is the one most concerned with truth. For this reason, and because he professes to be the Municipal President, he is referred to by the townspeople as *el loco*. However, at the instigation of Luchi, who recognises his intelligence, the prostitutes in the brothel where he lives address him as *Señor presidente*. There is clearly also a criticism here of the political reality of Ixtepec where there is no elected municipal president and the town is 'governed' by a ruthless general, a greedy landowner and his murderous henchmen; but only Luchi realises that Juan Cariño is aware of the possibility of a different reality for Ixtepec. Only she, until the arrival of Felipe, treats Juan Cariño with courtesy and consideration as she believes that were he not mad he would be a great man with a lot of power and the world would be 'tan luminoso como la Rueda de la Fortuna'.[8] Luchi thinks that Juan Cariño had perhaps once dreamt that he was the President but never awoke from that dream. For her, he represents another world beyond the baseness of her own life and the violence that exists in Ixtepec. In this way he is linked to that other world outside chronological time associated with the characters of Felipe, Julia, Isabel and Martín. More importantly, he provides Luchi, the marginalised prostitute without hope of a better life, with the pretext to allow herself to dream of one. She scrutinises Juan Cariño's eyes:

> creyendo descubrir en ellos al mundo asombroso de los sueños: sus espirales al cielo, sus palabras girando solitarias como amenazas, sus árboles sembrados en el viento, sus mares azules sobre los tejados. ¿Acaso ella no volaba en sueños? Volaba sobre unas calles que a su vez volaban persiguiéndola y abajo la esperaban unas frases. Si llegara a levantarse en la mitad de ese sueño, creería para siempre en la existencia de sus alas y las gentes dirían burlonas, 'Miren a la Luchi. Está loca. Se cree pájaro.' (62)

> (believing she might discover in them the amazing world of dreams: with its spirals to heaven, its words spinning like solitary threats, its trees sown in the wind, its blue seas over the roof tops. Did she not fly in dreams? She flew over streets which themselves were flying, pursuing her and down below a few phrases would await her. If she were to get up in the middle of that dream, she would believe forever in the existence of her wings and people would say mockingly, 'Look at Luchi, she's crazy. She thinks she's a bird.')

Luchi thus rebels against the official idea of the materialistic prostitute. She resembles Isabel in two ways: both straddle linear and cyclical time and both, when they attempt to participate in the historical process (by helping the priest escape), are punished with non-existence (being killed by Rosas' men and turning to stone respectively).

Garro's choice of a collective narrator which represents the élite of Ixtepec may, therefore, be a substitute for her autobiographical voice in order to distance herself from her position as part of such an élite. For although forming part of that élite in terms of class, Garro's own marginalisation as a woman,

---

8 Here the word *luminoso*, which is usually used in conjunction with Julia, is used to describe the Wheel of Fortune which in Golden Age Literature was associated with cyclical time. Garro was interested in and influenced by Golden Age Literature. This is reflected in one of her plays, *La dama boba*, which is based around the enactment of Lope de Vega's play with the same title.

and as a person born in Mexico yet denied the security of Mexican citizenship, made her even more sympathetic to the less privileged in society.[9] Garro has affirmed that she grew up playing with the children of the family's indigenous servants, as did Castellanos, and learnt to respect them (Toruño 1995: 2–3). This initiated an interest in their rights, and in her youth she wrote articles for newspapers and magazines in favour of land distribution for the peasants. This activity led to political problems in which she too was implicated.[10] Speaking about the reality in Mexico Garro stated: 'Creo que se pueden hacer las cosas y creo que mientras no se hagan ciertas cosas, México no tiene destino' (I believe something can be done and I believe that, as long as certain things are not done, Mexico has no future) (Toruño 1995: 57). Clearly then, the author's background and political sympathies are reflected in *Los recuerdos del porvenir*. However, Garro's awareness of gender as a political issue is also manifested in her writing on the nature of time and memory, as the following section attempts to demonstrate.

GENDERED TIME AND MEMORY IN IXTEPEC

The title 'Los recuerdos del porvenir', unlike the title of Proust's work *Remembrance of Things Past* (which Garro may well have read), immediately suggests a trajectory of time that is circular rather than linear. (How else might one remember things that are yet to come?) In other works by Garro, such as *La culpa es de los Tlaxcaltecas*, linear time exists side by side with circular time; events which take place in the past may be repeated in the future. The concept of time as a series of events that are repeated at a later date appears in pre-Columbian cosmology. As Richard Townsend's description of the Aztecs' notion of time reveals:

> Like many other peoples of antiquity in the New World and the Old, the Aztecs did not experience time as a succession of uniform movements, stretching monotonously from the indefinite past into the indefinite future. Nor was their time of indifferent uniform quality. It would be impossible to overstress the fact that time for the Aztecs was full of energy and motion, the harbinger of change, and always charged with a sense of *miraculous happening*. (Townsend 1992: 122 [my emphasis])

As Townsend affirms, the notion of time as non-linear is also found in the Old World. According to Christian belief, two distinct times exist: 'profane'

9   This was because of her father's Spanish nationality and in spite of her marriage to Paz. In Mexico, at that time, it was the father's and not the mother's nationality which determined that of the child, irrespective of whether she/he was born in Mexico or not.

10   Toruño describes how Garro wanted to speak to Cárdenas on the matter, but he refused until he found her lying on the road in the path of his vehicle outside the presidential residence, Los Pinos (Toruño 1995: 36).

time which refers to events in everyday life and which is both continuous and linear, and 'sacred' time, which is simultaneous, during which extraordinary things happen. Thus the two most important cultural/religious influences in Central Mexican culture, the Aztec and the Catholic, were familiar with these two concepts of time. However, it seems that linear time is associated by Garro with the historical process imposed by the alien 'masculine' conquering culture of Europe, and circular time with the 'feminine' and indigenous culture of the vanquished of America. Thus the male/female binary opposition appears once more as linear time/circular time.

The legacy of the Spanish Conquest includes the embracing of capitalism, which arguably began in sixteenth-century Europe, and continued with the modernisation programme which adopted US style capitalism, undertaken by the Mexican government from the 1940s onwards. This programme failed to benefit the majority of the population, particularly the indigenous people, and led to stagnation and backwardness in the Mexican provinces. This is characterised in *Los recuerdos del porvenir* by the profane time of Ixtepec. The apathy and inaction of the town's inhabitants, unable to react to the violent regime imposed upon them by the military occupation of the town which is, in turn, the cause of such apathy, continues until the arrival of Felipe Hurtado. His coming is epiphanic and results in the extraordinary events that take place during moments of sacred time. The inexplicable events associated with sacred time can also be seen as occurring in cyclical, feminine time ('feminine', because it is excluded from official history as was feminine and/or female discourse), which is, in turn, associated with indigenous culture and tradition.[11] Christian sacred time is not so unlike the Aztec notion of time, therefore, as both are associated with extraordinary events or miraculous happenings. In *Los recuerdos del porvenir*, extraordinary events occur during such moments, which are contrasted with the stagnant, apathetic nature of Ixtepec, symbolised by static time. However, Garro subverts the masculine–linear/feminine–circular time binary by having 'masculine' characters ruled by feminine time and vice versa. Many of these same feminine characters, though not necessarily female, have the attributes traditionally associated with 'the feminine' in the binary system, such as, imagination, passivity, emotion, sensitivity and a dark, secret side. Thus, by reference to this circular (sacred or monumental) time and through the characters of Martín, Felipe and Julia, in particular, Garro suggests that certain people have the ability to imagine alternative realities while others, such as Rosas, must struggle to conceive of any reality other than their own.[12] Isabel Moncada straddles the

---

[11] This dichotomy is more clearly presented in 'La culpa es de los Tlaxcaltecas'. See also Cynthia Duncan (1985: 105–120) and Amy Kaminsky, who, however, takes the view that Garro sees linear time as positive and cyclical time only as negative (Kaminsky 1993a).

[12] This idea is also found in Garro's play *Andarse por las ramas* (1958).

binary opposition in that she is aware of both circular and linear time. It is appropriate therefore that she should be in some ways androgynous, embodying what are seen as both male and female characteristics. She experiences the two types of time enunciated in the novel: linear and circular, as well as the state of stasis associated with both when they cease to pass, which is referred to in the novel as static time. Garro therefore suggests that the two kinds of time are not linked to any specific biological factors, and that the binary masculine–linear/feminine–circular is, at best, irrelevant and at worst, harmful, as it constrains women to inaction.

However, Francisco Rosas too, somewhat surprisingly, represents an alternative voice to the official discourse regarding male behaviour (and linear time) as he is unable to separate his love for the woman of his dreams from his role as a military officer. The ideals of the Revolution have been lost in the struggle for power and the successive assassinations, but Rosas no longer believes in the Revolution and is not even interested in power for its own sake. He only wants it as a tool to secure Julia's love – which he is unable to do; his failure, therefore, is both personal and professional. Like Martín, he is trapped in history and chronological time, but unlike Martín's, his is a world without imagination or ideals, apart from that of the ideal woman – Julia. He lives in static time, which for Martín is chronological time suspended, but which he perceives as being 'outside time'. For Rosas it is a world marked by frustration and impotence, 'También el general, incapaz de dibujar sus días, vivía fuera del tiempo, sin pasado y sin futuro' (The General too, incapable of delineating his days, lived outside time, without a past or a future) (15). The cause of his anguish is Julia, whose memories of other men are an inaccessible citadel to him and which he is unable to erase from her mind. Unable to control her memories, or change her past, his military power is useless. For him, memory is a curse as he knows that all gestures and actions persist in it. Although he feels trapped in static time his words reflect a notion of circular time, 'La memoria es la maldición del hombre. [. . .] Acaso el gesto que él hacía ahora no quedaría para siempre en el tiempo?' (Memory is the curse of man. [. . .] Would not the gesture he was making now remain forever in time?) (80). His actions are governed by his position in time and his role as a soldier and he believes he does not have free will.

Thus, unable to accept that Julia does not love him, and lacking Felipe's eloquence, he tries to win her over by buying jewels and clothes for her with the money obtained from the sale of lands expropriated by the revolutionary government; money paid to him by Rodolfo Goríbar to kill the Indians who occupy those lands. In this way, his corruption is a microcosm of what has happened in post-revolutionary Mexico, and one of Rosas' roles is that he embodies the failure of the Revolution (81). Rosas fails in his attempts to subject Julia to his will and his inability to control her mind adds to his frustration. Thus he is trapped in static time by his own memory, and the double realisation that Julia does not love him, and that the memories she has are of other men. He feels powerless and tormented by memories that are not even his own:

> No la entendía. ¿Por qué se empeñaba en vivir en un mundo distinto del suyo? Ninguna palabra, ningún gesto podían rescatarla de las calles y los días anteriores a él. Se sintió víctima de una maldición superior a su voluntad y a la de Julia. ¿Cómo abolir el pasado? Ese pasado fulgurante en que Julia flotaba luminosa en habitaciones irregulares, camas confusas y ciudades sin nombre. Esa memoria no era suya y era él que la sufría como un infierno permanente y desdibujado. (81)

> (He didn't understand her. Why did she insist on living in a different world to his own? No word, no gesture could redeem her from the streets and the days before the ones with him. He felt like the victim of curse that was superior to his will and that of Julia. How could he wipe out the past? That bright past in which Julia floated, luminous in irregular rooms, confused beds and nameless cities. That memory was not his and it was he who suffered it like a permanent, blurred hell.)

The anguish of Rosas who is unable to understand or accept the secret part of Julia – her memories – also provides a reminder that memory can be more powerful than brute force. He has the whole town in his power, including Julia's body, but has no power over her mind. (This is reminiscent of Pedro Páramo's love of Susana San Juan in Rulfo's homonymous novel). It is also a sharp contrast to Martín's tolerant attitude towards his wife's secret past (a tolerance viewed as unacceptable according to standards established by *machismo*).

Martín, another masculine character ruled by feminine time, inhabits as a child the dimension of cyclical time, but as an adult is unwillingly governed by the chronological time of the world of adults. Expected to put aside his childish dreams and illusions, he too feels trapped. The following quotation reveals both the sense of entrapment felt by Martín, and Isabel's reluctance to participate in his world of static time: 'Por las noches, sentada en el salón, no hablaba. Veía a Félix detener los relojes, y aquel gesto ilusorio para escapar al tiempo cotidiano la llenaba de piedad por su padre, preso en un sillón leyendo los periódicos' (At night, sitting in the drawing room, she didn't talk. She would watch Felix stop the clocks and that illusory act of escape from ordinary time filled her with pity for her father, prisoner in his armchair, reading the newspapers) (157). Memory and cyclical time are conflated in the mind of Martín, for whom memory is made up of past and future events and remembrances of things that have not yet happened (and herein lies the title of the novel):

> Nunca se decía: 'El lunes haré tal cosa', porque entre ese lunes y él había una multitud de recuerdos no vividos que lo separaban de la necesidad de hacer 'tal cosa ese lunes'. Luchaba entre varias memorias y la memoria de lo sucedido era la única irreal para él. De niño pasaba largas horas

recordando lo que no había visto ni oído nunca. [. . .] A medida que creció, su memoria reflejó sombras y colores del pasado no vivido que se confundieron con imágenes y actos del futuro. (22)[13]

(He never said to himself: 'On Monday I'll do such and such a thing' because between that Monday and him there was a multitude of unlived memories which separated him from the need to do 'such and such a thing that Monday'. He struggled between several memories and the memory of what had happened was the only unreal one for him. As a child he spent long hours remembering what he had never seen or heard. [. . .] As he grew up, his memory reflected shadows and colours from the unlived past which became confused with images and acts from the future.)

Martín also rejects the binary opposition (male) activity/(female) passivity. When Martín's wife comments that he has his head in the clouds because he tells his sons not to go back to work in the mine if they do not want to, even though the family needs the money, Martín justifies his passivity by implying that he is above the materiality of existence; man's days 'le parecían de una brevedad insoportable para dedicarlos al esfuerzo del dinero' (seemed to him of an unbearable brevity to dedicate them to the effort associated with money) (35). He feels alienated from the other people in Ixtepec society whom, he considers, waste their time with unimportant pursuits, forgetting their mortality. Given that Martín is an object of pity for Isabel, it is not surprising that she should rebel against the apathy, inaction and failure to face reality that she sees in her father as a 'lack' traditionally associated with the feminine. His idea of imagination – a refuge in the nostalgia of the past – is not hers. Her ideas about, and belief in, the importance of imagination are revealed in her reply when Dorotea tells her not to imagine things that do not exist: 'lo único que hay que imaginar es lo que no existe [. . .] hay que imaginar a los ángeles' (the only thing that should be imagined is what does not exist [. . .] we must imagine angels) (20). Her longing for the world of action and imagination is symbolised by the theatrical representation that takes place in Doña Matilde's summer house.

Finally, I will discuss the notion of circular (mythical, sacred) time as associated with Julia and Felipe Hurtado. Through the creation of such characters and the use of myth, Garro opens up to the reader different levels of reality. Julia is perceived by Rosas as other-worldy and ethereal, 'Julia no andaba en este pueblo. No pisaba tierra. Vagaba perdida en las calles de unos pueblos que no tenían horas, ni olores, ni noches: sólo un polvillo brillante en el que desaparecía cada vez que él encontraba la mancha diáfana de su traje rosa' (Julia was not in this town. She didn't walk the earth. She wandered lost in the

---

[13] Garro herself said, in an interview, that she began to write stories with happy endings because she believed it was possible to write one's own future. However, this is certainly not the case with *Inés* (1995), the ending of which is bleakly pessimistic.

streets of towns that had no hours, nor smells, nor nights: only shining dust
into which she disappeared every time he encountered the diaphanous smudge
of her pink outfit) (112). These characteristics of Julia's take on mythical
proportions as far as the people of Ixtepec are concerned:

> Sonámbula, caminó entre la gente encandilándonos con su piel translúcida,
> sus cabellos ahumados y en una mano su abanico de paja finísima en forma
> de corazón exangüe. Dio varias vueltas por la plaza para ir a sentarse
> después en la banca de costumbre. Allí se formó una bahía de luz. Julia en
> el centro del círculo mágico formado por ella, rodeada de las queridas y
> escoltada por los hombres de uniforme. (95)

> (Sleepwalking, she walked among the people dazzling them with her trans-
> lucid skin, her dusky hair and in one hand her fine straw fan in the shape of
> a bloodless heart. She took several turns around the square only to go and
> sit on her usual bench. There a circle of light formed with Julia in the centre
> of the magic circle surrounded by an escort of the officers in uniform and
> their lovers.)

It is only Felipe Hurtado who appears free of Ixtepec's spell. He also has a
mythical quality and is referred to as *El mensajero*.[14] Felipe's eloquence is
apparent from the time of his first meeting in Ixtepec with Julia, when he talks
to her at length while she '[lies] in the hammock, with her robe half open and
her hair tousled, listening to the stranger' (41). Felipe is also an illusionist. He
first appears as such to Don Pepe Ocampo, the owner of the hotel when he
produces two cigarettes out of thin air and offers one, already lit, to the hote-
lier (40). Further evidence of Felipe's unusual powers is given when, during a
rainstorm, he walks from the summer house to Don Joaquín's main house
through the rain and a wind so strong he thought it would 'carry him off to the
top of the trees in a neighbouring country', to arrive with his candle still
burning (106). It is only much later that Doña Matilde's guests ask themselves
how he had got through that storm with the candle still alight and his clothes
and hair dry, though at the time it seemed quite natural to them (109). He also
believes in the important part played by illusion in people's lives, and the
detrimental effect caused by its absence. It is he who first suggests the staging
of a play in order to stir the townspeople's imagination (76).

Thus, by having imagination, sensitivity and the mythical/circular notion
of time represented by the 'feminine' characters of Felipe, Martín, Juan
Cariño, Nicolás, Julia, and Isabel, and injustice, violence and oppression associated with characters such as Rosas and Rodolfo Goríbar, but also with those
who turn a blind eye to the suffering of others, such as Lola Goríbar, or Elvira

---

14 This is possibly an allusion to Hermes, whose many gifts include that of the ability
to persuade, 'The gods especially employed him as messenger, when eloquence was
required to obtain the desired object', and to create illusions (Smith 1889).

Montúfar, Garro subverts the binary oppositions that associate violence and brutality with men and tenderness and sensitivity with women.

THEATRE: LIFE AND DEATH

The binary pair active/passive referred to above in relation to time, whereby the active, modern male would be contrasted with the passive traditional female, is also subverted with the arrival of Felipe Hurtado to Ixtepec. The assumption by Don Ramón, the town's entrepreneur, that Felipe is, '¡Hombre moderno, de acción!' (A modern man, a man of action!) (39), does not correspond to the reader's images of the Felipe who spends his time reading under a tree in the country, or in the summerhouse at Don Joaquín's spacious residence. The irony of Don Ramón's comment, which reflects the official version of a country supposedly in the throes of modernisation and progress for all, is clear. Felipe suggests that what the people of Ixtepec (and, by inference, the people of Mexico) need, in the absence of progress, is illusion, and art is seen as a possible space for empowerment and change.[15] In the case of Ixtepec, illusion can be provided by theatre, in which the townspeople themselves participate. Theatre would take its spectators out of their closed, passive world by presenting them with alternative visions of reality and therefore, with the idea that not only is a different reality possible, but that they can be instrumental in actively changing their own lives. The suggestion that what is lacking in Ixtepec is *ilusión* (hope) is remembered by the narrator later on, '[. . .] sus palabras quedaron escritas en mi memoria con un humo incandescente que aparecía y desaparecía según mi estado de ánimo' (his words were engraved on my memory like incandescent smoke which appeared and disappeared according to my state of mind) (117). Before the theatre group is formed, the narrator comments, 'La vida en aquellos días se empañaba y nadie vivía sino a través del general y su querida. Habíamos renunciado a la ilusión' (Life at that time was gloomy and people only lived through the General and his girlfriend. We had renounced hope) (117–18). This contrasts with the change undergone following their involvement in the play, when they discover how sweet it is to think that they can be more than mere spectators of the violent life of the soldiers (122). The townspeople are strengthened by optimism through participation in the world of the imagination, which is given supernatural connotations, 'El encantamiento se rompió y por primera vez tuvimos algo que hacer, algo en que pensar que no fuera la desdicha' (The spell broke and for the first time we had something to do, something to think about apart from unhappiness) (122). However it is Isabel, desirous of action,

---

15 Indeed, this was the policy of the government in the years immediately following the Revolution, but by the late 1920s, Calles had to divert funding for the Arts to other priorities such as combatting the Cristero rebellion.

who actually gets her brothers involved in the theatrical project. Thus she too subverts the active/passive binary.

Finally, I will briefly describe the time associated with death. Catherine Larson writes of Garro that she 'has presented a multiplicity of temporal perspectives, but she has linked each of them to the creation of new and alternative ways of seeing the world' (Larson 1989: 6).[16] Among the latter is the view of death or nothingness as an alternative temporality and its significance as a feminine space. The women who die in the novel, including Luchi, the owner of the brothel, and the old woman, Dorotea, are marginalised – Luchi because of her profession, and Dorotea, because she is elderly and a spinster. Both die heroically for trying to save the life of the priest. Julia and Isabel, on the other hand, as far as we know, do not die, but are removed to another dimension, though they are effectively dead for those (readers and) people of Ixtepec who wish to believe so. Thus even the apparently fixed binary opposition life/death is subverted as is that of chaos/order.

The narrator expresses nostalgia for a better time when the ideals of the Revolution were still alive before the arrival of Rosas (14) and (ironical) references are made to the re-establishment of order by Rosas when he arrives in Ixtepec and hangs a few more Indians. However, this refers to an imposed, military and political order which goes against the natural one. Anita Stoll writes: 'Chronological or linear time represents the world of strife and struggle [chaos], while cyclical or eternal time is a mythic state of happiness and perfection' (Stoll 1990: 200–201). Garro also equates the notion of history and violence with linear time that can be arrested, so as to become static (64–65). This suggests a further set of binary oppositions: static time (as linear time arrested) is associated with negativity in the form of unhappiness, pain, darkness, cruelty, and violence; unlike circular or feminine time which can be seen as continuous and more positive (if less dynamic) than linear time. It appears that until the arrival of Felipe, Ixtepec itself is petrified in a world without hope, a world where linear time stands still and in which the people are trapped – excluded from the progress in which they should be participating. *Criollos* do not want to associate with *mestizos* who in turn do not want to associate themselves with the Indians (refusing to accept that they share the same origins). The condition of the so-called 'bastard race' is particularly difficult. Rejected by both *criollos* and indigenous people, they came to be considered the entrepreneurial class as, after the Conquest, they neither belonged to the land, as did the indigenous people, nor did the land belong to them, as they were forbidden from owning it (Tritten (1979)). Garro links this to their entrapment in static time, 'A los mestizos el campo les producía miedo. Era su obra, la imagen de su pillaje [. . .] Por su culpa mi tiempo estaba

---

[16] Catherine Larson was referring here to Garro's works written for the theatre (Larson 1989: 6), but I think it also applies to *Los recuerdos del porvenir*.

inmóvil' (The *mestizos* were afraid of the land. It was their work, the image of their pillage [. . .] It is their fault my time was immobile) (27).

Thus, General Rosas and Martín Moncada are both victims of, and responsible for, the torpid nature of time in Ixtepec. They are trapped, willingly or unwillingly, in chronological time which for them has become static. Martín Moncada is willingly trapped in a dream world of passivity through his refusal to face up to reality and Rosas is unwillingly trapped in a reality where he has no wish to be. Isabel tries to escape from Martín's unreality, to what she sees as Felipe's and Julia's world of illusion, via Rosas' world of reality and death. Evidence that she believes she succeeds in doing so is found in her words to Rosas towards the end of the novel, 'tenemos dos memorias [. . .] Yo antes vivía en las dos y ahora sólo vivo en la que me recuerda lo que va a suceder' (we have two memories [. . .] I used to live in both of them and now I only live in the one that reminds me what is going to happen) (251–52). However, the characters in the novel are not merely allocated a position in these different worlds according to their actions or their inaction. Garro is ambivalent about a facile separation of the different worlds as the characters of Isabel and Luchi reveal.

When Isabel becomes a stone at the end of the novel it can be read as an alternative to death, a traditional end for a nineteenth-century novel's heroine when she has transgressed gender boundaries. According to Moi, it is the inevitable outcome of the battle for supremacy between the oppositions, where activity is associated with victory, and passivity with defeat – the male always being the victor under patriarchy (Moi 1985: 104–5). Isabel's turning to stone happens, allegedly, because of her love for Rosas. However, as Amy Kaminsky has observed, this is only the explanation given by Gregoria (Kaminsky 1993: 106). Yet the description of Isabel's appearance before she disappears sounds more like a 'magical realist' elaboration designed to create an interesting tale than a factual account: 'De sus ojos salieron rayos y una tempestad de rizos negros le cubrió el cuerpo y se levantó un remolino de polvo que volvió invisible la mata de pelo' (Rays came out of her eyes and a storm of black curls covered her body then a whirlwind of dust blew up and hid the tangle of hair) (291). The narrator then adds that in her race to meet her lover, Isabel Moncada *se perdió* (was lost) (291); another fitting end for an anti-heroine?[17] On the other hand, if one is to suspend disbelief and accept Gregoria's story, the question arises as to why Garro should have her protagonist turned to stone. Several explanations have been offered for this, mostly related to myth. Robert K. Anderson considers it may be simply to leave a reminder in an act of revenge against the people of Ixtepec (Anderson 1985: 220).

---

[17] There is a similarity here with the fate of Isabel and the narrator's aunt Matilde in *Balún-Canán*, who also transgresses the rules of female sexuality. Both she and Isabel are 'lost' physically and morally (because they have lost their virginity).

Yet it appears that Isabel's destiny was already written, as is revealed when she reads a line from the play they are rehearsing in her aunt's house, 'Vuelvo al pabellón y escucho todavía flotantes las palabras dichas por Isabel y que provocaron su interrupción: "¡Mírame antes de quedar convertida en piedra!" ' (I return to the summerhouse and hear the words spoken by Isabel still floating up and which caused the interruption: 'Look at me before I end up turned to stone') (124). However, Isabel is also associated (by her mother) with rock in another, more dynamic form – as meteorite.

APPEARANCE/REALITY AND OTHER BINARY OPPOSITIONS

This final sub-section on time and memory looks at the binary opposition appearance/reality, in particular as it relates to Isabel Moncada. Isabel struggles to hold on to the reality of Rosas' world and resist the unreality of the world inhabited by her father, Martín; that other dimension outside chronological time which she associates with Julia and Felipe, is beyond her grasp. When her brothers leave to work in the mines at Tetela, Isabel, who said she wanted them to go, then finds herself lost without them. The two Isabels, 'una que deambulaba por los patios y las habitaciones y la otra que vivía en una esfera lejana, fija en el espacio' (one which wandered around the patios and the rooms and the other that lived in a distant sphere, fixed in space) (31–32), are conscious of each other and this is revealed by her efforts to keep hold of existence in the real world of chronological time by touching the material objects of that world (32).[18] Her relationship with Rosas is also an attempt to be part of the real world of historical time.

Isabel herself finally becomes a fixed part in a *mundo aparente*, when at the end of her story, and the beginning of the novel, she becomes *esta piedra aparente*. 'Aparente' is an ambivalent term that suggests both the word 'appearing' in the physical sense and 'apparent' in the sense that the physical world may be the world of *un*reality. Rosas Lopátegui argues that Garro uses the stone to symbolise the historic, social and economic paralysis of Ixtepec which, in turn, is a microcosm of the Mexico of the late 1920s, where reality often contrasts with the official rhetoric of progress and prosperity. There is

---

18 These two Isabels, male and female, physical and spiritual – again the stereotype is reinforced by Garro – are reminiscent of Jung's concept of the *anima,* man's unconscious image of the female and *animus*, woman's unconscious image of the male. Demaris S. Wehr explains the usefulness of this concept (while recognising Jung's misogyny in assuming the anima to be inferior) in the following quotation: 'Integration of the contrasexual image expands and broadens the personality, giving it access to qualities thought to belong to the other sex' (Wehr 1988). It is feasible that Garro was familiar with such ideas, given that the Society of Psychoanalysis was set up in Mexico in 1960, shortly after she wrote *Los recuerdos del porvenir,* which may explain her (probably) unwitting reinforcement of stereotypes.

further reference to the idea that the world of the imagination may be the real world in the second part of the novel, when Isabel is remembering her close rapport with her brother Nicolás: 'Se habían acostumbrado a la fealdad e inventaban un mundo irreal. Detrás de la *apariencia* de ese mundo estaba el mundo verdadero, el que ella, Juan y Nicolás buscaban desde niños' (They had become accustomed to ugliness and invented an unreal world. Behind the *appearance* of that world was the real world, the one that they, she and Nicolás, were searching for since they were children) (157 [my emphasis]). Isabel, unlike her father, is still able to move between chronological and cyclical time, in the real and the unreal worlds.

The creation of extraordinary characters such as Julia Andrade and Felipe Hurtado, both associated with illusion and the ideal, further opens up the possibility of alternative worlds or levels of reality. They also subvert the binary opposition illusion/reality which suggests that only two possibilities exist and, in so doing, provide an alternative discourse to the official positivist discourse about reality. The dimension outside chronological time where magical events take place is inhabited by characters who are either women – Isabel and Julia – or may be included in the category of 'feminine', such as Martín Moncada, Felipe Hurtado and Juan Cariño. Martín, for example, is criticised for his over-tolerant attitude towards the Indians, and for living in a world of his own, dominated by memories and nostalgia (traditionally considered the domain of women), unable to adhere to a linear concept of history and time. He is described as living 'outside time' by Doña Matilde (139). Therefore his is also a dissenting voice, as is that of Felipe Hurtado who does not conform to Señor Martínez's idea that he is 'hombre moderno, de acción' (39). On the contrary, Felipe inhabits the world of magic associated with the feminine, and is essentially passive until the end of Part One. Ironically, Martínez thinks Felipe Hurtado has come to the town to carry out modernising improvements which he fears may be thwarted by the retrograde General Rosas.

According to patriarchal logic, the positive characteristics of the binary oppositions reality/appearance, activity/passivity and progress/reaction are associated with the male, and the negative with the female. Isabel's endeavour to participate in the male domain by striving for the 'male' attribute of each pair, is another transgression of her position as a woman in society. Her desire to be active aligns the novel with the feminised *Bildungsroman* in which the protagonist, unlike that of the more traditional and conservative male *Bildungsroman*, who often relinquishes his ideals in order to finally become integrated into society, engages in 'oppositional activity', rejecting the passivity of her feminine role (Felski 1989: 133–138). Unlike most of the inhabitants of Ixtepec, Isabel is aware of alternative worlds but her attempts to abandon one and become incorporated in another are not entirely successful. She succeeds at certain moments but never on a permanent basis. However, if *Los recuerdos del porvenir* is read as a kind of female *Bildungsroman*, or novel of self-discovery, it is open to debate which of the two characters develops as a woman, or undergoes a 'transfiguration or illumination of consciousness' (Felski 1989: 143): Julia, who symbolically abandons her high-heeled shoes in a doorway along with her dependency on Rosas, or Isabel who abandons her role of 'muchacha decente' for voluntary subjection to Rosas' will.

One of the principal binary oppositions found in Mexican society regarding women – the Virgin/Whore dichotomy – is subverted, then, in the characters of Julia and Isabel. The novel is divided into two parts, the first with Julia as the centre of attention and the second, Isabel; the two women appear to be entirely different. Julia fulfils all the criteria of traditional femininity and beauty: she is acquiescent, silent, graceful and elegant, with a peach-like complexion and is usually dressed in a pink silk dress. Isabel, on the other hand, as a child is a tomboy, and as an adolescent she dances too wildly, laughs too raucously and is far too opinionated, thereby transgressing one of the women's 'commandments' of the nineteenth century in Mexico: not to speak in a loud voice or use bold mannerisms to call attention to oneself (Tuñón Pablos 1999: 59). Her physical appearance is characterised by her boyish face, her thick, black, curly hair and the red dress she wears to the party and thereafter until her demise. Yet, paradoxically, Julia escapes from her life as Rosas' doll, idol and sexual slave while Isabel appears willing to assume that role although she cannot successfully do so, given her very different nature. Indeed Rosas is afraid of her because he fails to understand her and even Martín, her own father, is afraid of her (239).[19] He believes she holds secrets (concerning the sexual relationship between himself and his wife, Ana). I would argue that it is in part the sexuality of Ana Moncada and the way Isabel has been mothered that lead her to adopt the rebellious, dissenting voice which characterises her. The mother–daughter relationship will be discussed in the section 'Good Mothers and Wicked Women'.

VIOLENCE AND LONGING: MEMORY AND THE SENSES

In this final section on time, I will discuss the relationship between the senses and memory. Individual memories, often tinged with nostalgia, are, more often than not, awakened by sensory stimuli. The nostalgia with which the time prior to Rosas' arrival in Ixtepec is imbued, is also found in the descriptions of the deserted Moncada residence. The abandoned house once

---

[19] Adrienne Rich's explanation about men's fear of women is useful here: 'A woman is for a man both more and less than a person: she is something terribly necessary and necessarily terrible [. . .] she is not simply the "other"; she is first of all the Mother who has to be possessed, reduced, controlled, lest she swallow him back into her dark caves, or stare him into stone' (Rich 1995: 112).

inhabited by the lively Isabel, now by plants and dust, is characterised by melancholy and stillness: 'Allí no corre el tiempo: el aire queda inmóvil después de tantas lágrimas [. . .] Sólo olvido y silencio' (Time does not flow there: the air is still after so many tears [. . .] Only oblivion and silence) (12).

Further evidence of nostalgia for a time of action, even though this be in the form of catastrophe, appears in Chapter V in the words of Ana Moncada, '¡Si tuviéramos siquiera un buen temblor de tierra!' (If we at least had a decent earth tremor!) (37). She compares the situation of stasis in Ixtepec with her memories of her childhood in the north, and the effect that the Revolution had on their lives: 'La premonición de una alegría desbarataba uno a uno los días petrificados. La revolución estalló una mañana y las puertas del tiempo se abrieron para nosotros' (The premonition of joy dissolved the petrified days one by one. The Revolution broke out one morning and the doors of time opened for us) (36).

Another instance connected with the Moncadas, of the petrifying effect of inaction, appears when Félix disconnects the pendulum of the clock in the living room, creating the illusion for Martín that he is able to stop time from passing. Here the negative aspect of memory is alluded to, wherein it imprisons people in nostalgia and the past, divorcing them from reality:

> El reloj quedó mudo [. . .]. 'Ya por hoy no nos va a corretear' comentó Martín mirando las manecillas inmóviles. [. . .] Sin el tictac, la habitación y sus ocupantes entraron en un tiempo nuevo y melancólico donde los gestos y las voces se movían en el pasado. Doña Ana, su marido, los jóvenes y Félix se convirtieron en recuerdos de ellos mismos, *sin futuro* [. . .]. (20)
>
> (The clock remained silent. [. . .] 'At least for today it's not going to hurry us up,' commented Martín looking at the immobile hands. [. . .] Without the ticking, the room and its inhabitants entered a new, melancholic time where gestures and voices moved in the past. Doña Ana and her husband, the young people and Felix became memories of themselves, *without a future*). (20 [my emphasis])

However, it was not always thus in Ixtepec. Don Pepe Ocampo, owner of Ixtepec's hotel, nostalgically tells Felipe of the days when Ixtepec was not in its present state of apathy and stagnation (caused by the political situation) but a thriving town, visited by many people (40).

The way the senses are used in *Los recuerdos del porvenir* differs some-what from the way they are used in the other novels studied here, as there is less emphasis on mother–child relationships. However, the fact that they are used in favourable descriptions related to previous better times, suggests the longing to return to the ideal pre-Oedipal phase of closeness and security experienced by children. This corresponds to the time before the arrival of Rosas and his men, before time became static.

Movement/stasis is mirrored in another binary opposition that opposes colour (life) with drabness (death). The lack of illusion among the people of Ixtepec is reflected in their lack of interest in the colours, sights and sounds of the natural world. Memory is often awakened by certain smells, sounds or colours; part of this analysis of time and memory must therefore include an examination of the link between smells, sounds, colours and memory. Attached to the importance of the senses are the more primitive/basic binary oppositions of light/dark, good/evil. The repeated use of words such as *sombrío* and *tinieblas,* therefore, has obvious connotations with regard to these binaries.

The narrator links the apathy and the lack of illusion among the inhabitants of Ixtepec with their insensitivity to the beauty of the natural world around them: 'Nadie se preocupaba de mirar al sol que caía envuelto en llamaradas naranjas detrás de los montes azules' (Nobody bothered to look at the sun that went down enveloped in orange flames behind the blue hills) (118). The narrator suggests that Felipe was perhaps the only person to worry about the apathy of Ixtepec's inhabitants. An insensitivity to the beauty of nature of those who deal in death appears much later when Rosas' men are waiting to execute the rebels (including Nicolás):

> Una raya naranja finísima se levantó del horizonte oscuro, las flores que se abren en la noche se cerraron y sus perfumes quedaron en el aire unos instantes antes de desaparecer. El jardín empezó a nacer azul de entre sus sombras moradas. Otra mañana pasaba inadvertida para los hombres que bebían café antes de ir a organizar más muertes. (275)

> (A fine orange line rose up from the dark horizon, the night flowers closed and their perfume hung in the air for a few moments before disappearing. The garden began to make a blue appearance among the purple shadows. Another morning was going unnoticed for the men who drank coffee before going to organise more deaths.)

Colours, sounds and smells evoke memories in the minds of the characters and also create images of great intensity. The sound of Julia's footsteps and the aroma of her perfume produce images in Rosas' mind of what he imagines to be Julia's memories, and of another world 'Le llegó su perfume y la oyó volver caminando descalza sobre las losetas rojas [. . .] Julia entraba en muchos cuartos y muchos hombres la oían llegar y aspiraban su perfume de vainilla que subía en espirales a un mundo invisible y perdido' (The smell of her perfume reached him and he heard her walking barefoot on the red floor-tiles [. . .] Julia entered many rooms and many men heard her coming and inhaled her vanilla perfume which rose in spirals to an invisible and lost world) (80).

Martín Moncada is particularly sensitive to the smells and colours around him. They awaken in him memories of his childhood and memories of 'things that never happened' during his childhood:

A medida que creció, su memoria reflejó sombras y colores del pasado no vivido que se confundieron con imágenes y actos del futuro. Había olores ignorados en Ixtepec que sólo él percibía. Si las criadas encendían la lumbre en la cocina, el olor del ocote quemado abría en sus otros recuerdos unas visiones de pinos y el olor de un viento frío y resinoso subía por su cuerpo hasta hacerse consciente en su memoria. Sorprendido miraba a su alrededor y se encontraba cerca del brasero caliente respirando un aire cargado de olores pantanosos que llegaban del jardín. (21)

(As he grew up, his memory reflected shadows and colours from a past not lived which became confused with images and actions from the future. There were smells in Ixtepec only perceived by him. If the maids lit the fire in the kitchen, the smell of the burning resinous wood opened up in his other memories visions of pine trees and the smell of a cold, resin-laden wind climbed up his body until it made itself felt in his memory. Surprised, he would look around and find himself next to an air heavy with swamp-like smells that came from the garden.)

Here the pleasant smell of the resinous *ocote* and the images of mountains and pine trees associated with it, which suggest happy memories, are contrasted with the heavy, damp smell of a low-lying swamp or lake which follows, and which suggests the horrendous events of the future which will take place. The 'memories of the future', produced by the smell, cause the five-year-old to feel disorientated and burst into tears.

The feeling of nostalgia related to past time and the binary life/death appear in the description of the now empty Moncada family house. The musty, heavy smells of plants and of abandonment and dilapidation become stronger and take on a sinister resonance in the large garden of Don Joaquín and Doña Matilde's house. The violence of the heat foretells the further violence that is to come and the sickly, penetrating smell of decomposition suggests death:

Un vapor se levantaba del jardín. Las plantas despedían olores húmedos y penetrantes. [. . .] El jardín que en la noche era luminoso y negro, cubierto de hojas misteriosas y de flores adivinadas por la intensidad de su perfume, durante el día se infestaba de olores y presencias amenazantes para la nariz del extranjero. Sintió nauseas. (55–56)

(A vapour rose from the garden. The plants gave off damp, penetrating smells. [. . .] The garden, which at night was black and luminous, covered with mysterious leaves and flowers which revealed their identity by the intensity of their perfume, during the day become infested with smells and presences that were menacing for the stranger. He felt nauseous.)

The narrator's positive view of the indigenous inhabitants of Ixtepec also reflects nostalgia for times past when they were uncontaminated by progress:

Mi gente es morena de piel. Viste de manta blanca y calza huaraches. Se
adorna con collares de oro o se ata al cuello un pañuelito de seda rosa. [. . .]
Los sábados el atrio de la iglesia, sembrado de almendros se llena de
compradores y mercaderes. Brillan al sol los refrescos pintados, las cintas
de colores, las cuentas de oro y las telas rosas y azules. El aire se impregna
de vapores de fritangas, de sacos de carbón oloroso todavía a madera, de
bocas babeando alcohol y de majadas de burros. (12)

(My people are dark skinned. They wear white cotton clothing and sandals.
They adorn themselves with gold necklaces or tie a pink silk kerchief
around their necks. [. . .] On Saturdays, the atrium of the church, sown with
almond trees is filled with buyers and sellers. The coloured drinks and
ribbons, the gold beads and the pink and blue material are bright in the sun.
The air is impregnated with the smell of fried food, sacks of charcoal still
smelling of wood, mouths dribbling alcohol and herds of donkeys.)

Colour is associated with the indigenous people as it is in *Balún-Canán*
(though not the same colours) and again has symbolic importance, as the
choice of colours used in relation to Rosas and his subordinates reveals. The
yellow and red in the following extract, for example, are related to the negative attributes of jealousy and blood usually associated with those colours,
due, in part, to the words – *violento* and *sombrío* – with which they are juxtaposed. Thus the effect produced by the yellow of Rosas' eyes and the red of
his second-in-command's scarf is sinister: 'Era alto y violento. Su mirada
amarilla acusaba a los tigres que lo habitaban. Lo acompañaba [. . .] Justo
Corona, también sombrío, con un paliacate rojo atado al cuello [. . .].' (He was
tall and violent. His yellow gaze betrayed the tigers that lived inside him. He
was accompanied by [. . .] Justo Corona, equally sombre, with a red kerchief
tied around his neck) (14). Jealousy and violence are suggested again in this
description of Rosas' eyes: 'Salió a la calle buscando con miradas amarillas al
forastero' (He went into the street, looking for the stranger with his yellow
gaze) (81); and again, later: 'El general parecía inquieto: los ojos amarillos
llenos de imágenes sombrías' (The general appeared uneasy, his yellow eyes
were filled with sombre images) (95). Finally, just prior to Nicolás' death,
Rosas sees his own reflection in the mirror, 'sus ojos amarillos eran manchas
de aceite' (His yellow oil-stain eyes) (270).

When Don Joaquín and Dona Matilde are waiting for Rosas to come and
take Felipe away, the colours and smells are again indicative that something
terrible might be about to happen. The colours reflected in Matilde's nightdress are the same ones used in association with the violence of Rosas and
Justo Corona: red and yellow (139). This use of colour is reinforced by reference to the other senses to imply foreboding. The smells and damp described
are suggestive of death and putrefaction and add to the sensation that the
events about to take place will soon become part of the bad memories associated with Ixtepec: '[. . .] el olor de las cucarachas gigantes llegó a través de las

rendijas de las puertas. Una humedad viscosa se untó a las paredes y a las sábanas' (the smell of the giant cockroaches came in through the cracks in the doors. A viscous humidity spread itself on to the walls and the sheets) (139–140). Even the sounds connote death: 'se oían caer las hojas podridas de los árboles. El ir y venir de los insectos produjo un ruido sofocante' (you could hear the sound of rotten leaves falling. The coming and going of the insects produced a suffocating noise) (139-40); and the amplification of the sounds gives the scene a nightmarish or cinematographic quality whereby tension is produced by the apparent slowing down of the passing of time.

The pervasiveness of violence in Ixtepec is introduced even earlier in the description of the sights and sounds of *fiesta* days (12). There is also, however, an element of resignation, as if the violence were a necessary outlet and part of a tradition. It contrasts with the form of violence established by the *mestizos*, frightened by the countryside because it is, 'su obra, la imagen de su pillaje' (the result of their work, the reflection of their plunder) (26–27), and by that perpetrated by Rosas and his men.

In Ixtepec most of the violence done to its people is under cover of dark. The hanged Indians are found in the mornings, as are the bodies of Dorotea and Damián Álvarez. The darkness in which Ixtepec is enveloped on the night that Felipe and Julia disappear is described by a muleteer arriving in the town. This darkness is the prolongation of night though it is dawning all around, because time is frozen in Ixtepec. But Ixtepec is 'un mar negro' (a black sea) from which the lovers escape into 'el resplandor de la luz rosada del amanecer' (the shining pink light of dawn) (146). Here the dark/light binary is blatantly obvious. Whether the lovers have actually escaped or are in fact dead is not the point; they have escaped the darkness of the soul associated with the violence of Ixtepec.

Light, in addition to particular colours and smells, is linked with those characters in the novel, in particular Julia and Felipe, associated with hope and imagination. The arrival of Felipe, uncontaminated by Ixtepec's misfortune, transforms the town. The reflections of light, the aromas and agreeable sound of the maids' chatter, contrast with the opacity and silence of the former Ixtepec and suggest a new hope:

El tiempo, por primera vez en muchos años, giró por mis calles levantando luces y reflejos en las piedras y en las hojas de los árboles; los almendros se llenaron de pájaros, el sol subió con delicia por los montes y en las cocinas las criadas comentaron ruidosas su llegada. El olor de la tisana de hojas de naranjo llegó hasta las habitaciones a despertar a las señoras de sus sueños inhábiles. La inesperada presencia del forastero rompió el silencio. Era el mensajero, el no contaminado por la desdicha. (65)

(Time, for the first time in many years, twisted down my streets bringing out lights and reflections in the stones and the leaves on the trees, the almond trees filled with birds, the sun rose with delight in the hills and in

the kitchens the servants commented noisily on its arrival. The smell of the
orange leaf tea reached the bedrooms and woke the ladies from their
clumsy dreams. The unexpected presence of the stranger broke the silence.
He was the messenger, the one uncontaminated by misery.)

Indeed, Felipe and Julia's presence produces a resplendence associated
with mythical beings or angels. When Julia and Felipe are in the summerhouse together on the afternoon before their disappearance, the group of
servants and Matilde 'buscaron en el aire las huellas brillantes que habían
traído a Felipe Hurtado hasta Ixtepec' (searched the air for the shining traces
that had brought Felipe Hurtado to Ixtepec) (134). Julia is given a mythical
quality by the use of the adjectives *irreal, efímera, translúcido, luminoso*, in
the descriptions of her. The pink of her clothes contrasts with her dusky
complexion and the jewellery she wears is always gold. As the 'sweat of the
sun', gold for the pre-Columbian indigenous people had a symbolic worth
equal to that which the blood of Christ has for Catholics. Worn by the ephemeral and mythically beautiful Julia, the gold assumes a symbolic quality and is
devoid of any sense of the vulgarity that such quantities of it might normally
accrue to its wearer. Early on, Julia is described, 'envuelta en una bata de
fulgurante rosa [. . .] los zarcillos de oro enredados en los cabellos' (wrapped
in a bright pink robe [. . .] the gold earrings tangled in her hair) (40). Dressed
up in a pink silk suit covered in white beads, and with gold jewellery to go out
in the evening, 'Parecía una alta flor iluminando la noche y era imposible no
mirarla' (She was like a a tall flower lighting up the night and it was impossible not to look at her) (41). Alone with Rosas in the hotel room, Julia's feet
in the last rays of the sun 'cobraron una vida efímera y translúcida, ajenos al
cuerpo envuelto en la bata rosa' (took on an ephemeral and translucid quality,
that did not belong to the body wrapped in a pink robe) (50). The image has a
fairy-tale quality. Julia is the archetypal young woman – beautifully dressed
and serenely elegant; or undressed, sleepy and smiling – she is every man's
dream, particularly the General's. But, like a dream, one moment she is there
and the next she is gone and is but a memory. Rosas, in trying to hold on to her
is therefore trying to do the impossible; hold on to the dream that such a
perfect woman could be his forever. Julia embodies the Virgin/Whore binary
as she is at once the ideal woman who is pure because she is unattainable (and
unattainable because such an ideal woman does not exist), and the whore, who
is seen by the *macho* as a necessary evil. Rosas, like Julia's previous lovers, is
condemned to become another of her memories. However, in her encounter
with Felipe at Matilde's house this image is literally shattered. While Julia is
trying to convince Matilde to send Felipe away or to let her see him, her presence is 'unreal' and her voice reaches him 'desde el centro de una tempestad
que partía del cuerpo luminoso de la joven' (from the centre of a storm that
began in the luminous body of the young woman). Then, her shining image
'se escindió y cayó en trozos de cristal' (split apart and fell to the ground in

shards of glass) (133–134). After this meeting with Felipe, Julia, in a symbolic act, abandons her high heeled shoes (her ideal womanhood) and, with them, the memories of past romantic encounters:

> Detrás de ella iban quedando sus fantasmas: se deshacía de su memoria y sobre las piedras de la calle iban cayendo para siempre sus domingos de fiesta, los rincones iluminados de sus bailes, sus trajes vacíos, sus amantes inútiles, sus gestos, sus alhajas. [. . .] Sintió que le estorbaban los tacones, se quitó los zapatos. Llegó descalza a los portales, caminando frente a un futuro que se alzaba delante de sus ojos como un muro blanco. (136)

> (Behind her she was leaving her ghosts, her memory was unravelling and on the paving stones of the street her festive Sundays, the brightly lit corners of dance-halls, her empty dresses, her useless lovers, her gestures, her jewels were falling away forever. [. . .] She felt her high heels got in her way and took off her shoes. She reached the arcade barefoot, walking towards a future that rose up before her eyes like a white wall.)

GOOD MOTHERS AND WICKED WOMEN

Ana Moncada sees the fate of Isabel as the result of her failure as a mother; she represents the ideas of the mother who tries to be good enough but feels she is not, and that of circular time. Intimations about her secret past life reveal that Isabel's overt sexuality is a repetition of her own. She reveals her position in cyclical time after Isabel goes to the hotel with Rosas and she repeats words she remembers being spoken by her own mother: '¡Martín, quiero saber qué fue de mis hijos!' (I want to know what happened to my children) (237). The importance of this mother–daughter link is that Ana's sexual behaviour (that is, enjoyment) as a young woman is correlated with Isabel's. The midwife's remarks on the birth of Isabel made Ana blush: ' "¡Qué viva! ¡Qué bonita! ¡Se ve que la hicieron con gusto!" Ana enrojeció desde su cama. [. . .] *Todos sabrían su lujuria gracias a la viveza de su hija.* [. . .] *Isabel había venido a denunciarla*' ('How lively she is! How pretty! You can see you enjoyed making her!' Ana blushed from her bed [. . .] *Everyone would know about her lust thanks to the liveliness of her daughter* [. . .] *Isabel had come to denounce her*) (238 [my emphasis]). Ana's guilt stems from her feeling that she is not the right kind of mother. As María Elena de Valdés writes:

> The institutionalized social symbol of the virgin mother is, of course, the Virgin of Guadalupe. As a social symbol she permeates all sectors and classes of Mexican society but, as a gender symbol rather than a religious one, she contributes to the denial of individuality to Mexican women [. . .]. [She is] the social symbol of the virgin mother, that is, maternity without

sexuality. This bifurcation of procreation and birth symbolically makes all women guilty of having been blemished by sexual intercourse in order to become pregnant and give birth. (de Valdés 1998: 53–54)

However, a factor that is overlooked or denied by the status quo is that between a quarter and a half of once 'decent' women – many of them mothers – engaged in prostitution during the Revolution in order to survive or, as Debra Castillo puts it, 'in that period of tremendous social upset, women were largely on the loose and on their own in Mexico' (Castillo 1998: 5). Of course, if this were not true, it would surely have been unnecessary for official discourse to promote the myth of the *madrecita santa* to cover up such 'slippages in gender conventions' (Castillo). Therefore, the behaviour of which Ana is now so ashamed, would have been normal eighteen years earlier when Isabel was conceived and the Revolution was still in its combative phase. However, it is partly the feeling of being denounced by her own daughter that makes the relationship between Isabel and her mother a difficult and distant one. Also, it is the assertion of the adolescent daughter's sexuality that is the most common cause of conflict between mothers and daughters. Shelley Phillips writes: 'Where attitudes encourage a female adolescent to believe her identity depends entirely on sexual partnership with a male, they create special problems for mother–daughter relationships. Autonomy for women, it is implied, involves escape from the mother to the protective custody of a male' (Phillips 1996: 63). Isabel rejects the idea that the only option open to her is protective custody as such in the form of marriage. But Ana, believing that Isabel's sexual nature is similar to her own and will lead to her downfall, wants Isabel to get married (23–24).[20] She later assumes that Isabel has gone with Rosas because of her uncontrollable sexual desire:

> '¡Es mala! ¡Es mala!' gritó Ana Moncada sintiéndose culpable de la mal-dad de su hija. Miró su cama con miedo y se oyó diciendo: '¿Vienes?' Con esa misma palabra había llamado Rosas a Isabel y su hija se fue con él en la oscuridad de los portales. Ella, después del nacimiento de Nicolás, había llamado a su marido cada noche: '¿Vienes?' Recordó aquellas noches; endulzaba la voz como Francisco Rosas y llamaba a Martín '¿Vienes?' Y su marido sonámbulo avanzaba hasta su cama, *hechizado por aquella Ana desconocida*, y juntos veían aparecer el alba. (238 [my emphasis])

---

[20] Phillips also explains that most daughters when questioned said that 'it was hard to reconcile awareness of their sexuality in adolescence with intimacy with their mothers. They claimed that sexual awareness made them feel more awkward – even distanced them from their mothers. There was little or no sense of a joint sexual heritage with their mothers, or of their sexuality as a continuity with the generations of women in their fami-lies' (Phillips 1996: 69).

('She's wicked! Wicked!' shouted Ana Moncada, feeling guilty for her daughter's wickedness. She looked fearfully at her bed and heard herself say: 'Coming?' With that same word Rosas had called Isabel and her daughter went off with him under the darkness of the arcade. She herself, after the birth of Nicolás had called her husband every night: 'Coming?' She remembered how, on those nights, she would soften her voice, like Francisco Rosas and call Martín 'Coming?' And her sleepwalking husband would approach her bed, *bewitched by that unknown Ana, and together they would watch the dawn.*)

Overt sexuality, unacceptable for any women other than prostitutes, is therefore explained away as the result of bewitchment.

The difficulties in this mother–daughter relationship, however, are also because Ana treats Isabel differently from her brothers. When she hears of the death of Ignacio, she shouts, '¡No lo cuenten delante de la niña!' (Don't talk about it in front of my little girl!) (84). As a result of her mother's attitude towards her, Isabel feels she does not love her mother. She turns away to avoid her goodnight kiss and tells Nicolás '¡no quiero a mi mamá!' (I don't love my mum) (156–157). This estrangement increases as she grows up. When Nicolás loses sight of Isabel in the garden and asks his mother if she has seen her, Ana's response is a further indication of their estrangement and Ana's guilt, '¡Déjala, es muy mala!' (Leave her alone, she's a very bad girl!) (13). This disapproval appears earlier when Isabel is dancing with Nicolás, 'Su madre la mira con reproche' (Her mother looks at her with reproach) (14). Ana understands only too well her daughter's restlessness but is reluctant to accept that this independent-minded young woman was once her little girl: 'Su madre no sabía cómo abordarla. "Es mi hija Isabel", se repetía, incrédula frente a la figura alta e interrogante de la joven' (Her mother did not know how to approach her. 'She's my daughter Isabel', she repeated, incredulous before the tall, questioning figure of the young woman) (31). Ana's sense of the difficulty involved in being a mother is summed up in her statement: '¡Es difícil tener hijos! Son otras personas [. . .]' (It's difficult having children! They're other people [. . .]) (20). Yet Ana herself is seen by her husband as 'un ser extraño y encantador' (a strange and enchanting being) who shared her life with him but 'guardaba celoso un secreto intransmisible' (jealously kept an untellable secret) (32). Her surprise at finding that her children are individuals is not uncommon. Nancy Chodorow suggests that many women see their children (daughters in particular) as extensions of themselves (Chodorow 1978: 103). Isabel, on the other hand, is consumed with adolescent self-obsession and frequently complains that she is alone and that no-one understands her (154: 162). Her resentment towards her mother is augmented by Ana's insistence that Juan and Nicolás should continue working in the mines. Isabel believes her mother insists deliberately to spite her, but Ana herself was deprived of such a relationship when her own brothers were killed in the Revolution before they were twenty-five years old (36).

Ana and Isabel also disagree over the question of religion. Isabel hardly believes in God and feels only indifference about what happens to the Church (161). She thinks her mother is a hypocrite for complaining to Rosas about the closing of the Church when she is constantly criticising the priests. Also, Ana's adherence to the Church clashes with her superstition and belief in witchcraft, producing yet another binary opposition (religion/superstition) in which the latter is traditionally presumed to be negative. This further alienates Isabel, who has little time for either type of belief. Ironically, though, she is seen by others as having 'powers' (13) and capable of bewitching Rosas. (Another allusion to the concept of *hechizo* is the one supposedly employed by Ana to seduce her husband, and so soon after the birth of Isabel, when it would be assumed she would normally devote her attention to her daughter.) When Gregoria, an elderly indigenous woman, is called upon to treat the bruises inflicted on Julia by Rosas, Gregoria assumes Julia has given him a love potion, even though it is obvious that by now Julia feels only indifference towards the General. (Indeed, it does seem as though Rosas is bewitched by Isabel, as he keeps her with him even though he does not really care for her.) As Amy Kaminsky points out, Gregoria cannot accept Isabel's sexuality, and even when the latter says she is going to confront Rosas saying, 'Mató a Nicolás, me engañó [. . .] Rosas me engañó' (He killed Nicolás, he deceived me [. . .] Rosas deceived me) (291), Gregoria assumes that it is due to Isabel's 'weakness of the flesh' (Kaminsky 1993: 105).

The alignment of the feminine with magic appears when Nicolás loses sight of Isabel in the Moncada's large garden and asks his mother if she has seen her, insisting that she has certain powers ('Tiene poderes') (13). By utilising this association of woman with magic, Garro emphasises the stereotyping of women in Mexico and, at the same time, *appears* to perpetuate the stereotype. However, elsewhere, what is perceived as magic (Julia's bewitchment of Rosas) by Gregoria (not necessarily a reliable source) is in fact only natural female sexuality. In the light of this, doubts are raised regarding Garro's perpetuation of stereotypes, and what is revealed is an ambiguity with regard to femininity, which incorporates the questioning of women's role in marriage and motherhood as well as their role outside these.

At the end of the novel Isabel is apparently turned to stone and the novel opens with the words of the narrator (Ixtepec) sitting on the stone, declaring, 'Sólo mi memoria sabe lo que encierra' (only my memory knows what it contains) (11). Many critical explanations have been given for Isabel's turning to stone. Garro, in condemning Isabel to eternal passivity, is merely writing her view of the reality for those marginalised beings who attempt to transgress. The Indians of Ixtepec who attempt to transgress are hanged. Julia who transgresses her role as the General's concubine, appears to have been rescued in the night by her saviour on his steed, as befits a romantic heroine, but the likelihood exists (it is left open to the reader) that perhaps they are both killed by the General. Right from the beginning of the novel Isabel's desire to escape her designated role is evident. By her unconventional behaviour she fulfils the role of the protagonist of a feminist novel who does not want to conform to the feminine ideal.[21] She dances wildly on her own, and for herself, in the gatherings at the family home; she spends her time in the company of her brothers; she declares that she has no intention of marrying and she indulges in 'unfeminine' pursuits such as climbing trees in the garden of the Moncada residence. Nicolás, who is closer to Isabel than anyone else, realises that his sister is different from the other women in the town. He also feels that Isabel has a certain power over him. Indeed their relationship verges on the incestuous: ' "Cualquier día no vuelvo más," prometió Nicolás con rencor' ('One of these days I won't come back,' promised Nicolás with resentment) (33), but he is afraid that one day he will return and find her married. Isabel feels the same bond with her brother which is possibly one motive for declaring that she will never marry. It may also be another reason for her relationship with Rosas, in spite of his actions towards the people of Ixtepec and her own brothers. Her apparent betrayal, as it would be seen by the other inhabitants, is as much an act of rebellion as of love or sacrifice. She is rebelling against the taboo on incest that prevents her from living with Nicolás, the person she most wants to be with.

That she has a certain power is confirmed by the strange effect she has on Rosas. The General does not love Isabel and still thinks of Julia, yet is unable to send her away. None of the reasons given for Isabel's affair with Rosas: her uncontrollable sexuality, her love for him, her desire to 'be Julia' are seen as valid by the townspeople (96). Isabel hopes that by taking Julia's place she will also take on the mythical, illusionary quality that she perceives in Julia, and be able to leave the claustrophobic provincialism of Ixtepec for that other world of magic, imagination and action that she believes Julia to inhabit. However, it is also the case that Isabel feels pity for Rosas and solidarity with him, because she feels herself to be, like Rosas, an outsider. The alienation she feels with regard to the other people in Ixtepec (because of her desire to participate in the historical process, and her potential breaking of the incest taboo in her desire for Nicolás), means that she is, in any case, condemned in their eyes. However, as the narrator explains: 'La memoria es traidora y a veces nos invierte el orden de los hechos' (Memory is treacherous and sometimes it changes around the order of things for us) (197). Isabel's relationship with Rosas gives the town a traditionally feminine transgression with which to brand her – la traición.[22]

---

[21] According to Toril Moi, feminist writing 'takes a discernible anti-patriarchal and anti-sexist position' and feminine writing, 'seems to be marginalised (repressed or silenced) by the ruling social/linguistic order' (Moi 1982).

[22] Garro was clearly very interested in the concept of 'betrayal' as she makes several references to 'los traídores de la patria' in her short story: 'La primera vez que me vi' in the collection Andamos huyendo, Lola (Garro 1980). I have dealt with this in an article (forthcoming) on that story.

Yet, a close reading of the text reveals that Isabel must have imagined that by sacrificing herself to Rosas, she would actually save the town and, above all, the lives of her brothers. At the party in Doña Carmen's house, ostensibly thrown in honour of Rosas, but in reality to keep him and his men busy while the priest (Father Beltrán) is being helped to escape, Isabel watches Rosas and his officers closely. When she sees Rosas looking at his watch repeatedly, she knows that something is amiss. Realising that the officers are about to leave early, Isabel tries to stop them, 'Isabel, muy pálida, fue en busca de la dueña de la casa. [. . .] "¿Qué hacemos niña?" preguntó asustada la señora. "¡Deténganlos!" suplicó Isabel' (Isabel, very pale, went to look for the owner of the house. [. . .] 'What shall we do child?' asked the lady, frightened. 'Keep them here!' begged Isabel) (200). Seeing that Rosas pays no attention to Doña Carmen's pleas for them to stay, she steps boldly in front of him and offers him her arm to dance. The band leader, instructed by Don Joaquín, plays one piece after another without pausing, to keep them dancing, but eventually the spell is broken by the appearance of Sergeant Illescas and Rosas follows him out of the room. Isabel's reaction is one of shock, 'Isabel buscó una silla y se dejó caer con los brazos colgantes y la mirada vacía' (Isabel looked for a chair and fell onto it with her arms hanging down and an empty gaze) (202). When Rosas returns and excuses himself, saying he will have to leave, his eyes come to rest on Isabel who watches him leave 'sin poder creerlo' (unable to believe it) (204).

Isabel's initial seduction of Rosas, therefore, is an act of subterfuge and heroism as well as a fulfilment of her own desire. Only she and her parents are given permission to leave the party, and she is anxious to leave immediately, *before* Rosas returns. Her fatalism is again visible when she reveals her belief that her fate with Rosas has already been sealed, 'Desde niños estamos bailando en este día' (We have been dancing on this day since we were children) (206). Later that night Rosas takes her to the hotel, and the other women there know therefore that something terrible must have happened (which suggests that she was the last person they expected to see there) (237).

Isabel, then, has more than one motive for becoming Rosas' lover. At the same time her own ambivalent feelings are displayed. She feels as though she does not belong to the static time she associates with the stagnation of Ixtepec, yet she has a fatalistic attitude which belongs to an idea of cyclical time. Her participation, first, in Felipe Hurtado's world of imagination and circular or sacred time (which allows him to time travel), and then, when Felipe disappears with Julia, in Francisco Rosas' real world of historical events, represents two attempts to escape Ixtepec and her fate as a wife and mother in a provincial town.

5

MOTHER/COUNTRY AND IDENTITY
IN ELENA PONIATOWSKA'S *LA 'FLOR DE LIS'*

> Few women growing up in patriarchal society
> can feel mothered enough; the power of our
> mothers, whatever their love for us and their
> struggles on our behalf, is too restricted.[1]

INTRODUCTION

The most internationally recognised of the four writers whose work is
discussed in this book, Elena Poniatowska, is best known for her journalism
and testimonial writing. Most of her writing deals with either extraordinary
people or events, which reveal her interest in Mexican society and her
empathy with those marginalised by poverty, class or disability.[2]

However, Poniatowska's fictional work is equally interesting. Her first
novel, *La 'Flor de Lis'* has received little critical attention compared with
Hasta no verte, Jesús mío (1969), translated as *Until We Meet Again, Jesus*,
Poniatowska's highly acclaimed testimonial novel based on the life of
Josefina Bórquez. *Hasta no verte, Jesús mío* both parallels and, in some ways,
is the antithesis of *La 'Flor de Lis'*. Both works follow a female narrator
through childhood and adolescence to maturity. However, the background of
Jesusa Palancares is as deprived as that of Mariana in *La 'Flor de Lis'* is privi-
leged. Other fictional works by Poniatowska include the children's story *Lilus
Kikus* (1954), a collection of short stories entitled *De noche vienes* (1979), and
the novella *Querido Diego, te abraza, Quiela* (1978) (*Dear Diego, Yours,
Quiela*), based on letters from Angelina Beloff to Diego Rivera. The irony and
humour found in *Lilus Kikus* reappear in *La 'Flor de Lis'* along with a fasci-

---

1 Adrienne Rich (1995: 243).
2 Those about people include her fictionalised biography of the photographer Tina
Modotti, *Tinísima* (1992), and that of the paraplegic Gaby Brimmer, who wrote poetry with
the aid of a typewriter and a single toe, published as *Gaby Brimmer* (1979). Those dealing
with events are: *La noche de Tlatelolco* (1971) about the massacre in the Plaza de las Tres
Culturas, Tlatelolco on 2 October 1968, when the army fired upon peaceful demonstrators,
killing hundreds of them; and *Nada, Nadie: las voces del temblor* (1988), in which
Poniatowska has gathered the testimony of the victims of the earthquake in Mexico City, in
September 1985.

nating insight into the life and mind of this important writer. *La 'Flor de Lis'*, though not published until 1988, was actually written in 1957, but Ponia-towska did not attempt to publish it as she considered the work to be of no literary worth and in no way 'useful'. In it, Poniatowska does what many writers (including Campobello and Castellanos) do in their first novels, she presents an autobiographical (albeit fictionalised) account of her childhood. In an interview with Agnes Dimitriou, Poniatowska states: 'Ahora va a salir una novela que se llama *La "Flor de Lis"*, que es una novela, es ficción' (Now a novel is coming out which is called *The 'Fleur de Lis'*, which is a novel, it is fiction). It is relevant here to try and categorise the genre into which *La 'Flor de Lis'* can be placed as I am attempting to explore the differences and simi-larities that exist between the works of the four writers and their motives for writing these particular novels from the perspective of a first-person narrator. This chapter also looks at the way in which multivocality in Poniatowska's text (as also in the works by Campobello, Castellanos and Garro) reveals the presence of a fragmented self, and shows the difficulty that occurs in the use of the first person. Mariana's ambivalence about her mother is a clear example of heteroglossia as is Luz's lack of conformity with her role as mother in Mexico.

Beth Jörgensen has accurately described *La 'Flor de Lis'* as a 'novel of development' which 'incorporates autobiographical elements'.[3] In other words, as well as being autobiographical fiction, the novel is also a type of female novel of awakening, similar in some ways to the novel of apprentice-ship, or *Bildungsroman*, as it narrates the awakening of the protagonist's consciousness (in this case regarding her position of privilege), and charts the process of her maturation and the evolution of her character (see Thorlby 1969).[4] Susan J. Rosowski writes:

> The novel of awakening is similar to the apprenticeship novel in some ways: it also recounts the attempts of a sensitive protagonist to learn the nature of the world, discover its meaning and pattern, and acquire a philos-ophy of life, but she must learn these lessons as a woman [. . .] The protag-onist's growth results typically not with an 'art of living', as for her male counterpart, but instead with a realisation that for a woman such an art of living is difficult or impossible: it is an awakening to limitations.
>
> (Rosowski 1983: 49)

It is important to consider this aspect of the work in view of Poniatowska's insistence that *La 'Flor de Lis'* is a work of fiction and of her belief, for thirty

---

3   '[. . .] and a limited use of documentary materials to create urban female protago-nists of the privileged and oppressed classes' (Jörgensen 1988: 476–477).
4   Poniatowska's novel *Paseo de la Reforma* (1999) is also about the awakening to the realisation of his position of privilege by a young man of upper-class society in Mexico City.

years, that her novels and stories 'no eran útiles para mi país' (Dimitriou 1990); in other words that autobiographical writing is tantamount to self-indulgence. Sara Poot Herrera writes of *La 'Flor de Lis'*: 'Si bien es cierto que las primeras palabras del libro corresponden a la madre del personaje de la ficción [. . .] también lo es que desbordan el texto y se acercan muchas veces a la madre de la autora' (While it is true that the first words of the book belong to the fictional character's mother, [. . .] it is also true that they spill out of the text and are often associated with the author's mother) (1996: 61). This chapter explores the relationship between Mariana, the protagonist and first-person narrator of *La 'Flor de Lis'*, and her mother, Luz. A parallel is made between mother/daughter and mother–country/writer as both mother and mother–country are found to be influential in the creation and perpetuation of gender roles and female identities. The significance of these relationships (between Mariana and her mother and Mariana and Mexico) is revealed by looking at the way Poniatowska explores the construction of gender through the use of binary oppositions.

As observed in earlier chapters, pychoanalytical studies on the mother–daughter relationship are helpful in ascertaining the effect a particular kind of mothering has on the behaviour and thought of young girls (such as the protagonist in *La 'Flor de Lis'*). I believe that relationship was influential in Poniatowska's coming to write and this claim is substantiated through the analysis of descriptions which rely on the senses and of the ways in which binary oppositions are used in the text. Once again, binary oppositions make their appearance in both a traditional 'essentialist' way (where the oppositions associated by patriarchy with male/female are reproduced) and in a transgressive way (in 'alternative discourse'). In Poniatowska's writing, such alternative discourse is used to criticise traditional gender stereotyping as well as the failures of the Mexican government to live up to its claims to progress for the nation. The process of Mexicanisation undergone by Mariana is paralleled by a similar process of Mexicanisation undergone by Mexico during the attempts by the governments of Miguel Alemán and Adolfo Ruiz Cortines to create an homogenous nation within a modern indus-trialised Nation State.[5] *La 'Flor de Lis'* reveals that industrialisation merely consolidated privilege in Mexican society, that progress remained a myth for the vast majority, and that modernisation little affected the status of women.

Women were still expected to play very precise roles in Mexico when Elena, the textual author, and Mariana, the narrator, were growing to maturity in the 1940s and 1950s. The way in which the protagonist of *La 'Flor de Lis'* both conforms to, and attempts to transgress, her role is comparable with

[5] I use the term 'Mexicanisation' to refer to the process by which Mariana/Elena adapted to her new country and came to consider herself, and to be considered by Mexicans of all classes, and not just her own (many of whom are of Old World descent), as Mexican.

similar behaviour by the female protagonists in the novels discussed in previous chapters. The transgression of such gender-constructed roles is linked to the mother–daughter relationship. In *La 'Flor de Lis'* the construction of gender roles centres around Mariana's mother and the priest, Jacques Teufel, who replaces her mother as a 'love object'.[6] This, in turn, is linked to the process of Mexicanisation undergone by the narrator as she affirms her growing love for her adoptive country in spite of the efforts of her francophile mother and anglophile grandmother to prevent it. The Mexicanisation of Mariana is paralleled by the consolidation of nationhood in Mexico, and its ambivalent position on the world stage. Just as Mexico attempts both to join the international capitalist system and to retain its identity, Mariana attempts to become a Mexican woman without conforming to the accepted stereotypes of woman as either Madonna, Malinche or Sor Juana. Thus the twin subject of mother and Mexicanisation and the tension produced by the pair are closely linked to gender roles as they are felt and perceived by Mariana. Poniatowska uses binary oppositions to deconstruct gender constructions, and sensory descriptions to express her feelings and perceptions.

Women's role in the twin processes of industrialisation and Mexicanisation in Mexico was, chiefly, that of exemplary mother. To this end, the myth of the *mujer abnegada y sufrida* was incorporated into the dominant discourse. Even the Adelita figure, the *soldadera* of the Mexican Revolution, who became the protagonist of films such as *Si Adelita se fuera con otro* (If Adelita were to go off with someone else) (Chano Urueta 1948) was depicted in a secondary role as camp follower or fighter going into battle to support her man. The *soldadera*, as well as, or more than, a fighter, was there to cook for her man, wash his clothes, carry his equipment and continue to bear his children. Poniatowska's own Mexicanisation is intimately connected to her vocation as a writer. At home she was brought up by a series of nannies, except for a period of two years which she spent as a boarder at the Sacred Heart Convent School near Philadelphia. All of these circumstances are shared by the protagonist, Mariana, in *La 'Flor de Lis'*. Finally, Elena learnt Spanish from her family's Mexican servants and thus acquired a profound emotional link with the Mexican people which is reflected in her socially and politically 'useful' writing.

BACKGROUND AND STRUCTURE

A brief look at Poniatowska's background and upbringing will reveal other parallels between herself and Mariana. To cite a few examples: Poniatowska

---

6 According to Freud's theory of Oedipal love the father becomes the girl's love-object. However, as indicated earlier, Object-Relations theorists, such as Chodorow, attach greater importance to the mother–daughter relationship.

was born in Paris (19 May 1933) to an aristocratic Polish–French father and a Mexican mother; she has a first cousin, Mariana, whose name she borrowed in order to present the work as fiction, and her family moved to Mexico when she was eight years old. There Elena, conscious of the fact that she was an outsider and a foreigner, strove to become Mexican in spite of being sent to a British-run school and having French as her first language. She revealed in an interview (with Gazarian Gautier in 1989) that she longed to be Mexican with all her heart. These details are mirrored exactly in the protagonist of La 'Flor de Lis'. Also, with regard to her becoming a writer, Poniatowska claims to have been a very solitary child, as did Campobello and Castellanos.

The novel is divided into twenty-eight sections, marked by a large capital letter at the beginning of the first sentence. These, in turn, are divided into sub-sections (as many as twenty-one), indicated by a small emblem. These take myriad forms including: a flower; a hand holding a pen; a pen-nib; a clover leaf; a fleur-de-lis; a heart; a club; a triangle; a quaver; a ship; an aeroplane; a suitcase; a crucifix; an ice-crystal; or a telephone and are clearly related to the content of the sub-section. The first section of the novel takes place in Paris and the first sub-section describes the home life and lineage of the narrator's family. This is followed by the narrator's account of life with her new nanny, Mademoiselle Durand, who is unfavourably compared with Nounou who took charge of them as soon as they were born. The sixth sub-section describes the care given them by Nounou and her dismissal when the girls' mother discovers that her children, playing at being dogs, regularly soil the nursery carpet.[7]

The second section sees the girls' move to the countryside safety of their grandparents' house. The sisters are introduced to the idea of Mexico by their grandmother Beth who playfully mocks their heritage by showing them photos of African 'cannibals' in the National Geographic magazine, telling them that they are Mexicans. The section ends with the journey by ship to Havana and by plane on to Mexico. There they are met by their maternal grandmother and Mariana wonders, '¿Dónde estarán las del hueso atravesado en la cabeza?' (I wonder where the ones with the bone through their heads are?)[8]

The third section, with the girls and their mother now in Mexico, describes the girls' sense of strangeness, 'Aquí todo es desaforado, la distancia, el Paseo de la Reforma [. . .] y la nueva abuela [. . .]' (Here everything is outrageous, the distance [. . .] the Paseo de la Reforma [. . .] and our new grandmother) (33). The girls are sent to a British-run school where they learn to use pounds, shillings and pence, and sing 'God Save the Queen'; and in their grand-

---

[7] Mariana and her sister's game of pretending to be dogs (referred to earlier in this chapter) parallels a similar game played by Garro and her sister, described in the short story, 'El día que fuimos perros' (Garro 1964).

[8] Elena Poniatowska (1988b: 32).

mother's house they discover her eccentric love of dogs. Sections 4 to 11
relate Mariana's life in Mexico with her mother, sister and friends, all of
whom are perceived by Mariana as more beautiful, more accomplished and
more self-assured than herself. Mariana observes and comments on her
mother's friendship with different sorts of people until her father's return
from the war, when her social life is curtailed. Mariana's interest in words and
her enthusiasm for Mexican history – part of the process of her mexicanisation – are expressed, and the sisters are sent to a convent school in the USA
to counteract this process and ensure their elite status and education.

In section 12, Mariana has returned to Mexico and she is sent to a retreat
where she meets the French priest, Jacques Teufel, the person who is to help
her complete her separation from her mother, her individuation and to develop
a social conscience. Her relationship with the priest takes over from that with
her mother, Luz, as the most important aspect of her life, though her love for
him remains unrequited. Sections 12 to 28 relate the influence the priest has
over Mariana's circle of acquaintances and the women in her family, particularly her mother, her Aunt Francisca and her sister, Sofía, as well as the effect
these women have on him. The priest's relationship with Luz is particularly
significant as not only does he displace her in Mariana's affections but, also,
she is so entranced by him as to further neglect her relationship with Mariana,
thus compounding the feelings of rejection suffered by her daughter. After a
period of influence and power over the well-to-do ladies of Mexico City's
French colony, Teufel falls into disfavour and disrepute and is obliged to
leave. Section 28 is retrospective, partly written in the third person and reveals
the state of self-awareness and confirmation of her identity as a Mexican that
Mariana has finally attained (261).

MADRE/PATRIA: MARIANA'S MEXICANISATION

Sara Poot Herrera has noted the importance of the mother for Mariana in
her quest for identity: 'en *La "Flor de Lis"* la madre representa el pasado, la
historia, la búsqueda de la identidad y de la nacionalidad' (in *La 'Flor de Lis'*
the mother represents the past, history, the search for identity and nationality)
(Poot Herrera 1996: 74). An analysis of the Mexicanisation of the narrator
reveals two processes. First, there is the young girl's construction of her
mother as an idealised figure to whom she wants to be close, which corresponds to her adaptation to her new environment. Secondly, there is the
parallel process of Mariana's desire to be more Mexican than her mother and
to be accepted as Mexican by the people. Thus a link is established between
madre and *madre-patria*, as the two become inextricably associated in the
(unconscious) mind of the protagonist. The move to Mexico of the textual
author and Mariana as young girls, and their desire to fit in in their adoptive

country, can be seen as a metaphor for the Mexicanisation of Mexico as a nation-state. This began in 1921 with an education programme devised by José Vasconcelos to incorporate the indigenous people as useful members of an homogenous nation. The realisation in the 1950s, following the era of modernisation and industrialisation, that many people, particularly the indigenous, had largely been left behind by progress is related to the concept of the novel of awakening. The 1940s and 1950s saw an awakening to the limitations of the possibility of an homogenous nation and the realisation that for a large section of the population, not just women, progress would remain elusive and marginalisation an inescapable fact of life. A brief explanation of the changes undergone in the social, political and economic climate of Mexico during Poniatowska's girlhood and adolescence (until she wrote the novel as a young woman) will throw light on the importance attached to Mariana's Mexicanisation.

During the 1920s and 1930s, the sustained effort by the Secretaría de Educación Pública (SEP) to explore, extol and reaffirm the indigenous roots of the Mexican people had led to the work of the Muralist movement with its great public homages to pre-Columbian culture. The ensuing movement became known as the Mexican Renaissance, and by the 1940s the Golden Age of Mexican cinema and music was taking place. Mexico's participation in the international capitalist system had led to the growth of the middle classes who were dissatisfied with being on the margins of international culture and contemporaneity (see Monsiváis 1981) so that, by the 1950s, Mexico was already beginning to lose much of its *mexicanidad*. 'Lo mexicano' was seen as commercialised folklore and though television did not arrive until 1957, a desire for the 'American way of life' already existed.[9] This process is parodied in Mariana's experience when she is sent to study in a convent high school in the United States. An analysis of the process of Mexicanisation undergone by the narrator, and how this is linked to the relationship with her mother, is therefore appropriate here.

To begin with, it is worthy of note that only during their sea-voyage together does Mariana begin to know her mother and find out she is Mexican. This suggests that not only is Luz less than proud of her origins but deems them of insufficient importance even to have them mentioned and she certainly does not consider her children to be Mexican. Furthermore, this is related in a section consisting of a single line, preceded by a black triangle, 'Sofía y yo no sabíamos que mamá era mexicana' (Sofia and I didn't know that Mamma was Mexican) (32). However, soon after their arrival in Mexico, the Mexicanisation of Mariana begins. Coincidentally, in the Era 1994 edition of *La 'Flor de Lis'*, Mariana arrives in Mexico on page 33, the year in which

---

[9]   This ambivalent attitude to the 'American way of life' reveals the discrepancy between official and alternative discourses and is also explored by Castellanos in her short story 'Domingo' from the collection, *Álbum de familia* (1971).

Poniatowska was born. Mariana's (and Elena's) arrival in Mexico is her
rebirth as well as the birth of her attachment to her 'mother-country'. She and
her sister, Sofía, are introduced to their 'new' grandmother (who speaks to
them in English) and to the sights, sounds and smells of the city and countryside. Mariana is fascinated by the vastness of the sky and the open country, by
the extreme heat and great hills – all on a much greater scale than the French
landscape to which she is accustomed.

Campobello, Garro and Castellanos all write about life in the provinces
where nature impinges more on daily existence than in the city. Poniatowska
is overawed by, and reflects upon, the power of nature (even though the novel
is, for the most part, set in Mexico City) during the family's excursions to the
countryside: 'Nos perdemos en la tierra infinita [. . .] las lomitas se agigantan
y avanzamos sobrecogidas por su inacabable demesura. Nada tiene fin. El sol
quemante amarillea y desolla los campos, nosotras somos una cucarachita que
avanza tatemándose' (We lose ourselves in the infinite land [. . .] the small
hills became huge and we advance overwhelmed by its endless enormity.
There is no end to anything. The burning sun yellows and flays the fields, our
car is a cockroach that advances, gradually getting toasted) (37). Mariana
recognises the distinctive nature of the Mexican countryside which she
already is beginning to love. She sees Sofía as dynamic, daring and wilful, and
herself as docile and uninteresting. But in the lines which follow, where she
gazes from the car window at the Mexican landscape, it is clear that she is
introspective, imaginative and observant, and, judging by her sister's
comment at the end of the following quotation, has a tendency – like her
mother – to be in another world:

> Amo los magueyes, los miro con detenimiento [. . .] vengan magueyes,
> vengan hasta la ventanilla, vengan hacia mí, vengan atentos, leales,
> severos, vengan guardianes, remonten las colinas, atraviesen los barrancos,
> vengan, soy su general, y ustedes mi ejército, el ejército más portentoso del
> mundo. 'Mamá, Mariana está otra vez hablando sola.' (37)

> (I love the magueys, I look at them carefully [. . .] come magueys, come up
> to the window, come to me, come attentive, loyal, severe ones, come
> guardians, climb the hills, cross the ravines, come, I am your general, and
> you are my army, the most extraordinary army in the world. 'Mamma,
> Mariana is talking to herself again.')

Mariana learns by heart the geographical data relevant to Mexico and her
awareness that her family is not interested enough in what is now their own
country leads her to proclaim in a loud voice when they are sitting at table
together, 'France fits more than four times inside Mexico, did you know that?'
(43). There is a lot of emphasis on nature and particularly on the flora of
Mexico in the descriptions Mariana gives of her new homeland. She is filled
with wonder at the variety of fruits and colours to be found:

[. . .] piso unas campanitas color azul tirando a lavanda [. . .] A su lado, unas vainas rojas que el colibrí abre en el árbol. Pero, ¿qué clase de país es éste que tiene árboles que producen flores? En Francia hay árboles frutales, sí, pero los árboles no se vuelven nubes, no incendian el cielo como aquí. Lilas y rojas, la calle es un tapete de flores. ¡Qué país. Dios mío, qué país!
(129–30)

(I step on some little blue, almost lavender coloured bells [. . .] Next to them, some red pods that the humming-bird is opening in the tree. But what kind of country is this that produces so many flowers? In France there are fruit trees, yes, but the trees do not become clouds, they do not light up the sky as they do here. The street is a carpet of flowers: lilac and red. What a country! My God, what a country!)

Luz had told them that it was a beautiful country but they were not prepared for such abundance:

Nunca nos dijo que veríamos montones de planetas en la esquina de la calle, que las naranjas rodarían aún tibias a nuestros pies como pelotas de luz, que en el desayuno nos tocaría un chorro de oro líquido llamado jugo de naranja [. . .] tampoco que en México atrincheraban los melones y las papayas ni que las sandías encimadas podían servir de Barricada o que los montones de pepitas a ras del suelo eran diminutas pirámides del Sol y de la Luna [. . .] No sabíamos que las piñatas chorreaban tejocotes [. . .].
(129–30)

(She never told us that we would see loads of planets from the corner of the street, that oranges would roll still warm to our feet like balls of light, that for breakfast we would get a stream of golden liquid called orange juice [. . .] nor that in Mexico the melons and papayas would be stuck on sticks, nor that piled up watermelons could serve as a barricade or that the mountains of pumpkin seeds on the ground were diminutive Pyramids of the Sun and Moon [. . .] We did not know that the *tejocote* fruit came pouring out of *piñatas*.)

Here she is comparing her new country with France by emphasising the plenitude in the New World contrasted with the (wartime) scarcity in the Old World. Elsewhere she ironically stresses the 'civilisation' of the Old World with the 'barbarity' of the New, thus subverting the binaries Old/New World and *civilización/barbarie* and the idea held by the social élite to which she belongs, that the Old World (Europe) is necessarily superior to, or more civilised than, the New (America). When her mother is surprised at her admiration for her new surroundings, Mariana quotes a little rhyme which shows how she is defensive about the country and critical of her mother's eurocentricity once again, 'Como si dijera, mira, mira cuánto apache, cuánto indio sin huarache'

(As if to say, look, look at the vandals, a lot of savages without sandals) (130).[10]

Another description of the abundance of nature appears when Mariana describes the garden of the *retiro*. She says she prefers grasses that, 'se atreven a crecer duras, con una coraza especial y adquieren ese color mate de todo lo sobreviviente' (dare grow hard, with a special shell and that matt colour of things that survive) (135). She relates how the English grass planted in her friend's garden grows – not into a soft carpet as it would in England – but into a 'víbora insistente y primigenia' (an insistent and primitive snake). Similarly, when the roses and azaleas are fertilised by the gardener, 'algo les sucedió en la tierra de México, demasiado vigorosa para su finura y crecieron descabelladas y voraces hasta adquirir el tamaño de un coliflor' (something happened to them in the Mexican soil, too vigorous for their delicate nature and they grew wildly and voraciously until they reached the size of cauli-flowers) (136).

The perfumes that emanate from the plants are also stronger, the pleasant mixing with the pungent, 'En el aire que huele a azahares, hay algo de pimienta, de chile, de pequeño incendio' (In the air that smells of orange-flower, there is a hint of pepper, of chilli, of little fires) and the noxious, 'Tras de los juncos descubro rincones que huelen a agua estancada, peor que eso, podrida, un olor casi obsceno que aturde y sin embargo me jala por indescifrable. Todo lo que no puedo domesticar me atrapa' (Behind the reeds, I discover corners that smell of stagnant, no worse, rotten water, an almost obscene smell that makes me giddy but draws me to it because it is indecipherable) (136).[11] The good and bad smells represent Mexico itself for Mariana. She is fascinated by what is untamed and this is what she loves about her new homeland. The smells also epitomise the struggle that is going on inside Mariana (and relate to the pre-Oedipal phase of close attachment to the mother when smell and touch are particularly important) as she attempts both to hold on to her and to separate from her, by forming an attachment with the priest. They also represent her recognition that both the priest and her mother are a mixture of good and bad.

Melanie Klein hypothesises that due to the fact that the 'infant's longing for an inexhaustible and ever-present breast' can never be satisfied, destructive impulses and persecutory anxiety occurs (Klein 1996: 237). This in turn 'result(s) in the feeling that a good and bad breast exists' and produces an 'innate conflict between love and hatred' (Klein). Minsky's analysis of Klein's theory extrapolates, 'that if our earliest experience as helpless infants was of loving care by our mother (or a substitute), then we will have been able to construct a sufficiently integrated sense of identity to allow us to break

10 Obviously this is a (European) cultural equivalent rather than a translation.
11 This is almost identical to the description of rotting garden vegetation in *Los recuerdos del porvenir*.

away from this primitive, binary mode of thinking to appreciate the complexity of ourselves and others' (Minsky 1996: 98).

Mariana's struggle to accept the complexity of human identities is revealed in her description of the sensual effect on her of the smells, like that of incense, 'ese humo pesado de la Elevación, que nada tiene de santo' (that heavy smoke when the Host is raised, that has nothing holy about it), and the way she attempts to purify herself by contact with the innocence of a child:

> [. . .] esos tufos dulces y lilas se expanden, suben a untarse en las cortinas de lona de las alcobas, macerando especies, girando sus perfumes lascivos entre los exámenes de conciencia, nos alucinan, son nuestra vigilia. Los inhalo malignos, más tarde, iré a besarle las manos a mi hermanito, Fabián, una y otra vez para purificarme. (136)

> (those sickly sweet, lilac smells, rise to cling to the sailcloth curtains around the beds, macerating species, their lascivious perfumes gyrating between examinations of conscience, they beguile us, they are our vigil. I inhale their malignancy, later, I will go and kiss my little brother Fabián's hands again and again, to purify myself.)

On page 54 the girls are handed over to the care of Magda who, unlike Mademoiselle Durand, replaces in their hearts their beloved Nounou. Magda is a *pueblerina* (village girl), who therefore not only represents the real Mexico for Mariana, but also the *madre-patria* (mother-country). Mariana persuades her mother to take on Magda without a letter of recommendation saying, 'Es que desde ahorita la quiero' (It's just that I love her already) (54), and although this relationship is not as intense as the one between the child-narrator and her *nana* in *Balún-Canán*, Magda plays a crucial role in the Mexicanisation of Mariana. She teaches Mariana her own colloquial Mexican form of Spanish and it is Magda who is responsible for showing Mariana and her sister 'the real Mexico' by taking them to markets, to the *zócalo* (main square), to the Basilica and to her village. Magda, who will stay with the family for years, does everything for them. Indeed, Mariana ironically describes how Magda is at her beck and call by alternating the general list of household chores with the games and (motherly) attentions she demands from her – which she is obviously not receiving from her real mother, 'Magda lava, chiquéame, plancha, hazme piojito, barre, hazme bichitos, sacude, acompáñame un ratito, trapea' (Magda, do the washing, spoil me, do the ironing, tickle me, sweep-up, do eensty weensty spider, do the dusting, play with me for a while, clean the floor) (54). Magda also introduces the girls to Mexican folklore by telling them far-fetched stories, such as the one about the girl whose hair grew inside her skull as well as outside because she rubbed green tomato into the roots; and by taking them to the *zócalo* on festive days such as 'el día de las Mulitas' (Thursday of Corpus Christi).

Magda is also instrumental in the creation of Mariana's social conscience.

Mariana realises, as they return from one such outing, that when they arrive
home they will be divided by class and social position, '[. . .] al regresar en el
camión siento un desconcierto cada vez mayor, una mano me aprieta las
tripas, la tráquea, no sé si el corazón. Porque nosotras pasaremos a la mesa,
con nuestra mamá y la visita en turno, y Magda irá a comer a la cocina' (going
home in the bus I feel an ever-increasing bewilderment, a tightness in my
belly, my throat, maybe my heart – I don't know. Because we will go to the
dining table, with our mother and that day's guest, and Magda will go and eat
in the kitchen) (58). Mariana also questions why it is Magda and not she, her
mother or grandmother, or her grandfather in France – 'tantas horas sentado'
(sitting down for hours) – who has to wash the dishes. She also questions the
lack of equal opportunities suffered by Magda because of her social position,
'¿Por qué no es Magda la que toma las clases de piano si se ve que a ella se le
ilumina el rostro al oír la música que tecleamos con desgano?' (Why is it not
Magda who has piano classes if it is *her* face that lights up when she hears the
music we so reluctantly play?) (58). She is aware that Magda (unlike Luz)
always puts their needs before her own, 'Ella siempre se atiende a lo último.
Para ella son los minutos más gastados, los más viejos del día, porque antes,
todavía encontró tiempo para venir a contarnos el cuento de las tres hijas del
zapaterito pobre' (She always sees to herself last. For her are the remaining
moments, the last ones left in the day, because she still finds time to tell us the
tale of the poor little cobbler and his three daughters) (59).

Magda fulfils, in fact, the role of *madre abnegada* which Luz is thus able to
eschew with impunity. Also, were it not for the close relationship with Magda,
Mariana's experience of Mexico would certainly, in view of her privileged
and cossetted upbringing, have been far more restricted. Mariana/Ponia-
towska would not have developed her love of the Mexican people and her
country, in spite of their failings, and her writing might have taken a quite
different orientation; one in which concern for her fellow citizens, particularly
the underprivileged, was not paramount.

References to Mariana's desire to belong and her insistence that she is
Mexican appear in short sub-sections where she has conversations with
people about her nationality and insists that even if she does not look
Mexican, she is: 'Soy de México porque quiero serlo, es mi país' (I am from
Mexico because I want to be. It is my country) (74). Sometimes the allusion is
limited to someone's remark to which she cannot even respond, 'Güerita,
güerita ¡cómo se ve que usted no es de los nuestros, no sabe nuestras costum-
bres!' (Blondie, blondie, it really shows that you are not one of us, you don't
even know our customs!) (74). Her pain at this rejection is evident in her reaction to the enjoiner by Nachita, one of the maids:

'Cochinas extranjeras, regrésense a los Yunaites, lárguense a su país.' De
azotea en azotea, entre las sábanas que chasquean resuena el grito y lo
recibo como una bofetada. ¡Qué vergüenza! Quisiera vender billetes de

lotería en alguna esquina para pertenecer. O quesadillas de papa. Lo que sea. (74–75)

'Dirty foreigners, go back to the States, buzz off to your own country.' Across the rooftops, between the crisp sheets, the shout echoes and comes back to me like a slap in the face. I feel ashamed. I would like to sell lottery tickets on some corner somewhere just to belong. Or potato pancakes. Whatever.)

Mariana's desire to belong in Mexico contrasts with Sofía's indifference and rebellious attitude. When, in the immigration office, they are thwarted in their attempts to obtain their residence permits and repeatedly kept waiting, Sofía's attitude towards the bureaucrats is not the stoical, patient one that is expected in that situation. There is also wry criticism of Mexico's bureaucracy and pretentious use of titles here. The Under Secretary of Immigration is referred to as 'su santidad' (his holiness) and the abuse of power is clear. Sofía, no longer able to put up with the disrespectful way they are treated just because they are foreigners says angrily, 'No vayan a creer que quise venir, me trajeron, bola de licenciados frijoleros y pedorros' (Don't think I wanted to come, I was forced to, you bunch of bean-eating, farty bureaucrats) (75). When finally, after hours of waiting, standing in queues, filling-in and signing forms they are told to return in two weeks, Mariana wonders whether even friends of the President would have to join the long queue, adding, in an apparently throwaway remark that reveals her awareness of the disparity in incomes, that the President has three hundred pairs of boots and twice as many pairs of shoes. This in a country where many wear only *huaraches* or go barefoot.[12]

MARIANA'S IDEAL MOTHER

The narrator's process of Mexicanisation – adaptation to the *madre-patria* – is related to Mariana's identification with Magda and the process of her individuation and separation from her mother. She needs to feel she belongs and that she is Mexican before she can let go of her mother. Her parents attempt to interrupt this process by sending Mariana and her sister to the convent school in Philadelphia where 'no-one talks about poverty' (98), along with the nieces of other members of the Latin American élite, such as the Presidents of Nicaragua and Cuba, the owners of business emporia and banana, sugar and coffee

---

[12] As the young Indian boy in Garro's short story 'El mentiroso' (The Liar) declares, 'Yo, al igual que todos uso huaraches, *cuando me va bien y ya sé que nunca tendré el gozo de ponerme unos zapatos*' (I, like everyone else, wear sandals, *when things are going well and I already know I'll never have the pleasure of wearing shoes*' (Garro 1980: 55 [my emphasis]).

plantations, they will concern themselves with problems suited to their gender and station in life, such as fashion and film stars: 'Our world is that of shampoos and ivory soap, cornflakes and hairdryers. We are the little goddesses' (99). They are sent to be educated in the belief that 'true' democracy, such as that of the USA and free trade, are the only suitable options for any country, and to be convinced that they are special and deserve their privileges: 'Es justo que sólo los mejores subsisten y nosotras estamos aquí porque somos the top of the top, la crème de la crème, la cereza en la punta, las dueñas del emporio' (It is right that only the best survive and we are here because we are the top of the top, the crème de la crème, the cherry on the cake, the owners of the emporium) (98). However, Mariana fails to be convinced of her innate superiority and this is paralleled in Poniatowska's recognition of her own privileged position and in her belief that she must write works that are useful to society.

Poniatowska attributed her coming to writing to the fact that her family was always moving around. She has affirmed that the only way she found not to feel afloat was to write.[13] In La 'Flor de Lis' Mariana says, 'Eramos unas niñas desarraigadas, flotábamos en México, qué cuerdita tan frágil la nuestra, ¡cuántos vientos para mecate tan fino!' (We were rootless as little girls, we floated in Mexico. What a fine thread stopped us from floating away. What a lot of wind there was for so fine a string!) (47). Janet Sayers writes that Klein explains art as 'reflecting our relations with others, in the first place with the mother' (Sayers 1991: 228).[14] Thus Poniatowska's art – her writing – which is mostly about the Mexican people and their problems, serves to connect her more firmly to her motherland. Her writing reflects what her unconscious mind perceives as a tenuous connection (un mecate tan fino), or an unsatisfactory relationship with her mother, and substitutes the relationship with the motherland for the one with the mother. This feeling of 'floating' is identical to that experienced by Mariana in the novel, coming from her unsatisfied desire to be mothered.[15] Her mother's absence acts as a catalyst to the narrator's imagination and fantasy. Sara Poot Herrera also equates the writer's experience with that of the protagonist. She writes:

> [. . .] es un homenaje que la narradora, la autora, Elena Poniatowska, hace a su madre. La ausencia de ésta sirve como detonador de la imaginación y la fantasía de Mariana. Luz es el sujeto de la fascinación que, al mismo tiempo que se le nombra con la palabra y se graba en la escritura, se vuelve inalcanzable, se volatiliza y se convierte en el objeto de la espera.
>
> (Poot Herrera 1990: 102)

---

13 Elizabeth Starcevic (1983: 72–77).
14 Unlike both Sigmund and Anna Freud who attribute art to sublimation of individual instinct.
15 Luce Irigaray suggests that 'love' is sublimated, idealised desire (Irigaray 1977).

(it is a homage that the narrator, the author, Elena Poniatowska, makes to her mother. The absence of the latter serves as a detonator for Mariana's imagination and fantasy. Luz is the subject of that fascination which at the same time as it is named with a word and recorded in writing, becomes unattainable, vanishes into thin air and becomes the object that is awaited.)

As is the case with Nellie, in *Cartucho* and *Las manos de mamá*, Mariana's attitude to her mother is ambivalent. She too both adores her mother and feels rejected by her. Monique Lemaître writes that throughout the narrative Luz's unconscious rejection of Mariana and the feeling of emptiness this creates inside her resurges again and again, 'Luz es el constante objeto del deseo del "sujeto" actante Mariana' (Luz is the constant object of desire of the acting 'subject', Mariana) (Lemaître 1990–91: 32). Beth Jörgensen also considers the relationship between Mariana and her mother as the central conflict of the novel, in spite of the importance of the protagonist's relationship with the diabolical priest, the aptly named Jacques Teufel.[16] Indeed, if analyst Hélène Deutsch's theory of loss is applied to Mariana, her relationship with the priest could be seen as a direct result of her unsatisfactory relationship with her mother. Mariana's idealisation of her mother and her subsequent obsession with the priest is identical to a case-history described by Deutsch and cited by Janet Sayers:

> An example was an aristocratic patient who, as a child, was brought up 'in accordance with ceremonial tradition' by three nurses who were frequently changed – just as Deutsch's were in her infancy. Initially, and also in common with Deutsch, the patient bolstered her self-esteem by idealizing her parents and developing a 'family romance' with them. But in the absence of any close relation with her parents the romance collapsed. Instead she devalued them and passively identified with the succession of different religious and sexual personae with which her convent school peers experimented. (Sayers 1991: 55)

In common with my analysis of the mother–daughter relationship in Campobello's work, Jörgensen's interpretation of the portrait of the mother owes much to Adrienne Rich's *Of Woman Born*. She observes how in *La 'Flor de Lis'* the 'terrible ambivalence – love, rivalry, rage, desire, rejection – which, according to Rich, a daughter feels towards her mother in patriarchal society, is clearly manifested. The novel is obsessed with the same feeling of abandonment and loss that Rich so painfully describes' (Jörgensen 1988: 119 [my translation]).[17]

---

16 *Teufel* meaning 'devil' in German.
17 Jörgensen quotes Rich: 'Few women growing up in patriarchal society can feel mothered enough; the power of our mothers, whatever their love for us and their struggles on our behalf, is too restricted' (Rich 1995: 243).

I have already shown in previous chapters how an analysis of the way the senses function in the text is useful when exploring the mother–daughter relationship. This relationship is significant, as is the more obviously influential one with the revolutionary priest, with regard to the awakening of Mariana's social conscience. That conscience is directly related to the testimonial and often socially and politically critical nature of Poniatowska's other writings (a product of her Mexicanisation) referred to earlier.

The relationship between Luz and Mariana is informed by allusions to the strong but ambiguous feelings Mariana has for her mother and by sensory descriptions related to her mother, which often incorporate references to nature. The first line of the novel begins with the pronoun *La* (her) – and refers to the first appearance of the narrator's mother, 'La veo salir de un ropero antiguo' (I watch her come out of an antique wardrobe). Mariana deifies her mother by referring to her as 'She/Her', as does Nellie, the narrator of *Cartucho* and *Las manos de mamá*. However, Poniatowska's narrator, unlike Campobello's, presents a view of the elegant, aristocratic figure, wearing a long white nightdress and a night cap such as the one worn by the Countess of Ségur in illustrated romantic stories (13). This is, at the same time, ironic and ambiguous, as she describes how her mother manages to pinch her nose in the closet door. Mariana, as well as seeing the door as destroying the image of elegance presented by her mother (which will be reiterated many times throughout the novel) sees it in personal and threatening terms: 'Ese miedo a la puerta no me abandonará nunca. El batiente estará siempre machucando algo, *separando, dejándome fuera*' (That fear of the door will never leave me. The closing door will always be crushing something, *separating, leaving me outside*) (13 [my emphasis]).

This first paragraph then, presents the central idea of the novel – the conflict between Mariana's adoration of her mother and the feeling that she is excluded by her. However, Mariana's idealisation of her mother does not allow that exclusion to be the fault of the beloved figure, but rather of some outside influence. In the case of Mariana and Luz, this takes the form of the narrator's father, her sister, Luz's friends and, finally, Teufel.

The tactical identification of girls with the image of their mother as strong or active is one aspect of the mother–daughter relationship that has already been remarked on. Such tactics are used both by Nellie in *Cartucho* and *Las manos de mamá*, and by Mariana in *La 'Flor de Lis'*, and have been described by Deutsch as a strategy for survival. Sayers writes:

> One of woman's main tasks, Deutsch stressed, is to preserve herself from the injuries to her self-esteem threatened by the masochism associated with mothering and woman's 'normal' social lot. Such self-preservation, she said, is helped by women identifying with an image of the mother as active and forceful. (Sayers 1991: 66)

Luz's physical fragility, as seen by Mariana, is contrasted by a strength of character and boldness of purpose that are traditionally seen as masculine attributes in Mexico. When Luz takes the girls to Acapulco by car, Mariana reveals her admiration for Luz's strength and independence. Luz decides to drive the girls to Acapulco in spite of having being told by others that it is imprudent, even dangerous, as they might be held-up by bandits, break down or have a flat-tyre. Luz appears to enjoy the criticism and Mariana evidently enjoys seeing this side of her mother, ' "¡Inconsciente!" Nos sonríe; hoy lleva puesta su cara de obstinación y *es la que mejor le sienta*. Su cara de que no pierde el tiempo. Su cara de que sabe' ('Irresponsible!' She smiles at us; today she is wearing her obstinate face and *it's the one that suits her best*. Her not wasting time face. Her knowing face) (44 [my emphasis]). After mile upon mile of driving through the heat in the rocky mountain ranges, reluctant to stop even when Sofía is sick, Luz, notes Mariana, seems to keep the car going, through pure willpower (44). After they arrive, Mariana describes how she watched out for the bandits so that she could warn her mother, 'que seguramente sabría qué hacer para que no nos asaltaran' (who would surely know what to do so that they wouldn't rob us) (46–47). Her faith in her mother's ability to deal with any situation is clearly revealed here. However, Mariana is able to appreciate that even for Luz it is not easy to be strong, even though she would never admit it (47).

Mariana's admiration of Luz's independence and strength of will contrasts with the view she has of her father, Casimiro. Poniatowska reverses the binary opposition that attributes strength of purpose to men and weakness or passivity to women. Elsewhere, she uses irony in her gentle mocking of these oppositions, as in this description of her grandfather walking ahead, 'El abuelo camina rápido; tiene un propósito, los hombres suelen tener un propósito. Por eso no camina con nosotros' (Grandfather walks quickly; he has a purpose, men usually have a purpose. That's why he doesn't walk with us) (26–27). Mariana's father, Casimiro, on the other hand, is not a 'typical' man. When he arrives in Mexico at the end of the war he is dressed as a soldier but he assures his family that he never killed anyone (91). He is unsure of himself and about what to do now that the war is over. Mariana says he only knows how to talk with his eyes (91) (again blurring the distinction between the senses). Although he plays the piano with great sensitivity he seldom plays a piece of music to the end, which suggests his lack of purpose. Mariana senses his weakness and observes that he is 'un hombre que tiembla; desde que se levanta a la vida, siempre algo lo desasosiega por dentro [. . .]. Se esconde de sus propósitos y cuando llegan, él ya no está [. . .]' (a man who trembles, from the time he gets up to face life, something always makes him uneasy inside [. . .]. He hides from his intentions and when they arrive, he is no longer there [. . .]) (91).

There are further references to Luz's active nature in the following exchanges which take place at Mariana's grandmother's house one afternoon. It is noteworthy for the women because it is unusual for someone of her class.

'Es una preciosura, y tan activa, no para ¿verdad?'/ 'Oye ¿que va a participar
en el torneo del Club de Golf Reforma?'/ 'Me contaron que hasta Cantinflas la
sacó a bailar la otra noche en una fiesta en su casa [. . .] salió en la revista
Social con un modelo de París [. . .]' (She's gorgeous, and so active, isn't
she?/Hey, I hear she's going to take part in the match at the Reform Golf
Club?/Someone told me that Cantinflas even asked her for a dance the other
night at a party in his house [. . .] she was in *Social* magazine in a gown from
Paris) (49). In reality Luz spends her afternoons playing gin rummy for
money, or at the *club hípico*, activities that to her are preferable to idling away
the hours chatting with the ladies of her class. The women also comment on
Luz's boldness, '¿Sabías que el otro día la vieron en Cuernavaca, sola,
manejando su coche? ¡Ah bárbara, tan audaz! ¿Qué así serán las europeas de
aventadas?' (Did you know that the other day she was seen in Cuernavaca, on
her own, driving her car? What a bold thing she is! Are all European women
so daring?) (50). They also help to perpetuate their own state of confinement
within the home by believing in the myths created to keep them there, 'Aquí
eso no se usa, deben tener mucho cuidado. Ustedes como se la viven en
Europa se les olvida que están en México, pero deben tener mucho cuidado.
Desde que se hizo la Revolución no puede uno de mujer andar sola' (That's
not done here, you should be very careful. The way you live in Europe you
forget that you are in Mexico, but you should be very careful. Since the Revolution a woman can't walk around alone) (50).[18]

It is during the trip to Acapulco that Mariana bares her soul about her feelings for her mother:

> Yo era una niña enamorada como loca. Una niña que aguarda horas enteras.
> Una niña como un perro. Una niña allí detenida entre dos puertas, sostenida
> por su amor. Una niña arriba de la escalera, esperando. Una niña junto a la
> ventana. El sólo verla, justificaba todas mis horas de esperanza. Claro,
> hacía otras cosas; iba a la escuela, me esmeraba, tocaba el piano, asistía a
> cuanta clase quería, hacía popo, me bañaba, me lavaba los dientes, quería
> merecerla, en el fondo, la esperaba y el sólo verla coronaba mis esfuerzos.
> Era una mi ilusión: estar con ella, jamás insistía yo frente a ella, pero sola,
> insistía cn mi ilusión, la horadaba, le daba vueltas, la vestía, hacía que se
> hinchara cada vez más dentro de mi cuerpo, como los globeros que de un
> tubito de hule hacen un mundo azul, rosa, amarillo, enorme. No me cabía
> en el cuerpo, me abarcaba toda, casi no podía moverme y menos en su
> presencia. (47)

---

[18] This is obviously a heavily ironic exposure of the *malinchismo* characteristic of the
Mexican upper middle-classes who praise anything European and criticise *lo mexicano*.
Another friend suggests that Mexican men are not good enough for glamorous, sophisticated women like Luz: '[. . .] no cabe duda de que el mundo se adquiere en el otro
continente, aquí somos todavía muy provincianos, Lucecita tenía que casarse bien, tan
linda ella' (there's no doubt that worldliness is acquired in the other continent, here we are
still very provincial. Lucecita had to marry well, lovely as she is) (50).

(I was a little girl madly in love. A girl who waits for hours. a girl like a dog. A girl kept there between two doors, sustained by her love. A girl at the top of the stairs, waiting. A girl next to the window. Just to see her, justified all my hours of waiting. Of course I did other things, I went to school, I played the piano, I went to as many classes as she wanted, I went to the loo, I bathed, I cleaned my teeth. Underneath it all, I wanted to deserve her; I waited for her and just seeing her, made the effort worthwhile. I had just one dream: to be with her. I never insisted on it when I was with her, but on my own, I stuck to my dream, I bore into it, I turned it around and around, I dressed it, I made it swell up bigger and bigger inside my body, like the balloon men who make an enormous pink, blue or yellow globe from a little rubber tube. She didn't fit in my body, she took me over completely, I could hardly move, even less so in her presence.)

The world of different colours created by the balloon artist is paralleled by that of Mariana's memories of her mother created by the different sensual impressions she receives.

One such impression during their early years living in France, is described by Mariana. At bed-time after she and Sofía have been bathed by their new nanny, towards whom they feel only hostility, she hears the sound of her mother's voice, which, for Mariana, is a voice in the wilderness of the incommunication that exists between the girls and their nanny. It reaches them, clear and bell-like, before she does:

> Nos miramos en silencio, dos pequeñas gentes y una grande, y en el desierto de nosotras tres oigo la voz, su voz de campana en el bosque; su rumor de bosque avanza por el corredor. Apresurada, empuja la puerta como suele hacerlo, con todo su cuerpo, de modo que la puerta la enmarca; cuadro viviente de si misma. (16–17)

> (We look at each other in silence, two small people and one big one, and in the desert between the three of us I hear her voice, her bell-in-the-forest voice; her rustle of the forest comes along the corridor. Hurriedly, she pushes open the door as usual, with her whole body, so that the doorway frames her; a living picture of herself.)

There are several points to note here regarding the relationship between Mariana and Luz. First, is the reappearance of the binary opposition culture/nature. The association between her mother and the good aspects of nature such as the rustling sound of the forest is a typically essentialist one which relates female to nature and male to culture. Secondly, Luz sweeps in dramatically, in a hurry as usual, inquires after her daughters, but does not wait for the answers. She chastises them for being grumpy – understandably so since they have been dumped with a new nanny they did not want, and whom, to add insult to injury, they find repulsive as she has a finger missing. Thirdly, she speaks loving words to them but leaves almost as soon as she has come in, which makes her words ring rather hollow: 'adiós mis chiquitas, buenas noches mis amores' (Good-bye my little ones, Good-night my loves). Finally, as she leans over to kiss them goodnight, Mariana describes her idealised figure. All of Mariana's senses come into play here as she sees the exaggerated whiteness of her mother's flesh, smells her perfume, feels the brush of Luz's hair against her cheek and hears the longed for words of endearment, '[. . .] veo sus pechos muy blancos, redondos, de pura leche, su piel de leche blanquísima, su perfume, el pelo que cae como una rama de árbol sobre mi cara fruncida, su cuello, oh mi mamá de flores' (I see her very white breasts, round, pure milk, her skin of whitest milk, her perfume, her hair that falls like the branch of a tree over my screwed-up face, her neck, oh my flower mother) (17).[19] Also, here, the binary oppositions civilisation/barbarism, black/white which have been so analysed by post-colonial theorists (especially Fanon and Bhabha) reveal the ambivalence of Mariana's later feelings about her *madre-patria*, for she idealises the white (European) mother but also loves her dark-skinned surrogate mother (Magda/Mexico). 'A mí la Santísima Virgen me tiene sin cuidado [. . .] Prefiero mil veces a la morenita de Magda, o a mamá' (I couldn't care less about the very holy Virgin [. . .] I prefer a thousand times little dark Magda, or mamma) (132–133). Mariana continues, 'me besa rápido llamándome "mi myosotis" palabra que guardo en mi mano' (she kisses me quickly and calls me 'my myosotis' a word which I keep in my hand) (17). Mariana treasures the term of endearment – *myosotis* is the botanical name for *nomeolvides* (forget-me-not) – which she keeps to diminish her feeling of loss.[20] Here it is the sense of hearing that is emphasised as she hears her mother's voice, the sound of her long evening dress trailing on the floor and the door closing between herself and her mother. The loneliness she feels is exacerbated, and the beat of her own heart (for which she substitutes that of the flower) accelerated, by the sudden emotion caused by her mother's presence: 'Oigo su voz a lo lejos. El vestido sigue barriendo el corredor. Se cierra una puerta. Me quedo sola con el nomeolvides aprisionado latiendo uno, dos, uno, dos, sus pequeños pálpitos azules' (I hear her voice in the distance. Her

[19] The whiteness of flesh is often associated with the (purity of the) Madonna, but here it seems to indicate Mariana's desire for her mother. The mother as erotic object is described by Freud as a normal part of the homoerotic relationship between mother and daughter (according to Lacan forbidden by patriarchy), which is later replaced by a male object, usually the father but in Mariana's case the priest. Christiane Olivier refers to 'that period in the life of little girls' in which '[. . .] bajo aspectos seductores y encantadores, nuestras hijas buscan inútilmente a alguien que "desee" su persona. Ellas se alejaron rápidamente de las faldas de la madre, comprendiendo que de allí no podían esperar ninguna salvación' ([. . .] under charming and seductive guise, our daughters search in vain for someone who will 'desire' them. They quickly distanced themselves from their mother's lap, understanding that they could expect no salvation there) (Olivier 1987: 131).

[20] However, according to the Collins Dictionary, 'Myosotis' is a plant with furry leaves, from the Greek *muos-otis* – mouse-ear. It may well be used with irony by Luz.

dress still sweeping along the corridor. A door closes. I'm left alone with the imprisoned forget-me-not, its little blue heart beating one, two, one two) (17).

The nature metaphor reappears in the following encounter between Mariana and her mother when they are on holiday by the sea. Her mother takes on the substance of water, a recurrent image – and one typically associated with the maternal figure – in much psychoanalytical theory.[21] However, here, the mother is unattainable, impalpable as the foam which disappears between Mariana's fingers, 'A traves del agua la veo a ella, su sonrisa, su aire de distracción. Quisiera abrazarla. Se me *deshace* en espuma' (Through the water I see her, her smile, her distracted air. I'd like to hug her. She dissolves in foam) (18 [my emphasis]).[22] This image of the mother juxtaposed with water recurs when the girls are taken to Vouvray on the Loire to escape from the shelling of Paris. This time her mother is commingled with the fine rain, but still unattainable. The words *inalcanzable* and *impalpable* are ones that are reproduced frequently in association with the narrator's mother:

> [. . .] mamá, de un día para el otro, viene a vivir con nosotras, dulce, inalcanzable como el agua dulce que cae del cielo. Se mezcla a la lluvia finita de Vouvray tan delgada que apenas se ve [. . .] Por la ventana veo caer una cortina de chorritos de agua, gota a gota; a través de un vidrio impalpable veo a mamá, longilínea, de cara al cielo con toda la lluvia cayéndole encima, dulce mi mamá de agua. Extiendo la mano para secar su rostro empapado. No la alcanzo. (23–24)

> (mamma, from one day to the next, comes to live with us, sweet, unattainable as the sweet water that falls from heaven. She is mixed with the fine rain of Vouvray – so fine you can hardly see it [. . .] Through the window I see a curtain of thin streams of water falling, drop by drop; through a pane of glass I see, untouchable, mamma, her figure lengthened, face turned to the sky with the rain falling on her, my sweet water-mother. I stretch out my hand to touch her soaking wet face. I can't reach her.)

---

[21] 'A large number of dreams often accompanied by anxiety and having as their content such subjects as passing through narrow spaces or being in water, are based on fantasies of intra-uterine life, of existence in the womb and of the act of birth' (Freud, *The Interpretation of Dreams* 1991: 524).

[22] Although quite different from the two words used in the following passage quoted (*impalpable* and *inalcanzable*), *deshacer* also connotes unattainability as her mother is seen as something without physical substance that cannot be held on to. Compare the way Poniatowska uses the sea here with Camus' use of the sea in 'La mère au plus près' (1953) as described by Ben Stoltzfus, '[. . .] his metaphorical exaltations barely veil a pre-oedipal longing for the mother. The pleasures he derives from proximity to the sea – *la mer* is a homonym for *la mère*, the mother – or embracing nature, although couched in the plenitude of presence, connote the nostalgia of absence, hence the coupling of love and death, joy and anguish, fulfillment and frustration that are manifest in the alternating of images of need and desire, failure and satisfaction' (Stoltzfus 1996: 105).

This interlude during which her mother is present is characterised by further references to nature, where the essentialist association between woman and nature is again presented as natural. When Sofía falls and hurts her arm while swinging on a door, the narrator wittily explains that in wartime it is not possible to pay so much attention to little girls as everything is in short supply, including parents – 'escasean las papas . . . , escasean los papás' – (potatoes are scarce, parents are scarce) and describes Sofía's injury in terms of the colours of nature. This time, therefore, it is her visual sense which takes precedence:

> [. . .] el brazo toma todos los colores de Vouvray; azul como los viñedos que se alinean en torno a la casa, morado como las hojas de parra, café de tierra, el mismo amarillo terroso de las cuevas en las que vive la gente [. . .] En el brazo de Sofía se dibujan paisajes, cielos oscuros antes de la tormenta, la grisura del Loire ancho y fuerte, los castaños pelones [. . .].
>
> (24)
>
> (her arm takes on the colours of Vouvray; blue like the vineyards lined up around the house, maroon like the climbing vine, earth-brown, the same earth yellow of the caves people live in [. . .] On Sofia's arm landscapes are drawn, dark skies before a storm, the greyness of the strong wide Loire, skinned chestnuts.)

When Mariana falls ill for the second time, Luz decides to take them to the south, to their grandparents' house. But no sooner do they arrive, than she abandons them and returns to Paris. The second section begins: 'Se va. Regresa a París. Nos deja con los abuelos' (She's leaving. She's going back to Paris. She's leaving us with our grandparents) (25). Life with the grandparents is characterised by going to Mass, delicious food, study under the tutelage of their grandfather (though Sofía refuses to participate) and games played with Sofía in which Mariana is the horse, whipped on by Sofía; or they are both dogs – but Mariana the one that seeks to be loved, petted and stroked. Here it is the sense of touch that predominates in Mariana's extremely poignant description:

> Yo dejo que me pasen la mano por el lomo, cosquillas, caricias, a todo me presto. Que me quieran, soy su perra, muevo la cola, que me quieran, que me rasquen la nuca, panza arriba, que me digan, que me tornen en torno a mis orejas largas y peludas, la trufa húmeda de mi nariz, mi cuello calientito, encimosa quiero más, panza arriba. (26)
>
> (I let them stroke my back, tickle me, caress me, I'm open to anything. Just so they'll love me, I'm their dog, I wag my tail, so they'll love me, so they'll scratch my neck, lying on my back, so they'll talk to me, twist my long furry ears around, the moist truffle of my muzzle, my nice warm neck, over-affectionate I ask for more, lying on my back.)

It is significant that Mariana is desirous of any attention at all, gentle or otherwise, as the rest of this paragraph reveals. Her sense of rejection as she compares herself with her primitive ancestors, surfaces once again:

> [. . .] acepto hasta la patada en el costillar, le saco sentido, todo tiene sentido hasta irme aullando con el mismo aullido de mi antepasado el pitecantropus erectus con su mazo en la mano, que se aleja, su cabeza aplanada, corre por el desierto, lejos de la manada que lo ha rechazado.
> (26)

> (I even accept a kick in the ribs, find meaning in it, everything has meaning even going off howling with the same howl as my ancestor Pithecanthropus Erectus with his club in his hand, who goes away, with his flattened head, runs through the desert, far from the herd that has rejected him.)

When her mother returns, Mariana's attention is directed once more to the sense of taste and she appreciates her food even more, savouring each mouthful, '[. . .] saca el chef un pollo que se derrite en la boca como mantequilla. Se acaba demasiado pronto. Nunca he vuelto a probar nada igual' (the chef takes out a chicken that melts in the mouth like butter. It's gone too quickly. I've never tasted anything like it since) (28); just as she does when they were holidaying together by the sea, 'Un helado praliné, con la galleta que lo acuchilla en una alta copa de plata perlada de frío. Me gusta encontrar con la lengua los trocitos de avellana' (A praline ice-cream, with the wafer stuck in the top in a tall silver cup frosted with cold. I like finding the little bits of hazelnut with my tongue) (18).

Luz is associated with light physically as well as metaphorically. On board the ship that is going to take them to Cuba, Mariana goes along the narrow passages and stairways, trying to find her way outside to the daylight which she compares to her mother. The purity of the fresh air, the clarity of the morning light, and the brilliance of the sea, together with the knowledge that she will be with her mother for several days, make her immensely happy. She compares Luz to various ethereal objects or gestures but they are also ephemeral and Mariana repeatedly makes felt her sense of loss in the following extract which also very poignantly describes Mariana's need to hold on to her mother, whom she feels is elusive:

> Esa mujer allá en la punta es mi mamá; el descubrimiento es tan deslumbrante como la superficie lechosa del mar. Es mi mamá. O es una garza. O un pensamiento salobre. O un vaho del agua. O un pañuelo de adiós al viento. Es mi mamá, sí, pero el agua de sal me impide fijarla, se disuelve, se ondea, vuelve a alejarse, oh mamá, déjame asirte. (29)

> (That woman at the end is my mamma; the discovery is as dazzling as the milky surface of the sea. It's my mamma. Or it's a heron. Or a salty thought. Or water vapour. Or a handkerchief waving farewell in the wind.

It's my mamma, yes, but the salt water prevents me from fixing her image,
she dissolves, ripples like a wave, becomes distant again, oh mamma, let
me hold on to you.)

The power of nature with which her mother is associated, is also responsible
for keeping mother and daughter apart in Mariana's eyes. She blames the sea,
the waves and the wind, but never Luz herself:

> La veo allá, volátil, a punto de desaparecer o de estallar en su jaula de
> huesos, a punto de caerse al mar; el viento se lo impide o la espuma más
> alta de la ola que va abriendo el barco; el viento también sostiene sus
> cabellos en lo alto; el viento ciñe su vestido alrededor de su cuerpo; ahora
> sí, alcanzo a ver como arquea las cejas y entrecierra los ojos para llegar
> más lejos. ¿Qué estará viendo? (29–30)

> (I see her there, volatile, about to disappear, to explode in her cage of
> bones, about to fall into the sea, the wind, or the foam of the highest wave
> made by the boat prevents her; the wind blows her hair up; the wind winds
> her dress tightly around her body; yes, now I can see how she arches her
> eyebrows and half closes her eyes to see further. What can she be looking
> at?)

This image of her mother with windswept hair and flowing garment is
reminiscent of paintings by Remedios Varo or Leonora Carrington (influenced by surrealism) who were painting such other-worldly images in
Mexico at the time La 'Flor de Lis' was written. Mariana again stresses the
other-worldliness of her mother, who, like the figures of such paintings,
appears to inhabit a different dimension, only occasionally crossing into that
in which Mariana and the rest of the people around her are situated. Mariana
attributes her unawareness of her daughter's presence to the noise made by
the ocean and the ship's engine. In an incident strikingly similar to that
found in Balún-Canán the little girl makes repeated efforts to gain her
mother's attention, including asking for divine intervention; the emphasis is
on sound:

> Ni siquiera me ha oído, no sabe que estoy parada junto a ella, en el mar no
> se oye el ruido que hacen los humanos, sus gritos se confunden con el
> chasqueo del agua, los motores se tragan la risa. Mamá estira el cuello
> hacia el mar, le jalo el vestido, voltea a ver sin mirarme. ¡Dios mío, dile que
> me vea! (30)

> (She hasn't even heard me, she doesn't know I am standing next to her, at
> sea you can't hear the noise humans make, their shouts become confused
> with the crash of water, the engines swallow the sound of laughter. Mamma
> stretches her neck out towards the sea, I pull at her dress, she turns to look
> without seeing me. 'Please God, tell her to look at me!')

Mariana finally makes her presence felt, and Luz takes her by the hand. But it is evident from her gratitude and the fact that she removes her hand when it becomes sweaty that she feels herself unworthy of her mother. Here the emphasis is on touch. She does not want Luz to feel any unpleasantness, knowing her to be unaccustomed to the realities of looking after children. The little girl's reaction is that of an inexperienced lover, immature and unsure of herself:

> 'Mamá.' Me toma de la mano sin decirme nada, y siento gratitud por su aquiescencia; nos quedamos las dos recargadas contra la barandilla, hasta que mi mano empieza a sudar y la deslizo fuera de la suya, maldigo esa mano que me falla cuando más la necesito. (29–30)

> ('Mamma.' She takes my hand without saying anything, and I am grateful for her acquiescence; we remain leaning on the railing, until my hand begins to sweat and I slip it out of hers. I curse that hand that lets me down when I need it most.)

This feeling of unworthiness is reiterated later when Mariana is watching her mother get ready to go out, wearing a different Designer dress each time, as well as 'different eyes'. Mariana is intimidated by her beauty and afraid to touch her and disturb her hair (38). Her feelings are not only (like those of the narrator of *Balún-Canán*) that she is unworthy of her mother, however; they are also destructive and stem from her belief that she is being abandoned each time her mother goes out. The juxtaposition of the feelings of love and hate experienced by Mariana towards her mother – a clear example of hetero-glossia – is nowhere more clearly presented than in the following extract. Here, emphasis is on the visual sense and the 'untouchable' quality of her mother and Mariana's idealisation of her mother's beauty contrasts with her violent fantasies about Luz's death:[23]

> La palidez de su rostro bajo la mata de pelo que parece pesarle en la nuca, echarle hacia atrás la cabeza, el cuello frágil de tan largo, el hueso en la nuca dispuesto a la guillotina; allí podría caer la pesada cuchilla, sangrarla, desnucarla, descerebrarla, descabezarla, separar su rostro de altos pómulos del resto del cuerpo volátil, intangible, intocable. (38)

> (The paleness of her face under the mass of hair which seems to weigh on her neck, pull her head back. Her neck, fragile in its length, the bone on the back of her neck ready for the guillotine; that's where the heavy blade could fall, make her bleed, cut her head off, decapitate her, separate that high-cheek-boned face from the rest of her volatile, unreachable, untouchable body.)

---

[23] According to much psychoanalytical data, such violent fantasies about the mother are quite common; see for example Mitchell (1990: 57).

The intangibility and unattainability of her mother is reiterated here by the narrator. Mariana's unrequited desire for physical contact with her mother leads her to make of Luz such a fragile icon, 'Porque nadie toca este cuerpo, nadie lo toma de la cintura; se volatilizaría, se rompería en el aire tan extremadamente delicado' (Because nobody touches that body, nobody takes it by the waist; it would evaporate, it would break up in the air it is so extremely delicate) (38). Touch and sight are juxtaposed, as they are by Nellie in *Las manos de mamá*, because Mariana, unable to touch her mother as much as she would wish too, substitutes that desire with her gaze, by looking. Thus, as in the description of her mother's milk-white breasts, her desire for her mother takes on sexual overtones, 'Entre sueños veo su falda al caminar; sus piernas bajo la levedad de la muselina; sus vestidos son ligeros, por el calor del trópico ahora que vivimos en le Mexique [. . .] Flota la tela en torno a su cintura' (Between dreams I see her skirt as she walks; her legs beneath the lightness of the muslin; her dresses are light because of the tropical heat now that we live in le Mexique [. . .]. The cloth floats around her waist) (39). Mariana recognises her own feelings of loss, and the fact that she is deceiving herself, when she imagines her mother is coming towards her, 'me hago la ilusión: "allí viene, viene hacia mí" ' (I convince myself: 'here she comes, she's coming towards me') (39). But, like Nellie, she is not even noticed by her mother, and her feeling of being left behind is again apparent, 'pero sus pasos la llevan hacia la puerta de la calle, la abre presurosa, *sin verme sale*, cierra tras ella, ya está fuera y *me he quedado atrás*' (but her steps take her towards the door of the street, she opens it quickly, *without seeing me she goes out*, she closes the door behind her, she's outside now and *I am left behind*) (39 [my emphasis]). This juxtaposition of Mariana's sexual idealisation of her mother's beauty and unattainability is restated in the following description of her playing a game with them: 'La miro saltar, joven, flexible, sus muslos de venado tembloroso, su cintura a punto de quebrarse, su pelo una riqueza caoba sobre el cuello. Al rato va a salir, siempre se va, no tenemos la fórmula para retenerla' (I watch her jump, young, flexible, her trembling deer thighs, her waist about to break, the rich mahogany hair on her neck. She's going to go out soon, she always goes, we don't have the formula to keep her here) (40). Mariana's voyeuristic behaviour is exacerbated by her mother's constant rejection of her daughter's demands for attention and affection, 'A veces la veo en su recámara, la riqueza caoba sobre la almohada, a punto de la somnolencia. Qué admirable su cuerpo delgado sobre la colcha. Se sabe mirada, vuelve la cabeza adormecida hacia la puerta, me adivina: "Déjame sola" murmura con una voz dulce "déjame sola" ' (Sometimes I see her in her bedroom, the rich mahogany on her pillow, on the point of drowsiness. How admirable her slender body is on the bedspread. She knows she is being watched, turns her sleepy head towards the door, guesses it is me, 'Leave me alone' she murmurs in a gentle voice 'Leave me alone') (40).

Mariana does not, however, think it is only she who is distanced from her mother. Even her father has to accept this strangeness in his wife who is always distracted or absent:

> A los que hablan con ella les desespera el hecho de que no parezca verlos, esa distancia que pone entre ella y los demás. Dan ganas entonces de sacudirla, 'Aquí estoy, veme.' Eso nadie se ha atrevido a hacerlo, ni siquiera papá. Hizo caso omiso de su distracción y se casó con la ausencia.
>
> (30)

> (It drives people who speak to her to despair that she appears not to see them, that distance that she puts between herself and others. You feel like shaking her then, 'Here I am, look at me.' No-one has dared to do that, not even papa. He ignored her absent-mindedness and married absence itself.)

This image of her mother as mysterious, absent, even when she is present, is found again later on in the novel; once more in the context of nature (surrounded by the green of the ferns). There is also an image of saintliness (the ferns form a halo around her). After several days away she has returned and sits with them, but by the third spoonful of food she is elsewhere again and although she looks at them, Mariana knows that she does not see them:

> Durante varios días no la vemos y de repente la presiento 'Allí viene'. La envuelve la soledad verde esperanza; la nimba el verdor de los helechos. Ni cuenta se da del misterio que representa. ¿De dónde viene? ¿En dónde estuvo? Se sienta a la mesa con nosotros y ya para la tercera cuchara está ausente, sé que ya no nos ve aunque ponga sobre nosotras su mirada. (48)

> (For several days we don't see her and then suddenly I sense her presence 'Here she comes'. Solitude green as hope envelops her, the green of the ferns forms a halo around her. She does not even realise how mysterious she is. Where does she come from? Where has she been? She sits at the table with us and already by the third spoonful she is absent, I know that she no longer sees us even when her gaze rests upon us.)

Not only does Mariana feel her mother does not see her, but also that she does not listen to her. She describes how they have to go to all kinds of after-school activities in the heat of the afternoons, travelling by bus with the *hoi polloi* when they would evidently prefer to be at home with Luz. As usual it is the bold Sofía who speaks up for them while Mariana says; 'Guardo silencio porque sé que no me oye' (I keep quiet because I know she doesn't hear me) (48).

The absence of physical contact, of *touch*, in her relationship with her mother compels Mariana – just like Nellie in Campobello's novellas – to *look* at her mother with admiration and also to compare her with other women, '*Ver*la caminar descalza sobre la alfombra y sentarse de pronto en posición de loto, las palmas hacia arriba, me hace *espiar* a las mujeres del mundo a ver si reconozco en ellas los mismos movimientos' (To see her walk barefoot on the carpet and sit suddenly in the lotus position, palms turned upwards, makes me spy on the women of the world to see if I recognise the same movements in them) (40 [my emphasis]). This looking makes her into an observer, like the girl-narrators of *Balún-Canán* and *Cartucho*. (Mariana's introspective nature is compounded by Luz's description of her and her sister (40) which emphasises Sofía's physicality and Mariana's propensity for intellectual pursuits.)

Mariana's idealisation of her mother's physical appearance is not total either, however. When Luz collects the girls from school, it is a special rather than routine event for Mariana, 'No todos los días viene por nosotras a la escuela, pero cuando lo hace tengo una golondrina en el pecho, sus plumas en la garganta. Me salta a la boca, no puedo hablar' (She doesn't come to school for us every day, but when she does I have a swallow in my breast, its feathers in my throat. It jumps into my mouth, I can't speak) (41). Mariana has mixed feelings of pride and embarrassment at the way her mother's appearance and behaviour make her stand out; so much so that she even 'hears' her perfume.[24] She remarks on the compliment directed at her mother's prettiness but also on the fact that her mother pays the school fees late and does not try to maintain a dignified appearance like the other mothers:

> Llega riente, fluye, 'oye, qué bonita es tu mamá', sacuda sus cabellos de piloncillo derretido, camina dando saltos hacia la Dirección, paga la colegiatura con retraso, fluye, florea sobre el pavimento del patio de recreo, da unos pasitos de baile, torea, escoge un avión pintado con gis y brinca del cuadro uno al tres, ríe y yo me avergüenzo, qué dirán, que ésa no es una mamá, que es un chango, oigo hasta su perfume. Las otras mamás atraviesan el patio derechitas, no tintinean como la mía. (41)

> (She arrives, laughing, fluid, 'hey, your mum is really pretty', she shakes her molasses-brown hair, walks and leaps her way to the secretary's office, pays the fees late, flows, makes a flourish on the tarmac of the playground, makes a few dance steps, bull-fighting moves, chooses a plane drawn with chalk and jumps from square one to three, laughs and embarrasses me, what will people say, that she's not a mother, she's a chimpanzee, I even hear her perfume. The other mothers cross the patio walking erect, they don't tinkle across like mine.)

The juxtaposition of the two animal images – one deer-like and the other ape-like (clearly positive and negative respectively) – mirror the confusion in Mariana's mind and the ambivalent nature of her feelings. This ambivalence is intimately related to Mariana's sense of loss at her mother's absence and

---

24 This is clearly an example of synaesthesia.

consequent feeling of 'lack'.[25] The expression of Mariana's sense of loss is expressed in a small sub-section, indicated by a single flower, towards the end of the third section, 'De pronto la miro y ya no está. Vuelvo a mirarla, la define su ausencia' (Suddenly I look at her and she is no longer there. I look at her again, she is defined by her absence) (42). Earlier in this chapter I referred to the idea that, for Mariana, Luz exists in a different dimension. This is a strategy adopted by the little girl to make sense of her feeling of loss, caused by her mother's elusiveness. Mariana consoles herself with the idea that even though Luz may not express her love overtly, she nevertheless needs Mariana's love. However, the strategy is overshadowed by the negative comments surrounding it:

> No puedo seguirla, no entiendo hacia qué espacio invisible se ha dirigido, qué aire inefable la resguarda y la aísla; desde luego ya no está en el mundo y por más que manoteo no me ve, permanece siempre fuera de mi alcance. Sé que mi amor la sustenta, claro, pero su ausencia es sólo suya y en ella no tengo cabida. (42)

> (I cannot follow her, I do not understand towards which invisible space she has gone, what ineffable air shields her and isolates her, clearly she is no longer in the world and as much as I wave, she does not see me, she always remains out of my reach. I know my love keeps her going, of course, but her absence is hers alone and there is no place in it for me.)

LUZ AND LUZBEL

In this sub-section I have juxtaposed Mariana's mother – *Luz* – signifying light, with the priest –*Teufel* – signifying devil, Prince of Darkness, *Luzbel* in Spanish. This suggests another binary opposition: good/evil and alludes to the way in which Poniatowska challenges, and even reverses, some of the binary oppositions fixed as 'male' and 'female', thus transgressing the hierarchy established by the patriarchal order. According to the traditional, patriarchal view, the dark and all that is associated with it: secrecy, sin, the night, the moon and witchcraft were considered the realm of women. In *La 'Flor de Lis'* however, Poniatowska turns this around not only by presenting her mother as the embodiment of beauty and light (a sort of Madonna figure – but less passive) and the priest as dark and sometimes almost evil, but also by making

---

25 According to Lacan, 'A little girl [. . .] is the *lack* itself due to her lack of a phallus (in spite of the bogus status of the phallus which lacks any justification for the power it confers, being merely a signifier)' (Lacan 1996: 274). Minsky writes that the system of binary oppositions associated with 'having' and 'not having', that is: positive/negative, power/lack, masculinity/femininity, etc. that has been produced, based on that status, is therefore arbitrary (Minsky 1996: 159–60).

both these figures more complex characters than their names would suggest. Teufel's physical appearance and influence over the girls suggests he is evil:

> Clavaba sus ojos hundidos y muy negros con mil alfileres dentro en el rostro del interlocutor, clavaba su cara blanca y su pelo negro, el levísimo sudor de su frente pálida, su olor a hombre (y francés) en la retina de la joven en turno y naturalmente todas solicitamos visita privada. (126)

> (He fixed his deep-set, very black eyes with a thousand needles in them on the face of his interlocutor, he fixed his white face and black hair, his pale forehead sweating slightly, his man's (Frenchman's) smell in the retina of the young woman whose turn it was and naturally, we all asked for a private visit.)

In fact he is a radical who tries to develop a social conscience in the girls. While Luz, with her white skin and fragile, Madonna-like appearance, neglects her family in order to devote herself to the priest with whom she is obsessed (not merely spiritually). The significance of this particular binary also emerges in Teufel's insistence on calling Mariana *Blanca*, even though she objects at least twice, and the fact that it is his dark, slightly Mephisto-phelean aspect that attracts Mariana to him. Her best friend Casilda is also dark-haired, 'Sus cabellos cortos, negros y azules envuelven su rostro y la hacen parecer un San Sebastián sonriente y sin saetas' (Her short hair, black and blue, frames her face and make her look like a smiling San Sebastián without the arrows) (127). This image is slightly erotic and clearly a seductive one for Mariana. At the same time, Mariana does not care for the Virgin Mary. Rejecting the different evocation (to the one describing Luz's breasts) of whiteness and goodness associated with the Madonna she declares, 'Prefiero mil veces a la Morenita de Magda, o a mamá. Luz, Luz, y Luz, ésa sí me enamora y no la estatua de ojos bajos' (I prefer a thousand times dark little Magda, or mamma. Luz, Luz and Luz, she inspires love in me not that statue with eyes cast down) (132–33). Clearly it is not so much the physical appear-ance, as the temperament associated with the Madonna that Mariana rejects. She chooses as her role-models women who are dynamic rather than saintly:

> Todavía si la Madona corriera como Luz o jugara o perdiera sus llaves, pero no hace nada, nada salvo poner cara de mustia, cara de víctima, cara de mártir. Para mujeres, mi mamá: Luz. O mi abuela. O de perdida tía Francisca o tía Esperanza que podría cargar Catedral sobre sus hombros'.
> (132–33)

> (If the Madonna at least ran like Luz or played about or lost her keys, but she does nothing, nothing except put on a gloomy face, a victim's face, a martyr's face. For women, give me my mamma: Luz. Or my grandmother. Or at least Aunt Francisca or Aunt Esperanza who could carry a Cathedral on her shoulders.)

Poniatowska plays again with the concept of light and darkness in the sub-section entitled EMITTE LUCEM TUAM ET VERITATEM TUAM. Engaged in her tasks as altar girl with her colleague Leticia, Mariana admits she only wants to look towards what for her is a forbidden space, the priest's bedroom. She can see a light in his room across the garden and the dark, ivy-covered house, to which she has no access, looks to her tantalisingly like 'la torre donde vive el mago' (the tower where the magician lives) (134). There is ambiguity about what happens to the girls who do go into his room, 'Entrar allí es una transgresión, sólo llama a las privilegiadas' (To go in there is a transgression. Only the privileged are called by him) (134). The suggestion is that they are not merely praying together, 'salen con las mejillas enrojecidas, el pelo alborotado, las faldas desarregladas, el olor y la mirada de quien acaba de aprender algo definitivo para su vida' (they emerge with their cheeks flushed, their hair untidy, their skirts awry, and the smell and the look of one who has just learned something that will define their life) (134). There is also a clear indication of the priest's inner struggle to maintain his religious vows, 'Hoy, sentado en medio del refectorio sobre una silla de madera, el sacerdote luchó con Luzbel' (Today, sat in the middle of the refectory on a wooden chair, the priest fought with Satan) (134). When Mariana, following the example of the other girls, does go into the priest's room, she finds the cave-like atmosphere heavy with tobacco smoke and the darkness of the room broken by a single lamp. She notices that his voice also is sometimes 'a cave' and his fingers so yellowed by nicotine as to be almost black, in fact she observes that, in some way, everything in the room is black (143–44). Her description compounds the image of the too-worldly priest.

Many of the sub-sections in the second half of the book concerning Mariana's relationship with Teufel are preceded by a heading in Latin.[26] These are an ironic allusion to the Catholic Mass, still said in Latin at that time, but also bear relevance to the content of the text. For example, the third sub-section from the end has the heading ERGO. MALEDICTE DIABOLE. RECOGNOSCE SENTENTIAM TUAM ET DA HONOREM DEO VIVO ET VERO (258).[27] This part is written with a retrospective, third-person narrator, 'Basta cerrar los ojos para encontrar a Mariana en el fondo de la memoria' (It is enough to close one's eyes to find Mariana in the depths of one's memory), rather than with the first-person 'yo' (I) and the present tense used throughout the rest of the novel, which gives a sense of immediacy and reflects Mariana's feelings at the time. This is another example of multivocality which, as in the works by Campobello, Castellanos and Garro, reveals the presence of a frag-mented self and shows the difficulty that occurs in the use of the first person. The eruption of an 'other' voice has, again, a distancing function which

[26] These are printed in capital letters.
[27] 'Therefore accursed Devil reconsider your intentions and honour the true and loving God.' I am indebted to my father, Terence Hurley, for his translations from the Latin.

renders that narrative more 'objective'. With Mariana's self-absorption
having been set aside temporarily, the third-person narrator here is able to
comment 'objectively' on the fragility and loneliness of women divorced
from reality and taken-in by so-called 'saints' like Teufel, so human in his
failings. The use of the retrospective and the other voice suggests that this is
an example of self-criticism by Mariana as much as a criticism of the other
women of her family or class. The change in narrator here is similar to the
change from first-person narrator in Parts One and Three to third person in
Part Two of *Balún-Canán*, where another (objective) voice describes the situation of the Argüello family. In *La 'Flor de Lis'* the priest's human imperfection is clearly stated in the following description of him by Mariana: 'Un
hombre que come carne y mastica y ronca, un hombre que bosteza y pregunta
suspicaz "¿En qué piensas?", y a quien le ha dado por añadir rencoroso a lo
largo de los años: "si es que piensas" [. . .]' (A man who eats meat, chews and
snores, a man who yawns and asks suspiciously 'What are you thinking
about?' and who over the years has taken to adding bitterly: 'if you do think'
(258–259). Seeing how the women of her family were taken in by this
unlikely 'saint' is the reason, explains the narrator, that Sofía is getting
married so young, 'quiere asir la mano del hombre, cercar la realidad, pertenecer' (she wants to hold the hand of a man, hold on to reality, belong)
(259). Once again her practicality contrasts with Mariana's more thoughtful,
romantic nature.

With reference to Mariana's (above-mentioned) unrequited love, one sub-
section has the heading QUIA TU ES. DEUS. FORTITUDO MEA; QUARE ME
REPPULISTI. ET QUARE TRISTIS INCEDO DUM AFFLIGIT ME INIMICUS?
(201).[28] In it Mariana reveals her feelings for the priest, her chagrin that he
does not repay the attention she pays him, or treat her like the woman she feels
herself to be, and her subsequent envy of the other women in her family whom
he does treat as women. She expresses her infatuation, '[. . .] Teufel va a
darnos una conferencia y lo amo, quiero oírlo, quiero verlo, quiero que me
hable, y después, regresar a casa con él, los dos juntos, él y yo, solos, sin Luz,
sin Francisca, sin Sofía, sin las advertencias de institutriz de Casilda, sin una
sola compañera del retiro' (Teufel is going to give us a lecture and I love him,
I want to see him, I want him to talk to me and then go back home with him,
the two of us, him and me, alone, without Luz, without Francisca, without
Sofía, without Casilda's schoolmarm warnings, without a single companion
from the retreat) (202).

The ambivalent feelings felt by Mariana towards her mother reappear in
her relationship with the priest. This ambivalence is discernible in the heading
AB HOMINE INIQUO ET DOLOSO ERUE ME (126).[29] The sub-section then

---

[28] 'Because you are God, my strength. Why have you repulsed me and why do I go
sadly when inflicted with hostility?'

[29] 'From the wicked and deceitful man, take me (away).'

begins with, 'Con el padre Teufel, desde el primer momento una expectación anormal nos invadió' (With Father Teufel, from the start, we were filled with abnormal expectations). The priest chastises the girls in mocking tones, for studying 'safe' subjects, such as History of Art and Literature that will keep them apart from the rest of the people in their cocoon of privilege, rather than something 'useful' such as nursing, teaching, dress-making or pharmacy that will enable them to serve humanity, 'Pobrecitas niñas empañadas en cavar su propio tedio. ¿Cuándo van a servir a los demás? ¿Cuándo van a perderse en los demás?' (Poor little girls, compelled to dig the hole of your own tedium. When are you going to serve others? When are you going to lose yourselves in others?) (120). The ambivalence in Mariana's attitude is due to the fact that she does not like what he says to them, but knows that what he says is true.[30]

'OTHER' VOICES

The use of psychoanalytical criticism is particularly appropriate with regard to La 'Flor de Lis' in view of Mariana's more objective comments about her feelings for her mother:

> No es que la extrañe, es que la traigo adentro. Hablo con ella todo el tiempo, hablo con ella en la lengua del sueño, me acompaña su pelo flotante, la expresión triste de sus ojos de agua profunda. Espero sus respuestas dentro de mí y sigo contándole todo hasta el momento de poner la cabeza sobre la almohada. Y todavía después sigo hablando con ella; espero a que me responda en el lenguaje del sueño. *Más tarde en la vida una psicoanalista argentina me dirá: 'Ya deje en paz a su madre, que ni la quiere como usted la quiere, olvide esa obsesión, no le conviene.*
>
> (95 [my emphasis])

> (It's not that I miss her, I just carry her with me. I talk to her all the time, I talk to her in dream language, her floating hair, the sad expression of her deep-water eyes accompany me. I wait for her answers in my mind and still tell her everything until I put my head on my pillow. And even then I carry on talking with her; I wait for her answer in dream language. Later in life, an Argentine psychoanalyst will tell me: 'Leave your mother in peace. She doesn't even love you the way you love her. Forget this obsession, it's not good for you.)

---

[30] It is no coincidence that Elena Poniatowska's ambition for her writing has been to serve people by giving a voice to those in Mexico who have no voice: 'Durante casi treinta años yo pensé que yo debía nada más estar al servicio de causas sociales' (For thirty years I thought I should only be at the service of social causes); at the same time believing that her fiction or more personalised writing was of no interest: 'que yo debía de olvidar totalmente las ideas que a mí se me ocurrían en la mañana acerca de tal o cual cosa' (that I should forget totally the ideas that occurred to me in the mornings about this and that) (Dimitriou 1990: 130).

Here, the retrospective (authorial) adult voice emerges to replace that of the teenager sent away to convent school. Mariana's obsession is such that it is as if she were haunted by her mother. The teenage voice has gothic overtones:

> Todo el tiempo pienso en ella; la veo mientras me baño, se atraviesa frente a mí, me raya el paisaje como la lluvia, se para frente al árbol negro que miro por la ventana. De pronto presiento que camina tras de mí; vuelvo la cabeza y se levanta la construcción opresiva del convento, sus muros enmohecidos, el musgo casi negro que los calza, qué húmedo país [. . .]).
>
> (97)

> (I think of her all the time; I see her while I am bathing, she crosses in front of me, she streaks my landscape like the rain, she stands in front of the black tree that I look at through the window. Suddenly I have a presentiment that she is walking behind me; I turn my head and the opressive convent building rises up, its walls covered in mildew, moss that is almost black, what a humid country [. . .].)

The multivocality of *La 'Flor de Lis'* lies not just in the voice of the textual author and the different voices of the narrator – as privileged European aristocrat, as lonely little girl, as self-obsessed teenager, as proud Mexican, but also in the appearance of 'other' voices. Mariana's story is, in many ways, an awakening, or a spiritual journey as she comes to learn, through the process of separation from her mother and individuation, that her situation is one of privilege and her self-importance absurd. Teufel, who is a mixture of Rasputin and a priest of liberation theology, can be seen as responsible for the fact that Mariana, in spite of her privileged, aristocratic background, became Poniatowska, a courageous and dedicated journalist who speaks out for those who are not permitted or supposed to speak out for themselves. However, according to Lemaître, who was a contemporary of Poniatowska's, Teufel (unlike many other characters in the novel) is a fictional figure (Lemaître 1990–91: 28) and symbolises the author's own ideology (Lemaître: 34); in which case, he provides further evidence of the multivocality in *La 'Flor de Lis'*. This ideology is expressed when Teufel harangues Mariana to reject her privileges and genealogy:

> 'El mundo tiene que renovarse. Hay que destruir a la sociedad a que usted pertenece, hacerla trizas con sus prejuicios, su vanidad. Su impotencia moral y física [. . .] Las únicas capaces de abolir las clases sociales son las mujeres, las mujeres que pueden tener hijos con quienes quieran y en donde sea.' (146)

> (The world has to be renewed. The society you belong to has to be destroyed, its prejudices and vanities cut to pieces. Its moral and physical impotence [. . .] The only ones capable of abolishing social classes are women, women who can have children with whom and wherever they like.)

Section 26 deals with the acute loneliness felt by Mariana as her mother becomes ill following Teufel's banishment. Luz's treatment of Mariana is designed to remind her of the fact that, in spite of her privileged position, she is only human. When Luz wonders out loud if the priest might not be a saint and Mariana naïvely asks her, 'Y yo también ¿algún día seré una santa?', her mother's reply puts her in her place, 'Tú, Mariana, tú eres una ranita hinchada de orgullo' (You, Mariana, you are a little frog puffed up with pride) (241).

Part of Mariana's process of growing up involves being able to see things from more than one point of view. When she finds that her interest in the Mexican Revolution is not shared by Luz, whose unexpected response when she tries to talk to her about the revolutionaries is, 'No me hables de ellos, son puros bandidos' (Don't talk to me about them. They are a load of bandits) (47), Mariana consults her grandmother's friend, Mr Chips. He explains the reason for Luz's reactionary attitude, 'Tu familia perdió todas sus haciendas' (Your family lost all their lands).[31] Poniatowska uses this incident – and others – to voice popular criticism of the Mexican government. She takes interest in the conversations between adults in other people's houses and discovers that they believe that, 'Los políticos son los mismos ladrones que hicieron la Revolución' (The politicians are the same thieves who fought the Revolution) (47–48).[32] Although here, this is the view expressed by society's élite, it is also one of the main themes of Poniatowska's books about the two disasters in Mexico which were caused by corruption in the political system: the massacre of innocent people in Tlatelolco by the *granaderos*[33] in 1968, and the collapse of the supposedly earthquake-proof buildings in the centre of Mexico City, resulting in 1985 in the death and homelessness of thousands of people.

Among the 'other' voices that emerge between the lines that represent Poniatowska/Mariana's voice, is that of Luz. Like the landowning people of Ixtepec who were left behind by progress and industrialisation, Luz (as the daughter of the Mexican landed aristocracy) should have become an anachronism in the modern 'democratic' nation but, in fact, she is merely restricted by what are seen as the norms of acceptable behaviour for someone of her gender and class. She is able largely to ignore these restrictions, however, until the arrival of Casimiro in Mexico, who, in spite of being a weak man, unsure of himself, is nevertheless *su señor*. Mariana describes the change, 'Desde que él está mamá es distinta; cuando dice algo aguarda su aquiescencia; los ojos de

[31] This is what actually happened to the family of Paula Amor – Poniatowska's mother.

[32] As explained in a previous chapter, those in power after the Revolution (many of the original idealists having been assassinated) were the ones who benefited most from the expropriation of good land, not the peasants.

[33] A specially formed and brutal brigade of riot police which was disbanded after the massacre at Tlatelolco in 1968.

azúcar quemada se han oscurecido; antes era más libre, su pelo flotaba más, su vestido, sobre todo su vestido' (Since he is here, mamma is different; when she says something she waits for his acquiescence; her caramel eyes have become darker; before she was freer, her hair floated more, and her dress, especially her dress) (88). Luz's story appears in the novel in written form, when Mariana reads her diary. She comments on her relationship with Casimiro, the lack of communication between them and her situation as a woman, 'mis diálogos sin respuesta con Casimiro, las preguntas que no nos hemos hecho, las palabras no dichas, a tal punto que parece que no tenemos nada que decirnos' (my dialogues with Casimiro that have no reply, the questions we haven't asked each other, the words left unsaid, to the point where it seems we have nothing to say to one another) (207). She reveals an awareness that class differences make women different.[34] 'Me pregunto si Lupe en el planchador se detendrá un solo momento a preguntarse: ¿Dónde estoy? ¿Quién soy? ¿Qué quiero realmente? o si simplemente amanece contenta con lo que hace' (I wonder if Lupe, when she is ironing, stops for a moment and asks herself, Where am I? Who am I? What do I really want? or if she simply gets up happy with what she does) (207). Finally, she comments on the way women of her generation are not encouraged to be independent and think for themselves or even exist for themselves but only to serve others, 'Las mujeres estamos siempre a la espera, creo, dejamos que la vida nos viva, no nos acostumbran a tomar decisiones, giramos, no damos la vuelta, regresamos al punto de partida, nunca he querido nada para mí, no sé pedir, soy imprecisa y soy privilegiada' (We women are always waiting, I think, we let life live us, we are not used to making decisions, we go around things, we don't change radically and we go back to the starting point. I've never wanted anything for myself, I don't know how to ask, I'm vague and privileged) (207).

If Luz is expected to be just a wife and mother, not a woman, Mariana and Sofía's freedom is also restricted by their father's presence. When they go again to Acapulco, this time it is Casimiro who drives, 'Él maneja. Hace bulto en el asiento. Es el hombre de la casa. Nos mira por el retrovisor. Sofía y yo tenemos papá. No vomitamos' (He drives. He fills the seat. He's the man of the house. He looks at us in the driving mirror. Sofía and I have a father. We don't throw up) (89). She adds with irony, 'A lo mejor vomitábamos por falta de señor' (Perhaps we threw up because we didn't have a man of the house). Similarly when he discovers the girls are climbing trees and showing their knickers he curtails that activity with the words, '¿Son niñas o son changos?' (Are you girls or are you monkeys?) (88). Mariana describes this loss of freedom, where spontaneity (Luz as a woman not just a mother) is replaced by

---

[34] One of the major criticisms of second wave feminism of the 1960s and 1970s was its lack of awareness of issues of race, class and ethnicity and its tendency towards a monolithic model. Critics of this model include: bell hooks, Bonny Zimmerman, Cherrié Moraga and Gloria Anzaldúa.

regimentation (Casimiro as soldier) thus, 'Antes vivíamos a la hora del recreo, el día entero era de los encantados, siempre en los árboles, ahora hemos bajado a la banqueta y las banquetas son serias, grises y monocordes, llevan a un lado, tienen una finalidad, no se les ocurre nada fuera del camino' (Before we used to enjoy life, the whole day was enchanting, always in the trees, now we have come down to the pavement and pavements are serious, grey and monotonous, they lead somewhere, they have an end, nothing out of the ordinary occurs to them) (88).

Mariana's relationship with and separation from, her mother, then, represent her links with Europe and her leaving behind of the Old World with its rigid class system and aristocracies. The perpetuation of gender roles that the mother–daughter relationship and a 'certain kind of mothering' implies, is enunciated by the use of binary oppositions and references to the senses. Mariana's strong feelings for her mother are heavily underscored by descriptions related to touch, smells, and sounds and by the almost voyeuristic visual images of Luz created by Mariana. Luz is the figure that, for Mariana, represents desire (that which can never be satisfied) and 'lack' (that which can never be attained).

Magda, the Mexican nanny and maid on the other hand, represents Mariana's adaptation to, and, eventually, acceptance by, her newly adopted 'mother' country. Mariana's separation from her mother and individuation is aided not only by Magda, but also by her Mexican friends (many of whom are also descendants of European families) and by the French priest. The jealousy aroused in Mariana by the priest's relationship with her mother is provoked both by her infatuation with the priest and by her obsession with her mother that continues into adulthood until the psychoanalyst tells her to leave her mother in peace as she does not even reciprocate the love. Perhaps it is more accurate to say that she does not smother Mariana with obsessive love, as it appears that Mariana survives her 'neglect' by her mother, just as Nellie and the niña of Balún-Canán do. It is arguable that Luz is a better mother to Mariana than to Sofía, as she is more concerned about her future. She does not want Mariana to be too Mexican, marry a Mexican, or marry too young (as she believes Sofía has done) but rather, thinks that she should be sent to Paris to see a bit of the world and lose her provincialism. Mariana, however, at the end of the novel, describes her feeling of being Mexican and her enjoyment of the sights, sounds, smells and tastes of the city. Mexico for her is many things; a stone bench, the slowness with which people move in the hot sun, violent emotion. The strong love she feels for Luz is matched by her feelings for Mexico, 'Me gusta sentarme al sol en medio de la gente, esa gente, en mi ciudad, en el centro de mi país, en el ombligo del mundo' (I like to sit in the sun amongst the people, those people, in my city, in the centre of my country, the belly-button of the world) (261). Mexico and her own mexicanness are represented in Mariana's mind by that distinctively Mexican delicacy – the *tamal*, made of maize meal, the staple of life for the people of Mesoamerica,

and chilli, which gives it its distinctive piquancy. The *flor de lis* of the restaurant name, also represents Mariana's aristocratic European ancestry. In order
to become more Mexican, however, she rejects the tame ideas of the European
aristocracy, 'lárguense con sus peinetas de diamantes y sus cabellos cepil-
lados cien veces, yo no quiero que mis ideas se amansen bajo sus cepillos de
marfil y heráldicas incrustadas' (get lost with your diamond combs and your
hair brushed a hundred times, I don't want my ideas to become meek under
ivory hair-brushes inlaid with your family shields) (260). The closest she
wants to come to aristocratic heraldry is the restaurant the 'Flor de Lis' where
she habitually goes to buy *tamales*.

The many voices that appear through the narrator and the other protagonists – Luz, Teufel, Casimiro, Sofía, Magda and Mariana's grandmothers –
represent the diversity of voices that make up her family background and
influences (and, at the same time, the diverse nature of the Mexican people) as
well as her own different identities as she seeks to find the one with which she
feels most comfortable.

CONCLUSION

The central concerns that have been addressed in this book are the ways in which gender, myths about women and the mother–daughter relationship are manipulated in patriarchal society in order to perpetuate them; and the ways in which the multivocal texts produced by Campobello, Garro, Castellanos and Poniatowska reveal this fact by giving a voice to those on its margins.

Given the importance of motherhood and multivocality in the novels of all four authors, my textual analysis has confirmed that gender is crucial to the position of these women writers as subjects in Mexico and that a serious study of writing by women must take gender into consideration.[1] An exploration of the myths about women is imperative, therefore, when exploring the concept of motherhood in patriarchal society, as the myth of the selfless mother, the *madre abnegada*, is one of the most powerful propagated by patriarchy. This particular myth has been emphasised during certain periods of occidental history. The years following the Revolution, when the Mexican government undertook its programme of nation-building as it attempted to incorporate Mexico into international capitalism, is one such period.

As regards multivocality, my objective in this book has been to explore and reveal the ways in which these writers present alternative discourses to the official discourse of the status quo. This included a discussion of the strategies adopted by those on the margins in Mexican society, in this case female children and adolescents, to overcome the barriers that stand between their subject-position and their search for an identity with which they can feel comfortable. My project entailed looking for insights into the reality of being female in Mexico during the first half of the twentieth century and disclosing the alternative realities regarding motherhood and childhood revealed in the semi-autobiographical novels of these four writers.

Analysis of the novels, conducted by means of alternative feminist criticism (which is multidisciplinary, incorporating readings from Bakhtin, psychoanalytical, literary, and socio-historical theorists) has revealed that the heteroglossia and polyphony in the discourses present in the texts offer alternative visions of the Mexican Revolution and its aftermath, of the mother–daughter relationship and of certain myths about women. The autobiograph-

---

[1]   For a discussion of writing and gender see Shaw (1997); Castro-Klarén (1985); Traba (1985).

ical character of the novels (detected through a combination of biographical and textual analysis, and psychoanalytical criticism to study the ways the authors use references to the senses) was also taken into consideration, where relevant, as I believe that all four writers: Campobello, Garro, Castellanos and Poniatowska, have used their fiction – to borrow Ramblado Minero's words – 'with the purpose of self-representation, and exemplification of the female condition' (Ramblado Minero 1999: 313). As regards writing by Mexican women at this stage in their literary development, the personal is indeed political (as is the case in general for women writing in Latin America, where prevailing myths about women are still accepted currency). Thus, in my exploration of the symbolic use of sensory description, I have given precedence to the unconscious over the poetic; however, the combination of the two clearly has transgressive potential, as I suggested earlier with reference to Kristeva.[2]

The freeing of unconscious desire and challenging of male-defined categories, occurs to varying degrees in the five texts discussed in this book. By approaching the problem from the mother/daughter perspective, I have attempted to reveal the ways in which motherhood – as defined by patriarchy – is used to perpetuate existing gender categories and stereotypes. My argument has also encompassed, therefore, the unconscious, socio-political and stylistic implications in the use of binary oppositions by Campobello, Garro, Castellanos and Poniatowska, to deconstruct myths about women – particularly mothers – and to challenge such gender stereotypes. The use of binary oppositions (a tool used by patriarchy to establish and maintain gender difference) is, according to Kristeva, a legitimate means of achieving such a challenge. Kristeva's argument that as women's only access to the Symbolic order is through the language of the father, they must in order to protect themselves from exclusion and marginalisation from patriarchal society repress identification with (the body of) the mother and use a double discourse which reflects the real state of all identity (both masculine and feminine, both inside and outside the boundaries of the Symbolic) is clearly applicable here.[3]

A similar double discourse emerges in the texts discussed in the patriarchal and alternative discourses, which appear in the alternative versions of the Revolution and in the ambivalence revealed by the female narrators in their feelings towards their respective mothers, and the mothers' revelations about themselves. Thus, the theoretical strategies employed for the writing of this

---

[2]   Minsky (1996: 179) confirms this when she writes: 'French feminist writers [. . .] suggest that unconscious desire, associated with the mother and imprisoned between the rational, binary categories of language, can be freed from patriarchal control through the use of a specifically poetic language which, because of its close involvement with the unconscious, must always challenge the arbitrary, male-defined categories through which we experience the world, which man must identify but which are imposed on women.'

[3]   Kristeva (1986: 152–56).

book, principally dialogism and feminist psychoanalysis, allow that mother-hood and multivocality are interrelated in several ways. Motherhood has been approached from the point of view of the mother–daughter relationship but is described by more than one voice. It is seen mostly from the child's perspec-tive, but also takes into consideration the often neglected maternal discourse, where this is present. The study of multivocality, therefore, has centred on two subordinate ideas: the way heteroglossia and polyphony appear in discourses about the Revolution in Mexico and the post-revolutionary eras, in which programmes of reform, nationalisation and industrialisation took place; and in discourses about the mother–daughter relationship which include the mother's role in those programmes.

   Although traditional psychoanalysis was considered by Luce Irigaray as patriarchal and phallocentric, feminist revisions of it – particularly ones that re-evaluate the maternal – are essential to a discussion of the mother–daughter relationship. The alternative discipline, that of the social sciences, while less often employed in discussions of literature, is also an essential tool when contemplating the realities of existence for women and other marginals. In a patriarchal culture, like that of Mexico, where motherhood is granted such a special status, an analysis of the mother–daughter relationship in texts written, and mostly narrated by daughters, is fundamental to a discussion of such texts. This is particularly the case in these novels where the writers not only write from the position of daughter (and three out of four with a girl-narrator) but also give a voice to the mother(s), which defies the convention that a good mother must only be a mother and not aspire to anything else.

   Psychoanalysis has been a useful, if flawed, tool for the analysis of the mother–daughter relationship. While bearing in mind that it developed from the model of the modern Western-European middle-class, I have found that psychoanalytical theory is nevertheless relevant to the discussion of the writing by these modern Mexican writers who have been educated in a society based on the ideas of that tradition and, moreover, at a time when psychoanal-ysis had attained unprecedented cultural influence.[4] Marianne Hirsch believes that from Freud to Chodorow to Irigaray what has hardly changed is 'the presentation of a mother who is overly invested in her child, powerless in the world, a constraining rather than an enabling force in the girl's development, and an inadequate and disappointing object of identification' (Hirsch 1989: 167). There is conclusive evidence in the five works discussed in this book that this is not always the case and that not only is there ambivalence in the representation of the mother but, by listening to the many voices that emerge from the text, it is possible, to use Hirsch's words again, 'to invest with speech the silence that defines maternal experience' (Hirsch 1989: 169). Thus,

   ⁴ As affirmed by the importance given to theories on child-rearing by psychoanalysts and child psychologists, and the influential nature of the Surrealist movement in art which appropriated the unconscious.

although in *Balún-Canán* both the *niña*'s mother-figures (Zoraida and *nana*) are distant and constraining, loving and enabling respectively, both are powerless. In *Los recuerdos del porvenir*, the mother-figures (and other women) are mostly seen as publicly conforming to their roles but have private memories, aspirations and thoughts that reveal them to be quite different people from those known to their husbands (or lovers) and daughters. In *Cartucho* and *Las manos de mamá* and in *La 'Flor de Lis'*, the mothers, although objects of adoration for the narrators and possibly disappointing in terms of the amount of attention they pay their daughters, are not inadequate in terms of identification. Both Nellie and Mariana admire the refusal of their mother to conform to the ideal mother myth, preferring their image of independence and individuality.

My argument has focused on the use of binary oppositions and references to the senses in the novels discussed. This is principally because these may be used both consciously by the writers, to make a certain point, or unconsciously, as a result of their conditioning as women in a patriarchal society that relies heavily on binary oppositions to maintain the status quo, by forcing women into certain roles. One of those roles, motherhood, emphasises the mother-child bond which is created during the pre-Oedipal phase of development and which is reliant on the senses, as the bond is strengthened by sensual stimulation whereby the child identifies the mother through smell, touch and the sound of her voice. According to some feminist psychoanalysts, as I have emphasised, under patriarchy women's power is restricted and the close relationship with daughters is curbed in order to perpetuate the subordination of women. The result of such manipulation is that sons are favoured over daughters who therefore can never receive enough mother-love. This, in turn, creates resentment and ambivalence in the mother–daughter relationship. Equally, the idealisation of the mother by society, creates unrealistic expectations of what mothers are capable of providing and denies women an identity beyond that of mother. Such expectations may be internalised by young girls who can only be disillusioned by the reality of their relationship with their own mothers. The writers whose work is explored in this book, present both sides of the mother–daughter argument by reflecting the internalisation of high mothering expectations by daughters and by including the mother's discourse in their portraits of mothers. In this way they subvert traditional ideas of motherhood and present alternative discourses which clash with the official discourse of patriarchy.

The discussion of multivocality and the mother–daughter relationship in my analysis of the texts has centred on the discourse of those marginals – which includes both mothers and daughters – denied a public voice for centuries in Mexico. Uncertainty as to the acceptability of their words has led these writers to subsume their dissenting voice into a multivocalic discourse which does not, however, conceal its heteroglossia. In *Cartucho* and *Las manos de mamá* as well as Nellie's dissatisfaction with her relationship with her mother that comes through the text (albeit semi-obscured by her adulation of *mamá*), Rafaela also claims a space for herself as a woman – and not just as a mother – in her relationships with the different men of the Revolution. In *Balún-Canán*, Zoraida breaks her silence with a monologue which reveals her reasons for being a less-than-perfect mother: she married and had children only because society left her no alternative if she wished to remain respectable. The other mother-figure, the *nana* is only able to express her dissent to those at the same level in the social hierarchy as herself or be punished. In *Los recuerdos del porvenir* the silence imposed upon women is turned around by those among the more well-to-do families of Ixtepec, to be used as a weapon of defence against interrogation by the military. Those at the other end of the social hier-archy – Luchi and the other prostitutes – break the silence expected of them and speak out against the General's brutality. Isabel Moncada, the only female in the novel who is accustomed to speak her mind, finally self-imposes the ultimate silence when she turns to stone and is thus silenced forever, without explaining her betrayal to the town of Ixtepec. In *La 'Flor de Lis'* Mariana expresses her desire for more mother-love and speaks out for herself by proclaiming her lack of conformity with the role(s) she is expected to play in Mexican society and with the identity that has been allotted her, while Luz writes of her own disappointment in her relationship with her husband in the diary read by Mariana.

As regards the link between the mother–daughter relationship and coming to writing, it is reasonable to conclude that it is the loneliness and sensitivity of the daughters, and a perceived unsatisfactory relationship with their mothers that contributes to producing the imaginative, creative child in each family who will grow up to become a writer. According to some psychoanalysts the mother–daughter relationship is influential in the formation of an artistic personality (Hirsch 1989: 100). Similarly, the bond with the indigenous mother figures in Poniatowska's *La 'Flor de Lis'* (of the two girl protagonists, it is Mariana who has the closer relationship with Magda) and Castellanos' *Balún-Canán* (where it is the little girl, rather than her brother who becomes close to the *nana*) leads the writers of these semi-autobiographical works to champion more overtly the rights of the underdog and of women generally, in spite of their awareness of the obvious racial differences and the social and cultural gulf that lies between them. I make this point to counter the argument that questions the ability of women from the privileged classes to empathise with indigenous (Indian) women (where 'Indian' connotes social class rather than race). The use of a child-narrator is one way of avoiding the obvious diffi-culties that these relationships imply.

To sum up, the main contributions of this book are to further the study of the question of gender and the questioning of gender categories. While many studies concentrate on the body as a manifestation of sexual identity and as a site of transgression, my analysis considers the body as the vehicle for uncon-scious responses and attitudes within a socio-historical reality, that is, without divorcing it from its status as a physical entity, a danger that might be incurred by using exclusively psychoanalytical theory, in which parts of the body are often used only symbolically. By emphasising the importance of the gender of the narrators/protagonists and of the socio-historical reality in which they are situated, I hope to have avoided such a danger. In combining an analysis of the work of these four pioneers of Mexican women's writing, my book opens up this hitherto relatively neglected field of study to further research.

The writing of this book has been very much a process of self-discovery as appears to be the case with the novels themselves. As the autobiographical nature of Campobello's novellas became increasingly evident it was easy to conjecture how the relationship between Nellie and her mother might have contributed to her extraordinary artistic career. Had Rafaela fulfilled Nellie's expectations of motherhood, it is plausible that Campobello would have fallen into the same role rather than trying to emulate her mother's self-sufficiency, earning her living as a teacher, writer and dancer. Poniatowska's autobiographical novel is the clearest example of the five works of a journey of self-discovery. It clearly reveals an important part of the process undergone by Poniatowska on her road to becoming a Mexican writer who will dedicate her life to writing for and about Mexican people from all the strata of society but particularly the less privileged. Similarly, my study of *Balún-Canán,* concentrating on the mother–daughter relationship, has emphasised the notion held by Castellanos herself, that women are in some ways responsible for the perpetuation of their own oppression and Hirsch's premise therefore justified (Hirsch 1989: 100). *Los recuerdos del porvenir* with its lack of a single protagonist, prevents it from being classified as a true novel of self-discovery. However I posit that it is a novel of self-discovery in the sense that it explores the limitations placed on women at the time of its writing, as well as at the time in which the novel is set. It also reveals how a woman's lot in life can be determined by her relationship with her mother as the fate of Isabel reveals. Thus these four writers who, though contemporaries, worked in isolation from one another, together contributed to the possibility of a different future for Mexican women writers: one in which their efforts and talent are recognised and celebrated and in which being female is no longer disadvantageous.

WORKS CITED

Where available, the date the work was first published will appear in square brackets preceding the date of the edition consulted.

PRIMARY SOURCES

Campobello, Nellie (1960), 'Prólogo', *Mis libros* (Mexico City: Cía. General de Ediciones)
—— [1931, 1937] (1969), *Cartucho* and *Las manos de mamá*, in Antonio Castro Leal (ed.), *La novela de la revolución mexicana* (Mexico: Aguilar), Prólogo, pp. 7–45
—— (1988), *'Cartucho' and 'My Mother's Hands'*, intro. Elena Poniatowska, trans. Irene Matthews (Austin: University of Texas Press)

Castellanos, Rosario (1950), *Sobre cultura femenina*, MA Thesis (Mexico City: Ediciones de America: Revista Antológica)
—— (1966), 'La novela mexicana contemporánea', in *Juicios Sumarios*, Cuadernos de la facultad de filosofía, letras y ciencias (Xalapa, Mexico: Universidad Veracruzana), 83–113
—— (1975), 'Carlos Monsiváis: asedio a México', in *El mar y sus pescaditos* (Mexico City: Sepsetentas)
—— [1964] (1988), 'Teoría y práctica del indigenismo', in *El uso de la palabra* (Mexico City: Editores Mexicanos Unidos), 123–26
—— [1965] (1988), 'El desplazamiento hacia otro mundo', in *El uso de la palabra* (Mexico City: Editores Mexicanos Unidos)
—— (1994), *Cartas a Ricardo* (Mexico City: Consejo Nacional para la Cultura y las Artes)
—— [1985] (1995*a*), 'Autorretrato', in *Meditación en el umbral* (Mexico City: FCE) 185–187
—— [1957] (1995*b*), *Balún-Canán* (Mexico City: FCE)
—— [1973] (1995*c*), *Mujer que sabe latín* (Mexico City: FCE)

Garro, Elena (1958), 'Andarse por las ramas' and 'La dama boba', in *Un hogar sólido* (Mexico: Universidad Veracruzana), pp. 9–27 and 171–246
—— (1964), *La semana de colores* (Xalapa, Mexico: Universidad Veracruzana)
—— (1980), 'La primera vez que me vi', in *Andamos huyendo, Lola* (Mexico City: Joaquín Mortiz), pp. 33–54

—— (1982), *La casa junto al río* (Mexico City: Grijalbo)
—— (1992), *Memorias de España 1937* (Mexico City and Madrid: Siglo XXI)
—— [1963] (1994), *Los recuerdos del porvenir* (Madrid: Ediciones Siruela)
—— (1995), *Inés* (Mexico City: Editorial Grijalbo)

Poniatowska, Elena [1954] (1967), *Los cuentos de Lilus Kikus* (First published as *Los presentes*) (Xalapa, Mexico: Universidad Veracruzana)
—— (1969), *Hasta no verte, Jesús mío* (Mexico City: Alianza/Era)
—— [1971] (1981), *La noche de Tlatelolco* (Mexico City: Era)
—— (1987a), *¡Ay vida, no me mereces!* (Mexico City: Planeta)
—— [1978] (1987b), *'Querido Diego, te abraza Quiela' y otros cuentos* (Mexico City: Alianza/Era)
—— (1988a), *Nada, nadie: las voces del temblor* (Mexico City: Era)
—— (1988b), 'Introduction to *Cartucho/My Mother's Hands*', Irene Matthews (trans.) (Austin: University of Texas Press)
—— (1989), *La 'Flor de Lis'* (Mexico City: Era)
—— [1992] (1993), *Tinísima* (Mexico City: Era)
—— [1985] (1995a), *De noche vienes* (Mexico City: Era)
—— [1985] (1995b), *Prólogo* to *Meditación en el umbral* (Mexico City: FCE)
—— [1996] (1999), *Paseo de la Reforma* (Barcelona: Lumen)

INTERVIEWS WITH AUTHORS

Bello Serrano, Vicente (1996), 'México va muy mal, económicamente y espiritualmente: Elena Garro', *Excelsior* (Friday 4 October 1996)
Dimitriou, Agnes (1990), 'Entrevista con Elena Poniatowska', *Letras Femeninas* 16: 1–2, 125–133
Gazarian Gautier, Marie-Lise (1989), 'Elena Poniatowska', in *Interviews with Latin American Writers* (Dalkey Archive Press, Illinois), 201–216
Muncy, Michèle (1986), 'Encuentro con Elena Garro', *Hispanic Journal*, 7–2, 65–71
Rojas-Trempe, Lady (1989), 'Elena Garro dialoga sobre su teatro con Guillermo Schmidhuber: entrevista', *Revista Iberoamericana*, 148–9, 685–90

SECONDARY SOURCES

Abel, Elizabeth, Marianne Hirsch and Elizabeth Langland (eds) (1983), *The Voyage in: Fictions of Female Development* (Hanover: University of New England Press)
Agosín, Marjorie (1995), 'From a Room of One's Own to the Garden', in *A Dream of Light and Shadow: Portraits of Latin American Women Writers* (Albuquerque: University of New Mexico Press), pp. 1–40

Anderson, Benedict [1983] (1991), *Imagined Communities: Reflections on the Origins and Spread of Nationalism* (London and New York: Verso), pp. 22–32

Anderson, Helene M. (1983), 'Rosario Castellanos and the Structures of Power', in Doris Meyer and Margarite Fernández Olmos (eds), *Contemporary Women Authors of Latin America: Introductory Essays* (Brooklyn, NY: Brooklyn College Press)

Anderson, R. K. (1985), 'Myth and Archetype in *Recollections of Things to Come*', *Studies in Twentieth Century Literature*, 9–2, 213–27

Anta San Pedro, Teresa (1994–5), 'El poder destructor de la palabra en la novela de Elena Garro: *Los recuerdos del porvenir*', *Explicación de textos literarios*, 23.1, 43–56

Aub, Max [1969] (1985), *Guía de narradores de la Revolución Mexicana* (Mexico: FCE)

Baker, Armand F. (1968), 'El tiempo en la novela hispanoamericana', Ph.D. Dissertation (University of Iowa, Ann Arbor, MI: UMI)

Bakhtin, Mikhail [1981] (1992), 'Discourse in the Novel', in Michael Holquist (ed. and trans.), *The Dialogic Imagination: Four Essays by M. M. Bakhtin* (Austin: University of Texas Press), pp. 259–422

Balderston, Daniel (1989), 'The New Historical Novel: History and Fantasy in *Los Recuerdos del porvenir*', *BHS*, LXVI, 41–46

Bartow, Joanna R. (1993), 'Isolation and Madness: Collective Memory and Women in *Los Recuerdos del porvenir* and *Pedro Páramo*', *Revista Canadiense de Estudios Hispánicos*, 18.1, 1–15

Benstock, Shari (ed.) (1987), *Feminist Issues in Literary Scholarship* (Bloomington: Indiana University Press)

—— (1988), *The Private Self: Theory and Practice of Women's Autobiographical Writings* (Chapel Hill: University of North Carolina Press; London: Routledge)

Beverly, John, José Oviedo and Michael Aronna (eds) (1995), *The Postmodernism Debate in Latin America* (Durham and London: Duke University Press)

Bhabha, Homi K. [1990] (1995), *Nation and Narration* (London and New York: Routledge)

Booth, Wayne C. [1961] (1968), *The Rhetoric of Fiction* (Chicago and London; University of Chicago Press)

Boullosa, Carmen (1989), *Antes* (Mexico City: Editorial Vuelta)

Bradbury, M., E. Mottram, J. Franco (eds) (1971), *The Penguin Companion to Literature 3: United States and Latin American Literature* (Harmondsworth: Penguin)

Brodzki, Bella (1988), 'Mothers, Displacement and Language', in B. Brodzki and Celeste Schenk (eds), *Life/Lines: Theorizing Women's Autobiography* (Ithaca and London, Cornell University Press)

Calmus, Ellen (1995), 'We are all Ramona: Artist, Revolutionaries, and Zapatistas with Petticoat', in Trisha Ziff (ed.), *Distant Relations* (New York: Smart Art Press), pp. 164–74

Campos, Julieta (1973), *Función de la novela* (Mexico City: Joaquín Mortiz)

Carballo, Emmanuel (1965), 'Nellie Campobello', in *Diecinueve protagonistas de la literatura mexicana del siglo XX* (Mexico City: Empresas Editoriales), pp. 327–38

Castillo, Ana (ed.) (2001), *La Diosa de las Américas: escritos sobre la Virgen de Guadalupe* (Mexico City and Barcelona: Plaza y Janés)

Castillo, Debra A. (1992*a*), 'Rosario Castellanos: "Ashes without a face" ', in Sidonie Smith and Julia Watson (eds), *The politics of Gender in Women's Autobigraphy* (Minneapolis: University of Minnesota Press), pp. 242–66

—— (1992*b*), *Talking Back: Toward a Latin American Feminist Literary Criticism* (Ithaca: Cornell University Press), pp. 216–59

—— (1998), *Easy Women: Sex and Gender in Modern Mexican Fiction* (Minneapolis; London: University of Minnesota Press)

Cázares, Laura H. (1996), 'Eros y Tanatos: infancia y revolución en Nellie Campobello', in Pasternac, Domenella, López González (eds), *Escribir la infancia: narradoras mexicanas contémporaneas* (Mexico City: Colegio de México)

Chakravorty Spivak, Gayatri (1993), 'Can the Subaltern Speak?', in Patrick Williams and Laura Chrisman (eds), *Colonial Discourse and Post-Colonial Theory: A Reader* (New York and London: Harvester Wheatsheaf), pp. 66–111

Chodorow, Nancy (1978), *The Reproduction of Mothering, Psychoanalysis and the Sociology of Gender* (Berkeley: University of California Press)

—— (1989), *Feminism and Psychoanalytic Theory* (Cambridge: Polity Press)

Cixous, Hélène (1975), 'Laugh of the Medusa', K. Cohen and P. Cohen (trans.), in *Signs* 1.4, 875–93

Clark d'Lugo, Carol (1997), *The Fragmented Novel in Mexico: the Politics of Form* (Austin: University of Texas Press)

Coe, Richard N. (1984), *The Grass Was Taller: Autobiography and the Experience of Childhood* (New Haven: Yale University Press)

Cohn, Dorrit (1978), *Transparent Minds: Narrative Modes for Presenting Consciousness in Fiction* (Guildford: Princeton University Press)

Cooke, Miriam, and Angela Woollacott (eds) (1993), *Gendering War Talk* (Princeton, New Jersey: Princeton University Press)

Crumley de Pérez, Laura Lee (1984), '*Balún-Canán* y la construcción narrativa de una cosmovisión indígena', *Revista Iberoamericana* 50.127, 491–503

Dauster, Frank (1980), 'Elena Garro y sus recuerdos del porvenir', *Journal of Spanish Studies, Twentieth Century* 8, 57–65

de Beauvoir, Simone [1948] (1972), *The Second Sex* (Harmondsworth: Penguin)

de Man, Paul (1979), 'Autobiography as Defacement', *Modern Language Notes* 94, 919–31

de Valdés, María Elena (1998), 'Identity and the Other as Myself: Elena Poniatowska', in *The Shattered Mirror: Representations of Women in Mexican Literature* (Austin: University of Texas Press), pp. 114–43

Dinnerstein, Dorothy [1977] (1991), *The Mermaid and the Minotaur: Sexual Arrangements and the Human Malaise* (New York: Harper Perennial)

Dore, Elizabeth (1997), 'The Holy Family: Imagined Households in Latin American History', in Dore (ed.), *Gender Politics in Latin America: Debates in Theory and Practice* (New York: Monthly Review Press), pp. 101–117

Duncan, Cynthia (1985), ' "La culpa es de los Tlaxcaltecas": a Reevaluation of Mexico's Past Through Myth', *Crítica Hispánica*, 7.1, 105–20

Dybvig, Rhoda (1965), *Rosario Castellanos, biografía y novelística* (Mexico City: Andrea)

Fanon, Franz (1994), 'On National Culture', in Williams and Chrisman (eds), *Colonial Discourse and Post-Colonial Theory: A Reader* (New York, London: Harvester Wheatsheaf), pp. 36–52

Felski, Rita (1989), *Beyond Feminist Aesthetics: Feminist Literature and Social Change* (Cambridge, Mass.: Harvard University Press)

Finnegan, Nuala (2000), *Woman as Monster: Projections of Femininity in the Prose Works of Rosario Castellanos* (Lampeter: The Edwin Mellen Press)

Forna, Aminatta (1998), *Mother of All Myths: How Society Moulds and Constrains Mothers* (London: Harper Collins)

Franco, Jean (1969), 'The Mexican Revolution and Literature', in *An Introduction to Spanish American Literature* (Cambridge: Cambridge University Press), pp. 194–208

—— (1989), *Plotting Women: Gender and Representation in Mexico* (London and New York: Verso, Columbia University Press)

—— (1994), 'Beyond Ethnocentrism: Gender, Power and the Third-World Intelligentsia', in Williams and Chrisman (eds), *Colonial Discourse and Post-Colonial Theory* (New York, London: Harvester Wheatsheaf), pp. 359–69

Franco, María Estela (1984), *Rosario Castellanos: una semblanza psicoanalítica: otro modo de ser humano y libre* (Mexico: Plaza y Janés)

Freud, Sigmund [1900] (1991), *The Interpretation of Dreams*, The Penguin Freud Library, Volume 4

—— [1933] (1996), 'Femininity', in Rosalind Minsky (ed.), *Psychoanalysis and Gender: An Introductory Reader* (London and New York: Routledge)

Friday, Nancy [1979] (1988), *My Mother/My Self: The Daughter's Search for Identity* (London: Fontana)

Frischmann, Donald H. (1985), 'El sistema patriarcal y las relaciones heterosexuales en *Balún-Canán* de Rosario Castellanos', *Revista Iberoamericana*, 132–33, 665–78

Fuentes, Carlos (1997), *A New Time for Mexico* (London: Bloomsbury)

García, Kay (1990), 'Comunicación y silencio en *Los Recuerdos del porvenir* de Elena Garro', *PNCFL Selecta*, 11, 97–101

—— (1994), *Broken Bars: New Perspectives from Mexican Women Writers* (Albuquerque: University of New Mexico Press)

Gilbert, Sandra M. and Susan Gubar (1986), 'Tradition and the Female Talent', in *The Poetics of Gender* (New York and Oxford: Columbia University Press)

Gilmore, Leigh (1994), *Autobiographics: A Feminist Theory of Women's Self-representation* (London: Cornell University Press)

Gonzalez, María R. (1996), *Imagen de la prostituta en la novela mexicana contemporánea* (Madrid: Pliegos)

Grant, Catherine (1991), 'Authorship and Authority in the Novels of Rosario Castellanos', Ph.D. Thesis (University of Leeds)

—— (1993), 'Women or Words? The Indigenous Nodriza in the Work of Rosario Castellanos', in Catherine Davies (ed.), *Women Writers in Twentieth*

Century Spain and Spanish America (Lewiston; Queenstown; Lampeter: The Edwin Mellen Press), pp. 85–100

Griffin, Clive (1993), *Azuela: Los de abajo* (London: Grant and Cutler)

Gubar, Susan (1986), ' "The Blank Page" and the Issues of Creativity', in Elaine Showalter (ed.), *The New Feminist Criticism: Essays on Women, Literature and Theory* (London: Virago), pp. 292–309

Guerra Cunningham, Lucía (ed.), (1990), *Splintering Darkness: Latin American Women Writers in Search of Themselves* (Pittsburgh, Pennsylvania: Latin American Literary Review Press)

—— (1994–5), 'Invasión a los cuarteles del silencio: estrategias del discurso de la sexualidad en la novela de la mujer latinoamericana', *INTI: Revista de Literatura Hispánica*, Vol. 40–41

Gusdorf, Georges [1956] (1980), 'Conditions and Limits of Autobiography, in James Olney (ed. and trans.), *Autobiography: Essays Theoretical and Critical* (Princeton: Princeton University Press), pp. 28–48

Gúzman, Martín Luis [1928] (1969), *El águila y la serpiente* (Mexico City: Cía. General de Ediciones SA)

Heilbrun, Carolyn G. (1988*a*), 'Non-Autobiographies of "Privileged" Women: England and America', in Brodzki and Schenk (eds), *Life/Lines: Theorizing Women's Autobiography* (Ithaca and London: Cornell University Press)

—— (1988*b*), *Writing a Woman's Life* (New York: Ballantine)

Hirsch, Marianne (1981), 'Mothers and Daughters', *Signs* 7.1, 200–22

—— (1989), *The Mother/Daughter Plot: Narrative, Psychoanalysis, Feminism* (Bloomington and Indianapolis: Indiana University Press)

Humm, Maggie (1989), *The Dictionary of Feminist Theory* (New York and London: Harvester Wheatsheaf)

—— (1995), *Practising Feminist Criticism: An Introduction* (London: Prentice Hall/Harvester Wheatsheaf)

Irigaray, Luce (1981), 'And the One Doesn't Stir Without the Other', *Signs: Journal of Women in Culture and Society*, 7.1, 60–67

—— [1974] (1985), 'Any Theory of the "Subject" Has Always Been Appropriated by the "Masculine" ', in Gillian C. Hill (trans.), *Speculum of the Other Woman* (Ithaca, New York: Cornell University Press), pp. 133–46

—— [1980] (1993), 'Body Against Body: in Relation to the Mother', in *Je, Tu, Nous* (A. Martin trans.) (London: Routledge)

Jacobus, Mary (1987), 'Freud's mnemonic: women, screen memories, and feminist nostalgia', in *Women and Memory: Special Issue, Michigan Quarterly Review*, XXVI.1, 117–40

Jelinek, Estelle (1987*a*), 'Introduction', in Jelinek (ed.), *Women's Autobiography: Essays in Criticism* (Bloomington: Indiana University Press)

—— (1987*b*), 'Women's Autobiography and the Male Tradition', in Jelinek (ed.), *Women's Autobiography: Essays in Criticism* (Bloomington: Indiana University Press)

Jordan, Glenn and Chris Weedon (1995), *Cultural Politics: Class, Gender and Race in the Postmodern World* (Oxford and Malden, Mass.: Blackwell)

Jörgensen, Beth E. (1988), 'Perspectivas femeninas en *Hasta no verte, Jesús mío* y *La 'Flor de Lis'* ', *Texto-Crítico*, 14, 110–123

Kaminsky, Amy (1993a), *Reading the Body Politic: Feminist Criticism and Latin American Women Writers* (Minneapolis: University of Minnesota Press)
—— (1993b), 'Residual Authority, and Gendered Resistance', in Steven M. Bell (ed.), *Critical Theory, Cultural Politics and Latin American Narrative* (Paris: University of Notre Dame)
Kandiyoti, Denis (1994), 'Identity and its Discontents: Women and the Nation', in Williams and Chrisman (eds), *Colonial Discourse and Post-Colonial Theory: A Reader* (New York and London: Harvester Wheatsheaf), pp. 376–91
Kauffman, Linda (1989), *Gender and Theory: Dialogues on Feminist Criticism* (Oxford: Blackwell)
Klein, Melanie [1956] (1996), 'A Study of Envy and Gratitude', in Rosalind Minsky (ed.), *Psychoanalysis and Gender: An Introductory Reader* (London and New York: Routledge), pp. 236–52
Kristeva, Julia, [1977] (1987), L. S. Roudiez (trans.), 'From One Identity To An Other', in *Desire in Language: A Semiotic Approach to Literature and Art* (Oxford: Blackwell), pp. 124–47
—— [1974] (1984), Margaret Waller (trans.), 'The Semiotic and the Symbolic', in *Revolution in Poetic Language* (New York and Oxford: Columbia University Press), pp. 19–106
—— (1990), 'Without Time', in Toril Moi (ed.), *The Kristeva Reader* (Oxford: Blackwell), pp. 152–6
—— [1991] (1993), 'Women's Time', in Robyn R. Warhol, Diane Price Herndl, *Feminisms: An Anthology of Literary Theory and Criticism* (New Brunswick, New Jersey: Rutgers University Press)
Larson, Catherine (1989), 'Recollections of Plays to Come', *Latin American Theatre Review*, 22.2, 5–17
LeMaître, Monique (1990–91), 'La identidad asumida y el texto subversivo en *La 'Flor de Lis'* de Elena Poniatowska', *Explicación de Textos Literarios*, 19.1, 27–37
—— (1996), 'La historia oficial frente al discurso de la "ficción" femenina en *Arráncame la vida* de Ángeles Mastretta', *Revista Iberoamericana*, LXII, 174, 185–97
León-Portilla, Miguel (1992), *The Broken Spears: The Aztec Account of the Conquest of Mexico* (Boston: Beacon Press)
Lerner, Gerda (1986), *Women and History: Vol.1 The Creation of Patriarchy* (New York and Oxford: Oxford University Press), pp. 212–29
Lloyd, Genevieve [1962] (1993), *Being in Time: Selves and Narrators in Philosophy and Literature* (London: Routledge)
López Morales, Berta (1990), María Teresa Marrero (trans.), 'The Language of the Body in Women's Texts', in Guerra Cunningham (ed.), *Splintering Darkness: Latin American Women Writers in Search of Themselves*, Latin American Literature Review Press, pp. 123–30
Magaña Esquivel, Antonio (1965), 'Las visiones de Rafael F. Muñoz y Nellie Campobello', in *La novela de la revolución: 2* (Mexico: Instituto Nacional de Estudios Históricos de la Revolución Mexicana), pp. 135–44
Marting, Diane E. (ed.) (1990), *Spanish American Women Writers: A Bio-Bibliographical Sourcebook* (Connecticut: Greenwood Press)

Mastretta, Angeles [1990] (1995), *Arráncame la vida* (Barcelona: Seix Barral)
—— (1998), *Mal de amores* (Mexico City: Alfaguara)
Matthews, Irene (1993), 'Daughtering in War: Two "Case Studies" from Mexico
    and Guatemala', in Miriam Cooke and Angela Woollacott (eds), *Gendering
    War Talk* (Princeton, New Jersey: Princeton University Press), pp. 148–73
Maynard, Mary (1995), 'Beyond the "Big Three": the Development of Feminist
    Theory in the 1990s', *Women's History Review*, 4.3, 259–81
Menton, Seymour (1990), 'Las cuentistas mexicanas en la época feminista 1970–
    1985', *Hispania*, 73.2, 366–70
—— (ed.) [1964] (1992), *El cuento hispanoamericano: Antología crítico-
    histórico* (Mexico City: FCE)
Meyer, Doris (1985), 'Nellie Campobello's *Las manos de mamá*: A Rereading',
    Hispania, 68, 747–52
—— (1996), 'The Dialogics of Testimony: Autobiography as Shared Experience
    in Nellie Campobello's *Cartucho*', in Brooksbank Jones and Davies (eds),
    Latin American Women's Writing: Feminist Readings in Theory and Crisis
    (Oxford; New York: Clarendon), pp. 46–65
Meyer, Doris and Margarite Fernández Olmos (eds) (1983), *Contemporary
    Women authors of Latin America: New Translations* (New York: Brooklyn
    College Press)
Meyer, Lorenzo [1976] (1981), 'El primer tramo del camino' and 'La
    encrucijada', in Daniel Cosío Villegas (ed.), *Historia General de México:
    Tomo 2* (Mexico City: Colegio de México), pp. 1185–1355
Miller, Beth (ed.) (1983), *Women in Hispanic Literature: Icons and Fallen Idols*
    (Berkeley: University of California Press)
Millett, Kate [1977] (1991), *Sexual Politics* (London: Virago)
Minsky, Rosalind (ed.) (1996), *Psychoanalysis and Gender: An Introductory
    Reader* (London and New York: Routledge)
Mitchell, Juliet [1973] (1990), *Psychoanalysis and Feminism* (London: Penguin)
Moi, Toril 1982, 'Feminist Literary Criticism', in Ann Jefferson and David
    Robey (eds), *Modern Literary Theory: A Comparative Introduction* (London:
    Batsford)
—— (1985), *Sexual/Textual Politics: Feminist Literary Theory* (London:
    Methuen)
Monsiváis, Carlos [1976] (1981), 'Notas sobre la cultura mexicana en el siglo
    XX', in Daniel Cosío Villegas (ed.), *Historia General de México: Tomo 2*
    (Mexico City: Colegio de México), pp. 1485–1531
—— [1970] (1986), 'Imágenes del tiempo libre', in *Días de guardar* (Mexico
    City: Era), pp. 145–63
—— [1977] (1995), *Amor perdido* (Mexico City: Era)
Morris, Pam (ed.) (1994), *The Bakhtin Reader: Selected Writings of Bakhtin,
    Medvedev and Voloshinov* (London; New York; Melbourne; Auckland:
    Edward Arnold)
Mulvey, Laura [1975] (1989), 'Visual Pleasure and Narrative Cinema', in *Visual
    and Other Pleasures* (Basingstoke and London: Macmillan), pp. 14–26
Muncy, Michèle (1990), 'La escritora a través de su obra: *Mis libros,
    Balún-Canán, Poesía no eres tú*', in Erro-Orthmann and Cruz Mendizabal
    (eds), *La escritura hispánica: Actas de la decimotercera conferencia anual de*

literaturas hispánicas en Indiana: University of Pennsylvania (Miami: Universal), pp. 121–30

Nickel, Catherine (1990), 'Nellie Campobello (b.1900) Mexico', in Diane E. Marting (ed.), *Spanish American Women Writers: A Bio-Bibliographical Sourcebook* (Connecticut: Greenwood Press), pp. 117–27

Olivier, Christiane [1980] (1987), *Los hijos de Jocasta: La huella de la madre* (Mexico City: FCE)

Olney, James (ed.), (1980), *Autobiography: Essays Theoretical and Critical* (Princeton, New Jersey: Princeton University Press)

Oyarzún, Kemy (1993), 'Literaturas heterogéneas y dialogismo genérico-sexual', *Revista de crítica literaria latinoamericana*, XIX, 37–50

—— (1996), 'Identidad femenina, genealogía mítica, historia: *Las manos de mamá*, de Nellie Campobello', *Revista de Crítica Literaria Latinoamericana*, 22, 181–99

Parle, Dennis J. (1985), 'Narrative Style and Technique in Nellie Campobello's *Cartucho*', *Kentucky Romance Quarterly*, 32, 201–11

Paz, Octavio [1950] (1982), *El laberinto de la soledad* (Mexico: FCE)

—— [1970] (1985), *Posdata* (Mexico City: Siglo Veintiuno)

Phillips, Shelley [1991] (1996), *Beyond the Myths: Mother–Daughter Relationships in Psychology, History, Literature and Everyday Life* (Harmondsworth: Penguin)

Pollock, Griselda (1988), *Vision and Difference: Femininity, Feminism and the Histories of Art* (London and New York: Routledge)

Poot Herrera, Sara (1990), '*La 'Flor de Lis'*, códice y huella de Elena Poniatowska', in López González, Malagamba and Urrutia (eds), *Mujer y literatura mexicana y chicana 2: culturas en contacto* (Mexico City: Colegio de México), pp. 99–105

—— (1996), Del tornasol de *Lilus Kikus* al tornaviaje de *La 'Flor de Lis'*, in Poot Herrera (ed.), *Escribir la infancia: narradoras mexicanas contemporáneas* (Mexico City: Colegio de Mexico), pp. 59–80

Pozas, Ricardo [1952] (1996), *Juan Pérez Jolote* (Mexico: FCE)

Price, Derrick (1997), 'Surveyors and Surveyed: Photography out and about', in Liz Wells (ed.), *Photography: A Critical Introduction* (London: Routledge), pp. 55–105

Ramblado Minero, María de la Cinta (1999), ' "Notebooks that B[ear] Witness to Life": The Autobiographical as a Source of Literary Inspiration in the Fiction of Isabel Allende and Kate O'Brien', Ph.D. Thesis (University of Limerick, Ireland)

Ramírez, Santiago [1959] (1968), *El mexicano: psicología de sus motivaciones* (Mexico City: Editorial Pax Mexico)

Ramos Escandón, Carmen (1992), 'The History of Women in Latin America', in S. J. Kleinberg (ed.), *Retrieving Women's History: Changing Perceptions of the Role of Women in Politics and Society* (Paris: Berg/Unesco)

—— (1995), 'Mujeres y género en México: A mitad del camino de la década', *Mexican Studies/Estudios Mexicanos*, 11.1, 113–30

—— (1997), 'Reading Gender in History', in Dore (ed.), *Gender Politics in Latin America: Debates in Theory and Practice* (New York: Monthly Review Press), pp. 149–60

Rand Morton, F. (1949), *Los novelistas de la revolución mexicana* (Mexico: Editorial Cultural)

Rich, Adrienne [1976] (1995), *Of Woman Born: Motherhood as Experience and Institution* (London: Virago)

Riding, Alan (1987), *Mexico: Inside the Volcano* (London: I. B. Tauris & Co., Ltd)

Roberts, Graham (1994), 'Glossary', in Pam Morris (ed.), *The Bakhtin Reader: Selected Writings of Bakhtin, Medvedev and Voloshinov* (London; New York; Melbourne; Auckland: Edward Arnold)

Romberg, Bertil (1962), *Narrative Technique of the First-Person Novel* (Lund: Almqvist and Wiksell)

Rosas Lopátegui, Patricia (1995), 'Los espacios poéticos y apoéticos en *Los recuerdos del porvenir* de Elena Garro', *Hispanic Journal*, 16.1, 95–107

Rosinsky, Natalie M. (1980), 'Mothers and daughters: Another Minority Group', in Davidson and Broner (eds), *The Lost Tradition: Mothers and Daughters in Literature* (New York: Frederick Ungar Publishing Co.), pp. 280–90

Rosowski, Susan J. (1983), 'The Novel of Awakening', in Elizabeth Abel, Marianne Hirsch and Elizabeth Langland (eds), *The Voyage in: Fictions of Female Development* (Hanover; London: Dartmouth College; University Press of New England), pp. 49–68

Rowe, William and Vivian Schelling (1994), *Memory and Modernity: Popular Culture in Latin America* (London and New York: Verso)

Rulfo, Juan [1955] (1988), *Pedro Páramo* (Madrid: Cátedra)

Rutherford, John (1971), *Mexican Society During the Revolution: A Literary Approach* (Oxford: Clarendon Press)

—— (1972), *An Annotated Bibliography of the Novels of the Mexican Revolution* (New York: Troy)

Sarmiento, Domingo F. [1845] (1970), *Facundo: Civilización y Barbarie* (Madrid: Alianza)

Sayers, Janet (1991), *Mothering Psychoanalysis* (London: Hamish Hamilton)

Schaefer, Claudia (1992), 'Rosario Castellanos and the Confessions of Literary Journalism', in *Textured Lives: Women, Art and Representation in Modern Mexico* (Tucson and London: University of Arizona Press), pp. 37–60

Scott, Reneé (1992), 'Las paradojas del mundo de los adultos en *Balún-Canán*', *South Eastern Latin Americanist*, 36.1, 22–30

Shaw, Deborah (1997), 'Problems of Definition in Theorizing Latin American Women's Writing', in Elizabeth Dore (ed.), *Gender Politics in Latin America: Debates in Theory and Practice* (New York: Monthly Review Press)

Skidmore, Thomas E. and Peter H. Smith (eds) (1989), 2nd edn, *Modern Latin America* (New York: Oxford University Press)

Smith, Paul Julian (1992), 'Rosario Castellanos and Hélène Cixous', in *Representing the Other: 'Race', Text and Gender in Spanish and Spanish American Narrative* (Oxford: Clarendon Press), pp. 128–60

Smith, Sidonie and Julia Watson (eds) (1987), *A Poetics Of Women's Autobiography: Marginality and the Fictions of Self-Representation* (Bloomington: Indiana University Press)

—— (1992), *De/Colonising the Subject: The Politics of Gender in Women's Autobiography* (Bloomington: Indiana University Press), pp. 242–66

Smith William (1889), *A Classical Dictionary of Biography, Mythology and Geography* (London: John Murray)

Soto, Shirlene Ann (1986), 'The Mexican Woman: A Study of Her Participation in the Revolution', in *Twentieth century Mexico 2: Women in the Revolution*, pp. 17–32

Stanford Friedman, Susan (1988), 'Women's Autobiographical Selves: Theory and Practice', in Shari Benstock (ed.), *The Private Self: Theory and Practice of Women's Autobiographical Writings* (Chapel Hill: University of North Carolina Press; London: Routledge), pp. 34–62

Starcevic, Elizabeth (1983), 'Elena Poniatowska: Witness for the People', in Doris Meyer and Margarite Fernández Olmos (eds), *Contemporary Women Authors of Latin America: Introductory Essays* (Brooklyn, NY: Brooklyn College Press), pp. 72–77

Steele, Cynthia (1985), Manuel Fernández Perera (trans.) *Narrativa indigenista en los Estados Unidos y México* (Mexico: Instituto Nacional Indigenista, Investigaciones Sociales, 15)

—— (1992), *Politics, Gender and the Mexican Novel 1968–1988: Beyond the Pyramid* (Austin: University of Texas Press)

—— (1993), 'Indigenismo y posmodernidad: narrativa indigenista, testimonio, teatro campesino y video en el Chiapas finisecular', *Revista de Crítica Latinoamericana*), XIX, 249–60

—— (1994–5), 'María Escandón y Rosario Castellanos: feminismo y política personal en el "profundo sur" mexicano', *INTI: Revista de Literatura Hispánica*, 40–41, 317–25

Stoll, Anita (1990), 'Elena Garro (b. 1920) Mexico', in Diane E. Marting (ed.), *Spanish American Women Writers: A Bio-Bibliographical Sourcebook* (Connecticut: Greenwood Press), pp. 199–207

Stoltzfus, Ben (1996), *Lacan and Literature: Purloined Pretexts* (Albany: State University of New York)

Strickland Nájera, Valeska (1980), 'La obra de Nellie Campobello', Northwestern University, Ph.D. Dissertation (Ann Arbor, MI: UMI)

Thorlby, Anthony (ed.) (1969), *The Penguin Companion to Literature 2: European Literature* (Harmondsworth: Penguin)

Toruño, Rhina María (1995), 'Tiempo, destino y opresión en la obra de Elena Garro', Ph.D. Dissertation (Indiana University, Ann Arbor, MI: UMI)

Townsend, Richard T. (1993), *The Aztecs* (London: Thames and Hudson)

Tritten, Susan (1979), 'The Social Quest of the Mestizo', Ph.D. Dissertation (University of New Mexico, Ann Arbor, MI: UMI)

Tuñón Pablos, Julia (1999), Alan Hynds (trans.), *Women in Mexico: A Past Unveiled* (Austin: University of Texas Press)

von Hauffstengel, Renate (1966), *El México de hoy en la novela y el cuento* (Mexico: Andrea)

Walby, B. S. (1990), *Theorising Patriarchy* (Oxford: Blackwell)

Weedon, Chris (1987), *Feminist Practice and Poststructuralist Theory* (Cambridge, Mass.:, and Oxford: Blackwell)

Wehr, Demaris S. (1988), *Jung and Feminism: Liberating Archetypes* (London: Routledge)

Williams, Linda Ruth (1995), 'Mothers and Daughters: Pre-Oedipal and Other

Feminisms', in *Critical desire: Psychoanalysis and the Literary Subject* (London and New York: Edward Arnold), pp. 116–21

Wittig, Monique (1986), 'The Mark of Gender', in *The Poetics of Gender* (New York; Oxford: Columbia University Press)

Woolf, Virginia [1929] (1995), *A Room of One's Own* (London: Penguin)

Zamudio Rodríguez, Luz Elena (1996), 'Los personajes infantiles en *Balún-Canán*', in Poot Herrera (ed.), *Escribir la infancia, narradoras mexicanas contemporáneas* (Mexico City: Colegio de Mexico), pp. 127–44

INDEX